Who Do We Think We Are?

Race and Nation in the Modern World

Who Do We Think We Are?

Race and Nation in the Modern World

Philip Yale Nicholson

M.E. Sharpe
Armonk, New York
London, England

Copyright © 2001 by M. E. Sharpe, Inc.

All rights reserved. No part of this book may be reproduced in any form
without written permission from the publisher, M. E. Sharpe, Inc.,
80 Business Park Drive, Armonk, New York 10504.

Library of Congress Cataloging-in-Publication Data

Nicholson, Philip Yale, 1940–
Who do we think we are? : race and nation in
the modern world / Philip Yale Nicholson.
p.   cm.
Includes bibliographical references and index.
ISBN 0-7656-0391-8 (hardcover : alk. paper)
ISBN 0-7656-0392-6 (paperback : alk. paper)
1. Racism—History. 2. Nationalism—History. I. Title.
HT1521.N56   1999
305.8—dc21   99-11650
CIP

Printed in the United States of America

The paper used in this publication meets the minimum requirements of
American National Standard for Information Sciences—
Permanence of Paper for Printed Library Materials,
ANSI Z 39.48-1984.

BM (c) 10   9   8   7   6   5   4   3   2
BM (p) 10   9   8   7   6   5   4   3   2   1

For

My wife, Linda

My sister, Linda

Jennifer and Brett

Andrew and Karin

Peter

and

Hannah

Contents

Preface

The worst physical beating I have ever taken was, according to my attackers, because I was a "dirty Jew." I was six years old and in the recess-energized yard of the Thomas G. Morton Elementary School in Philadelphia. It was in the autumn of 1946. I was knocked down running and slid, face to cement, with two of my five attackers on top of me. I wasn't feeling Jewish earlier that morning when I strapped on the khaki green U.S. military-issue wrist compass that had been given to me by my war hero uncle, Gene, that weekend. My mood was patriotic, a bit euphoric. I had not seen my father's youngest brother since he had gone into the Army Air Corps before I was old enough to remember him. The only image I had of him came from a big photograph that stood on my grandmother's mantel; in the photo, he was standing under his bomber's wing in full leathers with a scarf flying in the breeze. After they chased me down, my attackers kicked and punched and ripped the compass away from my arm. My right eye became swollen and closed, and my face and clothing were bloodied by the open abrasions on my forehead and the raw wound down my face from cheekbone to chin.

I didn't think about the loss of my prized compass until I got into bed later that night. I realized it was gone when I wanted to put it in its special place on the table near my bedside lamp where it stayed with the Japanese coins and worthless paper money that First Lieutenant Eugene Nicholson had brought back from the Pacific War for me. All I could think about until then was being a Jew and the beating I took for it. I knew that other Jews had endured and lost more at the hands of far worse tormentors than mine, and I was too embarrassed to tell the school nurse and later the doctor the reason for the beating. To them and to my parents I had slipped running and had fallen on my face. The compass I would later confess was simply lost. I know now that all kids at a certain age, not too different from mine, learn an extra lesson about their identity in the bigger world outside than what they had previously learned at home. None start out that day as a despised object vulnerable to physical abuse—or worse—and expropriation. What happened that day has puzzled me ever since and helped to lead me here.

Jews we were. Exactly what that meant, and means, has never been completely clear to me or to those who actually determine such things. If some folks were more Jewish than others, why were all hated so equally? Where did this peculiar egalitarianism come from? Bigotry and democracy do not appear on their faces to be congenial sentiments. Were there qualities that united bigots? I knew that even within families there were big differences about these questions. There are at least two sides to every family. Mine had a somewhat unusual, I was told, English-Irish side. My father's nonreligious immigrant parents got their upbringing and name in the British Isles. An Eastern European Jewish Orthodoxy came with my mother's parents. The only things these two groups seemed to have had in common besides my parents were Yiddish and poverty. My father's secular influence dominated our family life. He was smart and ambitious and exuberant about everything in America. On his occasional wartime day off he proudly took me to see the great ships he was helping to build at the Sun shipyards of the Bethlehem Steel Company in Chester, Pennsylvania. One other thing about my parents: they always got into trouble with friends and relatives about what was called "the Negro question." I didn't know why they were always accused of starting trouble when they dissented from the prevailing racist jokes and remarks that invariably were a part of social or family gatherings. I associated my father's patriotism with a democratic and universalist outlook. His authority conveyed to me the idealism of a nonracially conscious America, but I was wrong, and so was he. Our nation, its ideology, and our identity in it were racially formed.

The other great dividing line at the Cousins' Club or Thanksgiving dinner, besides racism, was the State of Israel and the destiny of the Jews. To a kid these debates were very serious. The adults meant business. The outcome of the argument, it seemed, might actually determine the fate of the Jews. Would someone leave the table and call the president with the decision? War or peace? Homeland now or Diaspora forever? Personally I always liked the idea of Jews spread out everywhere, a synagogue in every great city in the world as an emotional haven for any Jew. The religious side of my family included the meanest racial bigots and the staunchest Zionists. The other, more secular side, was less enthusiastic and more wary of the dangers of a Jewish state, and never used the word *schwartze* (German and Yiddish for "black") with any kind of anger. Was there some connection between religious, national, and racial zealotry?

My curiosity and uncertainty about who I was eventually led me to study history. A doctorate and thirty-four years of teaching have allowed me to continue to reflect on those childhood questions. When I completed my doctoral dissertation, "George Dewey and the Transformation of American Foreign Policy" (The University of New Mexico, 1971), a troubling point reminiscent of my youthful ruminations continued to puzzle me. My subject, Commodore George Dewey, went to the Philippine Islands late in 1897 to prepare to confront the Spanish fleet there. He entered into an informal alliance with the Philippine rebel nationalists led by Emilio Aguinaldo. When the two met, they became friends. Dewey wrote letters to his brother Edward that described his new pal in glowing terms. He expressed his belief that the Filipino people were more capable of self-government than the Cubans, on whose behalf the war was to be fought. Dewey and Aguinaldo ate and drank together and shared plans to fight against Spain. After his victory at Manila Bay on May 1, 1898, Dewey gave Aguinaldo captured Spanish weapons, honored his national flag, praised his accomplishments in cables and letters to friends and authorities in Washington. Then the U.S. policy changed. It took several months, from about June to December. The Treaty of Paris finally gave the islands to the United States with no regard for the Republic of the Philippines established by Aguinaldo. Now the people became the "little Filipinos." Dewey disparaged and vilified his former buddy, and the people were similarly degraded by President William McKinley's "little brown brother" remarks, as well as by the temporary use by American soldiers of the borrowed term "nigger." New terms of derision were found after fighting became serious and the United States had increasingly to rely on regular, all African American units taken from western frontier posts. The Filipinos became "slopes," "chinks," and "yo-yos." Dewey returned home a hero, while the ugly Philippine-American War dragged on even after the capture of Aguinaldo in 1901. Dewey's former cordiality toward Aguinaldo was permanently displaced by racial contempt.

My lost compass, those overheard childhood debates about race and nation, and the disturbing place of race in American history have been pointing and pushing me toward finding my way ever since. The journey has taken some unexpected turns, raised new problems, but the issue stays as fresh and real as current national and international events unfailingly confirm. The conclusion I have reached is that race and nation are entwined as interdependent irrational intimates, the chief makers of public identity in modern history. Readers can test that hypothesis against their own experiences and in the discussion that is the rest of this book.

Acknowledgments

Every author has many debts, and I am no exception. I was also the benefi-ciary of some good luck. My parents, Samuel and Gertrude Nicholson, were unique and brave in their condemnation of every kind of bigotry. They made our household an enlightened oasis on the matter of race, not an easy thing in the world in which we lived. During the years of my graduate education big subjects were still undertaken by big historians, and I had the good fortune to hear and discuss the fresh and provocative ideas of William McNeill, Stringfellow Barr, and Roy F. Nichols, among many others.

Professor John Dower's important book *War Without Mercy; Race and Power in the Pacific War* tilted me toward this project when I was asked to review it in 1986. My colleagues at the time, Professors Robert Devlin and Lester Baltimore of Adelphi University's History Department, turned my complaints and criticism of the field of study of race and racism into a challenge to comment on the then current historical literature for a faculty and graduate student seminar. Soon after that, my former student, now a professor of sociology, Earl Smith, encouraged me to go further with the project and not let it languish when it might have.

Nassau Community College has a collective bargaining agreement with its faculty that provides sabbatical leaves for proposals deemed worthy by one's peers. I was able to use the time mine provided for most of the writing of this book. Our college library has a wonderful staff, and Charles Owusu and Marilyn Rosenthal were especially patient and helpful with all my searches and inquiries. Because of the breadth of this historical survey, I have relied on the primary research and scholarship of hundreds of authors. The interlibrary loan service took care of every one of my requests and always tracked me down when they knew that something important had arrived.

As president of our faculty union, I could not have taken a leave from my duties without officers who took on all the responsibilities of our orga-nization. Aaron Seligman, Robert Karmon, Barry Fischler, and Lawrence

Cohen did their work as well as mine while I was in "China" for a semester writing this book. Carol Farber's diligence accounts for the elimination of a large number of grammatical and stylistic mistakes. Those that remain are not her fault. Ken Jenkins urged me to write something that our students could and would read. I hope the result is worthy of the generosity of spirit he and so many others have bestowed on it.

No one did more for me as a reader, critic, fan, and friend than my sister, the renowned feminist and philosopher Linda Jane Nicholson of SUNY, Albany. It is hard for me to imagine this project's completion without her. She read and offered important critical suggestions for every chapter. Her editorial skills kept me on track when I would have strayed innumerable times. Remaining errors or deficiencies are probably because I didn't follow her suggestions when I should have, not because of any shortsightedness on her part. Sam Wellbaum, Michael Ferlise, Steve Seidman, Richard Panken, and Eli Zaretsky read some or all of the manuscript and offered many important suggestions along the way. They will see their heeded and un-heeded suggestions, as Linda will, throughout this work. They, too, deserve no criticism for what remains.

The students who engaged me in a dialogue about this subject for the past several years in a variety of courses were always the best testing ground for the ideas and conclusions that ultimately emerged. I am not the first author, nor will I be the last, to discover that one of the best ways to learn more about something is to try to teach it to someone else.

Who Do We Think We Are?

Race and Nation in the Modern World

Chapter 1

Introduction

The mass media have a natural commercial interest in focusing public attention on catastrophes that are current or potential. Hurricane warnings, plane wrecks, and fires are always at the top of the news. Epidemics, famine, and war attract the same concentrated focus of public interest. When these dramatic phenomena pass from immediacy, some of them become the subject matter for scholars or experts to pick over and explain. The findings of these scholars sometimes help to provide closure, but some catastrophes defy the routine. They will not go away, and they are not satisfactorily explained.

The destructive power of racial mythology has been the most deadly human phenomenon in the modern age; it is another horseman of apocalyptic dimension. Racial mythology is no less virulent now than it was a hundred years ago when Mark Twain wrote *King Leopold's Soliloquy* to condemn the Belgian government's extermination policies against an African colonial population. In his satirical essay "To a Person Sitting in Darkness," Twain similarly pierced the allegedly benevolent policy of the United States toward civilians in pursuit of American goals in the Philippine Islands. Professor John Dower, a Stanford University specialist on East Asian and Japanese history, has estimated that of the more than 55 million fatalities in the course of World War II, most were civilians who perished after the outcome was certain, and whose loss was justified or deliberately carried out under officially sanctioned, national vilification policies built on racial, cultural, or ethnic mythologies.[1] Today, in North and South America, Africa, the Middle East, Europe, and the Far East, nations regulate and control the residential practices of their populations and define or limit their legal and political rights based on racial mythologies that have been condemned by biological and anthropological science as worthless and by most human rights advocates in and outside the United Nations as in defiance of all their basic codes.[2] People struggling to establish new nations in the former Soviet Union, Yugoslavia, and the contested remnants of old colonial empires rely on these same discredited beliefs to sustain murderous assaults on their neighbors.

The scale of suffering, of human agonies unimaginably vast, makes the subject an emotional powerhouse. Language itself is a hotly contested terrain. Are American citizens of African descent Negroes, people of color, black, African Americans, or what? Why is any such term needed? The term *Holocaust,* for all its dramatic grandeur, is probably too small to capture the enormity of the events it seeks to encompass. Perhaps human consciousness itself rejects emotional information that would be too maddening to absorb fully.

The topic of racism is never casual in everyday conversation. A newspaper reports that in Austria today many quite ordinary citizens suffer a physical revulsion at the thought of touching the hand of a Jew. The same intensity of feeling affects the victims of racism and those who empathize with their plight. In Germany, the United States, and Japan, fifty-year-old emotional debates and legal battles take place over national war reparations, guilt, responsibility, and the origin of racially based destructive decisions against their own or foreign populations during World War II. Hundreds of millions of people have sharply etched living memories of personal horrifying losses, lynchings, assaults. More still experience everyday insults, slights, and abuses, legal barriers, and economic injustices as a consequence of racial categorization.

Never far beneath the surface, racially divisive issues and emotions are as ubiquitous in the United States today as they were when the Kerner Commission released its famous warning in 1968 that the country was becoming dangerously divided into two unequal nations, one white and one black. In spite of massive executive, judicial, and legislative government intervention since then, little has changed what has turned out to be more of a prophecy in the commission's report than a prescription for remediation. The Milton S. Eisenhower Foundation issued a report to coincide with the thirtieth anniversary of the Kerner Commission report. The study, "The Millennium Breach," found that "the racial divide in the United States has not only materialized (as predicted in 1968), it's getting wider" (*New York Times,* March 1, 1998, p. A25). Legally enforced segregation in the United States according to race, or jim crowism, is gone from public life. That was a mighty achievement. Nonetheless, during the final three decades of this century increased racial ghettoization, impoverishment, and imprisonment have not been offset by the modest and sometimes questionable gains of affirmative action programs, school busing, and the creation of political "minority districts." Race plays no less a powerful part in the social and political life of the United States today than it ever did. In most of contemporary

Western Europe, immigration from the colonial periphery has brought renewed passion to old racial modes of thinking.[3] When the economic pie
shrinks or grows inequitably, racism comes into the political foreground. In
Ireland, Israel, South Africa, Australia, and throughout formerly colonized
Africa and Asia, forceful reminders of old racial wounds refuse to heal, and
new battles are still being fought over racially contested national issues.

In spite of the pervasiveness of race throughout the modern history of
nations, too little attention has been given to its foundations or causes. To
understand these limitations requires a brief overview of how race was
regarded during most of this period. From about the 1750s to the 1940s,
informed thinking about race and racism went through a period of established scientific legitimacy. Enlightened empiricism upheld racial categories of human differentiation. Criticism of slavery, including the stridency
of most abolitionists, did not typically decry racism. Antiracist arguments
came principally from victims or from those few who spoke or wrote on
their behalf. Benjamin Baneker, David Walker, Frederick Douglass, So-
journer Truth, and W.E.B. Du Bois were occasionally joined by some
Quakers or extraordinary individuals. For more than two centuries, high
scholarship provided little support for the creation of a nonracially conscious human society in the United States or elsewhere in the world of
enslaved or colonized populations.

In the United States the great historical works on slavery by Ulrich B.
Phillips, *American Negro Slavery* (1918) and *Life and Labor in the Old
South* (1929), presented a benign portrait of that institution, and no critical
analysis whatsoever of racism. It was the colonialists' and slaveowners'
commonplace view that their stern control was a necessity for bringing the
blessings of Christianity or civilization to backward people, the "white
man's burden." Professional historians were not far ahead of (or behind)
their dominant cultures' sentiment on race. While usually deploring brutality, historians rarely condemned the segregationist policies enforced by federal and state agencies in the United States or the racial practices of colonial
powers in their far-reaching domains. Journalistic, humanitarian, religious,
or radical-left critics of racial inequities found few allies in government or
the academy. President Woodrow Wilson's expansion of racial segregation
of government agencies after 1913 aroused almost no intellectual outcry or
popular protest. The complex and elaborate system of apartheid was established in South Africa after the racial depredations of World War II, in the
midst of Nazi war-crimes trials, and coincidental with the condemnation by
the newly formed United Nations of its racially theoretical underpinnings.
The historical profession, like most, was not nearly as democratically accessible as it later became. The conservative cultural and class bias of nearly

all pre-1940 American scholarship, and a great deal that followed, contributed to a distinct lack of critical concern about the conditions prevailing among the poorest Americans, particularly those in the rural South, and no critical examination of the idea of race.

Not everyone had accepted the prevailing outlook over these centuries. John Stuart Mill's humanism, not scientific evidence, prompted the following observation on the racism of the nineteenth century: "Of all the vulgar modes of escaping from the consideration of the effects of social and moral influences on the human mind, the most vulgar is that of attributing the diversities of conduct and character to inherent natural differences."[4] But it was not until Julian Huxley and A.C. Haddon's book, *We Europeans: A Survey of "Racial" Problems* (1936), followed soon after by Ashley Montagu's famous lecture, "The Meaninglessness of the Anthropological Conception of Race," presented to the American Association of Physical Anthropologists in Chicago, April 1941, and then Montagu's brilliantly titled book, *Man's Most Dangerous Myth: The Fallacy of Race* (1942), that the debate among social scientists was dramatically changed. The concept of race itself was now deemed bogus. There was no genetic evidence to support it, and, as Montagu argued a few years later, it would be "better if the term 'race' were altogether abandoned."[5] Biological science gave up the term first. *A Dictionary of Biology* (1951), while continuing to define species and subspecies, for the first time never mentions the word "race" anywhere.[6]

Though delegitimized by science, for most people racism remains an acceptable pseudo science, a rationale for the irrational, an explanation for the otherwise inexplicable. No established religious institution condones racism, yet none has been able to confront or counteract successfully its ethical and moral consequences in the modern era. Which church, mosque, or synagogue has excommunicated a racist? Too often, religious leaders seem acquiescent to, or complicit with, its offenses. In the age of private property rights, racism has allowed the expropriation of land, labor, and resources that would otherwise seem arbitrary and irrational. Modernity places an emphasis on individualism and individual rights, yet racism assumes and imposes collective human categories. Governments continue to make racial boundaries and distinctions by statute. Courts reaffirm racial divisions by creating categories of "protected" persons or groups, by granting immunities (in South Africa) based on political assumptions. Political decisions are made (and unmade) to establish racially defined "minority" voting districts. Banks, police departments, prison authorities, and insurance companies routinely employ racial categories in policies and practices. Murderous struggles for national civil power are racially genocidal current events. Many otherwise intelligent people shrug as they maintain that racism is simply a part of human nature, fear of the stranger, an expression of natural alienation from the Other. Unfortunately, the same pseudo-scientific reasoning is still found in much of the writing and serious thinking about race. Racism, the notion of innate biologically determined human differences, continues to find empirical defenders in spite of the overwhelming scientific evidence against it. Criticism of racism has been primarily moralistic or even economistic: it is wrong, and it doesn't pay. Then why, we must ask, does it hang on with such virulence or reemerge from the cultural cellar so fiercely?

This book is devoted to seeking the answer to this question. My answer is based on four related themes. The first of these is that race and nation are interrelated phenomena. Most historians regard the emergence of the expansionist Western nation-state in about 1500 as the beginning of a new era, the modern era. Few have thought about racism as an interrelated, defining part of that same era. In spite of the dangers inherent in any "grand narrative," a more accurate perspective than the one we have about race and nation will be realized only by looking at the big historical picture. The most important limitation of most studies on the issue of race is their extremely narrow focus. It is a problem typically depicted in the isolation of a single national experience, such as Hitler's Germany, South African apartheid, or jim crowism in the United States. My contention is that race is not simply a peculiarity of certain nations; it is a phenomenon of expansive nations and the emotional borderlines set by the laws that define and constitute nations. People were turned into races when nations extended and defined their political hegemony through conquest and expropriation. Race and nation were born and raised together; they are the Siamese twins of modernity.

The second theme is the place of territorial conquest or colonialism in the formation of national identity. The nation-state makes an innovative kind of war, neither traditionally religious and feudal nor dynastically imperial. The war-making nation in the modern world generates powerful emotional ties to its secular power centers. National and racial pride is linked to conquest by loyalty to coercive military authorities on the frontiers of an expanding state. Racism legitimizes not only external wars of conquest but also internal wars of conquest or extraordinary forms of expropriation by the same national authorities, though usually in different uniforms. Like war, and often as part of war, racism legitimizes confiscatory and exploitative practices beyond the scope of existing national laws. Slavery and mass murder are among the most obvious examples of national law legitimized by racism in peace and war. Religious institutions and authorities have not fared well, for the most part, on the issue of race because of their modernist dependency on and relationship with the authority of the nation-state. At times, religious authorities have been able to temper the abuse of subject populations by military powers; for example, in the early semifeudal phases of the Spanish and Portuguese overseas empires. As religious authorities gave up their temporal power, however, they either lent their support to the nation and enjoyed its protection or suffered its wrath.

The third theme is the process of vilification of the victim. In almost every account of the first meeting of two historically unconnected people, Henry Hudson and the Canarsies or Europeans in the South Pacific, for example, we find no opprobrious or defamatory descriptions. Often the native people are described as wondrous, exotic creatures. Conflict is not part of these first encounters. Only after the expropriations of land, labor, or other forms of wealth and the conflict that followed were derisive terms applied to those who were forced to give up what they had. Material expropriation yields human degradation among its practitioners. What is taken by coercion requires rational explanation. This is not to say that prejudicial dislikes or xenophobic suspicions about cultural or ethnic differences cannot exist outside national frameworks or exploitation. But it is the nation-state that turns such sentiments into racism with legally enforced and institutionally encoded national practices of expropriation, coercion, displacement, and death of the formally vilified people.

The fourth theme is the dialectical relationship between those who are racially vilified and those doing the vilifying. Prevailing national sentiments about virtue and vice become racial divisions. Notions of purity require concrete examples of that which is impure. Sexual fear and anxiety are typically projected. The conquered are endowed with the imagined negative behavioral fantasies of their oppressor. Those who become acculturated and accept the codes, laws, and institutionalized practices must adapt to the odd behavioral dichotomies on both sides of the line. Malcolm X often condemned racism not only for treating people as if they were inferior but also for making so many of them truly believe they were. A peculiar duality or divided identity has been described by many, including W.E.B. Du Bois, who called it a "double consciousness"; this is the outlook of those who achieved the cultural standards of the dominant society but still experience the stigma of racial vilification. On the one hand, they reach or exceed the norms set for respect and inclusion into the national culture; on the other hand, aspects of who they are, their full identity, remain either invisible or negated. Those who construct the racial dichotomy and enjoy its benefits deceive themselves as well by assuming a smug though false superiority or an erroneous belief in their racial purity. Sometimes, those who have been racially vilified have been said to possess unusual talents or abilities, intellectual or physical. Jews were maligned for being too clever, others for their imagined extraordinary sexual prowess or physical strength. These fantastic attributes and deficiencies emerge from the emotions and psyche of the oppressor. The racinated (those turned into a race against their will) are described as impure, as lacking civilization, and consequently they are introduced to things like water torture, plantation slavery, or genocide. Similarly, they are permitted to participate freely only in those practices and occupations that reinforce the prevailing racial sentiments.

Within the several broad historical periods I examine in this volume, different nations emerge and stand out for a time as prominent and as innovators. They take the lead in the development of national institutional codes and practices that others adopt and modify. Hence, the narrative follows shifts in those centers of authority where innovation and leadership are preeminent. The discussion begins with an examination of ancient and medieval manifestations of social and cultural division. Early in this study, the Portuguese, Spanish, and Dutch are my main focus of attention. They were the innovators in exploration and conquest. Later, my attention shifts toward Great Britain, the United States, and the European nations. Finally, the United States becomes the center of the discussion. This is a story of the interrelationship and interdependency of race and nation, not a complete portrait of one or the other. Both are the artifices of modern mythology. Both undergo change and development consistent with dominant institutions and beliefs through the various historical periods. Hence, the chapters are formed to coincide with prevalent themes and place emphasis on preeminent nations. The chapters are built around large historical epochs in which the four themes or hypotheses are elaborated in terms of well-known events and developments.

Chapter 2 looks at human society over the long era before there were any nation-states. We find many forms of social organization among preliterate, ancient, classical, and medieval societies. Human groups have created a wide range of structures from nomadic clan-type formations to elaborate dynastic empires, with much in between. Murderous rampages and brutal wars of conquest certainly existed before the emergence of the modern nation-state system, which took place after about 1500. The chapter seeks answers to the following questions: Were very early human societies racist? Why is there confusion and so much conflict about group distinctions and skin hue in ancient Egypt or India? What, if anything, did Alexander the Great think or do about race? How were cultural distinctions and prejudices a part of early human history? In all the great civilizations in Asia, Africa, and every part of the world there were outsiders, foreigners, and cultural subdivisions now commonly called ethnic groups. Were there racial laws, codes, and beliefs? How were differences in skin hue, physiognomy, and culture accommodated or rejected prior to the secular laws and institutional practices of the modern Western state? A large part of the rest of this book depends on the answers to these questions.

The concept of the nation, of a people unified by certain common adherence to the authorities and boundaries of law, language, geography, or politics external to traditional feudal or universal religious controls, begins in the Western world around 1500. The state came first, before the nation, as a secular administrative structure that facilitated and gave legitimacy to the trading cities that generated their prosperity outside the feudal commune of the Middle Ages. These city-states were antecedent to the nation-state. Chapter 3 explores the correlation between the new nation-states and the emerging concept of race as the Europeans defined their national borders and themselves as distinct from one another. These distinctions emerged in treaties made among themselves in war, and in their colonial conquests of foreign populations abroad. National laws, like the Poor Laws in England, defined and described the political status and the rights of internal populations as colonial laws and codes described conquered peoples. National borders were made in treaties among relative equals; racial boundaries differentiated the conqueror from the conquered. Explorers preceded their national armies and navies and established friendly initial contacts with almost every human group they encountered without regard to either the culture or appearance of those they met. Conquest and subsequent imperial administration brought into place the new laws that defined colonial boundaries claimed by one nation-state over its rivals, and laws within the colonial territory that set apart the conquered from their conquerors. Race and nation were made together in secular war and coercion in what was soon referred to as Europe, and overseas from Ireland to the Americas, and in Africa and Asia, where those same Europeans staked out their imperial claims.

Trade displaced the simple exploitation of resources and agriculture as the chief engine of national economic power after the Thirty Years' War (1618–48). Chapter 4 describes the expansion of national and racial law into new areas of human relationships. Soaring commercial interactions required a vast expansion of laws at the same time as empirical scientific enlightenment brought forth detailed explanations of "race." Color, or skin hue, was added to equally unscientific notions about blood, culture, and physical appearance as a component of race as European scientists began the impossible and ultimately fruitless task of seeking to classify the human species. The ancient nonracially structured practice of slavery became a racial institution in the overseas empires of the great nations. At the same time, and right alongside the legal structure of slavery, the political concept of liberty gained its greatest momentum and found some of its most eloquent spokesmen among slaveowners. Popular democracy played no role in the complex formation of race and nation in the age of mercantile empires; hence the terms *racism* and *nationalism,* which refer to the wider public emotional embrace or loyalty to these ideas, were rarely if ever used. Race and nation were formed by laws made by small military and administrative elites, sometimes at a distance from royal and aristocratic authorities. The Age of Mercantilism gave to nation and race a foundation in secular law and empirical science. The accumulation of wealth among those who were a part of the mercantile world built new loyalties and emotional bonds. In the next century the stirrings of democracy, the discoveries of science, and the wonders of new industrial technology enlarged the public sphere for these sentiments and practices.

The American and French revolutions sparked more than a century of expansion of national and democratic aspirations and achievements. Chapter 5 follows this great epoch of European national power and racial arrogance as it was extended throughout the world. Race and nation were now formalized by laws that enjoyed the popular consent of those (male) citizens included in the body politic and were imposed (for their own good, it was said) over the excluded. Now the nation evoked a patriotic identity and racial differentiation in law that brought forth a consensual public racism. Citizenship and racial identity were legally linked. The Irish became "white" when they became citizens in America. Passionate public loyalties shifted away from religious, aristocratic, and royal authorities to the more inclusive mythologies of national ideals such as *Liberté, Egalité, Fraternité,* or, as Abraham Lincoln put it, "One nation conceived in Liberty. . . ." Frontiers fell everywhere on earth to the onslaught of these European and American powers. In spite of rivalries among these powers, their national and racial interests sometimes coalesced, as in the suppression of the Boxer Rebellion in China in 1900. They quarreled among themselves as well and disputed over imperial claims wherever weakness was perceived. They inherited and redefined one another's racial and national codes from the Philippine Islands to South Africa, in Asia and the Middle East.

The nineteenth century was an age of monumental achievements in science and technology. The legitimacy of both nation and race was reinforced by explanations from the highest and most revered intellectual authorities in every nation. Dissent was marginal and came inconsistently from such social critics as Karl Marx, often eloquently from victims, and from a few humanitarian skeptics such as John Stuart Mill and Mark Twain. In the mercantile Age of Reason, race and nation were established by legal authority; in the more democratic age that followed, they won popular assent as prevailing mythologies in every Western capital, on their frontiers, and in colonial settlements throughout the world.

Race and nation were never more obviously unified than in the era that followed World War I and came to an end in the ashes of World War II. Stripped of overseas colonies and racinated subjects, Germany created an interior European colony and race from ethnic Jews. It was a shocking process and somewhat synthetic and forced, like the fuel oil Germany was driven by circumstances to make from coal. Chapter 6 examines and compares the parallel victimization and racination of European Jews with Irish, Native American, African, and Asian people. Anti-Semitic bigotry became racism when national and then imperial laws stripped Jews of their rights as citizens, brought about the complete confiscation of their property, and subjected them to brutal coercion, slave labor, transportation, and death. Briefly, in just one generation near the middle of the twentieth century, nationalistic Germany demonstrated that race and racism were never benevolent, not really about color and physiognomy, or about inferiority or superiority of cultures, or imposed only on geographically remote or alien populations. The events of this era starkly confirm what earlier times and other people had undergone when the interrelated force of race and nation held sway over their destinies. The delusional powers of race and nation were not confined, of course, to Germany. World War II tested every participant's national and racial consciousness, just as it exposed their deep and contradictory consequences. But Hitler really did give racism a bad name.

Nation building replaced retreating colonial empires in Africa, Asia, and the Middle East, and the essential features of race and nation were sustained during the Cold War in spite of Nazism's horrific depredations. Innovations in law accompanied new racial identities and divisions amid struggles against old colonial formulations and structures. Political conflicts for national power prompted fresh racial and national responses in emerging nations. Chapter 7 also takes up the paradoxical termination of formalized federal, state, and local segregation practices (jim crowism) in the United States with the continuation of a no less racially divided nation. Immigration issues, their relationship to citizenship and national/racial identity in Europe, are also part of the discussion of the postcolonial period. The Israeli-Palestinian paradox is a particularly poignant part of the tenacity of racial and national mythology and their brutally real consequences. In South Africa the complex racial system of apartheid was born; it also flourished and perished during these years. The final irony may be that the real struggle of the Cold War years was not between communism and democracy, but instead for the global achievement of the Western racial and nation-state system.

Chapter 8 looks at the increasingly globalized economy and culture of an electronic world of instant communications. International markets for multi-nationally produced goods might offer the prospect of diminished national authority and the possibility of a corresponding weakening of racial identities. This chapter is the least historical and raises some speculative considerations as a conclusion to the book. For example, it is no secret that a more powerful United Nations might offset the traditional power of nation and race. Global human and civil rights, along with living standards, could be established that might take the functional utility away from race and nation. As administrative structures, nations remain, nonetheless, the key political units of authority. The collapse of the Soviet Union and Yugoslavia are shown to reveal heightened appetites for more and smaller units of national political power. The conversion of ethnic prejudice to racial laws and practices, including genocide, accompanies most of these national struggles. After 500 years, race and nation appear alive and well.

In history nothing is static. Race and nation have been dynamic evolving forces. They elude precise delineation because they change over time and in different places. The institutions and practices associated with racism and nationalism are never exactly alike, but common threads are interwoven among them. The nation-state that emerged over the past 500 years displaced religious and dynastic institutional mythology and came to be the prevailing system of political authority in the world. Racism shared the twists and turns of this modern world system of human organization with the nation, as its other half, in one double helix. Race and nation are inseparably linked and interdependent. One claims the devotion and loyalty of most of the world's people. The other contributes to that devotion by denying the humanity of most of the (rest of the) world's people. Racism sleeps when expropriation is missing or dimly perceived; it awakes in war, in conquest, and as a reaffirmation of irrational loyalty to national authority. Leaders explain what is real; their power to decide the fate of others confirms their truths, and those who accept and depend on their authority internalize those truths as the prevailing mythologies. When Oedipus walks, the nation wakes, the earth shakes, brave men and women tremble, and somebody pays the price.

Chapter 2

No Nations, No Races: Premodern Formations of Authority and Cultural Identity

Before Civilization

How can we know how preliterate, ancient, and medieval people formed their identities, responded to authority, related to those they were not, knew who they were? It is hard enough to get a grip on these questions, let alone find good answers to them in our own age. Historians like to deal with literate people. Written records are grist for their analytical mills. Nonliterate cultures leave things behind for anthropologists to sift through, so there are some conclusions that can be drawn about them, their sources of authority and identity. Anthropologists have journeyed to and lived among such societies in our own times. We also have the records of explorers and travelers throughout history who encountered people in nonliterate societies. Captain Meriwether Lewis and Lieutenant William Clark, for example, during their explorations of 1804–6, encountered and described in their journals more than forty distinct tribal groups of Native North Americans, most of whom had never seen or been seen by Europeans.

Material circumstance has a great deal to do with the nature and extent of the organization of everyday life. Fishing or farming cultures, nomadic or seminomadic followers of wildlife depend upon leaders whose memories of the seasons, tides, and animal habits give them some authority, though that may be shared with religious figures whose role includes overseeing the codes and folklore that have to do with family, life and death, and pleasing the gods. Musical and artistic expression captures and reflects the essential

14

elements of the culture. In short, in this respect, nonliterate cultures are not so very different from societies that keep written records. Preliterate human communities spanned a wide range that included basic hunters and gatherers to highly sophisticated and agricultural people who kept domesticated animals and had refined metalworking skills. The interaction of members of such communities with outsiders varied from cautious timidity to friendly curiosity, and sometimes included hostility. There is no evidence of racial awareness, identification, conflict, or restrictive codes unless or until they were introduced by others. Lewis and Clark had not a single hostile racial encounter. As with Christopher Columbus and Henry Hudson, European first meetings with Native Americans were universally friendly. No expression of hostility based on physical appearance or difference is noted among the tribal people toward the Europeans. When hostile behavior is noted, it is not based on real or mythologized physical differences. Cannibal behavior, for example, seems to take place without regard to race, creed, or religion. When Magellan and forty of his people were killed in the Philippine Islands in 1521, it was because they had taken the side of one local group in its war with another. Many instances of foreign children raised as equals or adult aliens absorbed into such societies are further evidence of the lack of any racial mythology or consciousness. Europeans disapproved of the assimilation of their nationals with tribal or colonized people. They referred to it in the expression "going native," but aside from a generalized xenophobia about customs and language, tribal and preliterate people were never racists. Those who spoke with or wielded authority were those who interpreted the signs in nature and guided or made decisions about life and death and sacrifice. None of them used the concept of race for any purpose, though gender and age often played a part in decision making. Leaders combined spiritual and secular authority and took on paternal or maternal roles. Newcomers were usually regarded with cautious curiosity.

Early Civilization

Civilizations developed in many parts of the world with little or no contacts among those people who wrote down the social codes, civil laws, and religious beliefs and gave them transgenerational staying power. The ancient civilizations founded in Asian, African, and Middle Eastern river valleys more than 5,000 years ago provide us with information about varied expressions of authority, social divisions, relationships with neighbors, and the practice of slavery. These ancients also recorded their observations of and reactions to foreigners when there were contacts, and they noted gossip and hearsay about faraway people and places from travelers they met. Conscious of their own achievements, they universally regarded those without them as backward and uncivilized. None of these ancient civilizations conformed to our modern way of thinking of ourselves as one culture, nation, or civilization living in a world of other cultures, nations, and comparable civilizations. They inhabited total worlds, complete to themselves, which incorporated vast varieties of subgroups, cultures, and tribes under a dominant hegemony. Authority came from the foundations of the culture itself, with proximity of identity to its religious faith or gods, its language and lore. Leaders were those who could interpret the mysteries of existence with the cultural tools at hand. Oedipal dynastic empires and aristocracies were formed with intimate ties to the god or gods who helped form the uncertain destinies of all.

Ancient Egyptians, Chinese, and Greeks all shared a common term or character for those who could not read their language: they were "barbarians." Many cultures have made their written texts sacred and revered objects. Language is so fundamental a part of collective identity that it has been both art and icon to Hebrews, Arabs, Chinese, Egyptians, and many others. Before printing presses could standardize valued texts in large numbers, those responsible for the painstakingly drawn characters, encoded symbols, or finely written ideographs or hieroglyphics were at the very center of authority itself, or were their closely supervised employees. Myths were the explanation and elaboration of these sacred stories by the authorities to the nonliterate rest of the population. A large measure of cultural identity grew out of the acceptance by the faithful of this explanation of reality by the authorities. Authorities could be, and often are, accused of turning the tale to suit or advance their own aims. More typically, the authorities, as elites, created their own internal subculture with the aid of scribes who helped fix hierarchical relationships within the culture through formal titles and positions. Control of the actions or behaviors of elites was internally imposed, as in social classes, and drawn as much from the cultural demands of their positions as required for the control of others. The printed or drawn word itself imposes a cultural unity from top to bottom. Artful Arabic selections from the Koran adorn the walls of mosques everywhere that the Moslem faith is followed, just as sacred Hebraic torahs are celebrated and reverentially kissed by religious Jews. Mullahs and rabbis are as devoted as any in their congregations. Once the written word drawn as picture, idea, or alphabetic code separated a culture from the uncivilized, it became the center of that community's emotional identity, loyalty, and authority; not hue or physiognomy.

Differences in physical appearance were always noted in the ancient world, along with habits and practices, and both favorable and negative

reactions to people within and outside their realms were frequently recorded. In none of the diverse systems of culture and authority, from the
Indus Valley of India to the Mediterranean world, do we encounter legal
forms of discriminatory practice constructed on what we now understand as
racial theories or mythologies. In none of the ancient sacred texts are there
exclusive racial or physiological categories established to limit participation
in the faith or culture. The peculiar curse on Canaan, the innocent son of
Ham, condemned in Genesis 9 and 10, to be a "servant of servants," though
widely cited by defenders of slavery, makes no mention whatsoever of skin
color or anything like race.

The centrality of written language among the ancients is nowhere more
important than in China. The art of calligraphy and all that knowledge of
the finely crafted characters conveyed was the mark of the civilized human
being. All others were grouped together with contemptual nondiscrimina-
tory clarity as "barbarians," including those in "peripheral states" who
would later become incorporated into a greater China.[1] The Chinese readily
described the differences they saw in foreigners and commented on various
aspects of their appearance, often with a sense of arrogance and disdain, but
created no internal or overseas categories in speech or action built on physical or alleged inherited behavioral characteristics. The Chinese were the
"Middle Kingdom," and everyone else was perceived as living on the
fringes of their reality and their civilization for most of the 5,000 years of
that culture's enduring strength. The invaders and occasional conquerors of
China, the Mongols of the thirteenth century and the Manchus of the seventeenth, were absorbed by the Chinese culture and became as ardently Chinese as the Chinese they overran. It was language, spoken and written, not
physiognomy or hue, that divided human groups in the ancient world.

The ancient Indus civilization, sometimes known as the Harappa culture
from one of its most important sites—with Mohenjo-Daro—is described by
some historians as having been a more vast and highly developed urban
complex than either Egypt or Mesopotamia during the period 2300–1600
B.C.E. From skeletal remains, figurines, and statuary, historians conclude
they were "of mixed groups," and physical anthropologists contend "that
they were made up from a mixture of racial types."[2] During 1500 to 1200
B.C.E., their declining culture was gradually overrun by a series of waves of
immigration from the regions comprising the steppes of southern Russia
east of the Caspian Sea. The immigrants found their way through Iran and
the passes in northwestern India. They were tall, fair-haired, straight-nosed,
long-headed people and were called Aryans. They overwhelmed the deca-
dent and settled people of the Indus Valley and, over several hundred years,
most of the rest of India. These Aryans are always described as patriarchal

and warlike, and similar to Bronze Age, or Homeric-era Greeks. When they were not fighting, which seems to have been an activity from which they took only the briefest of respites, they enjoyed hunting wild boar and lions. They described all their opponents with hostility and used disparaging references to their physical differences, including color. The Aryans expressed contempt for the dark-skinned, flat-nosed, short Dravidians of central and south India, whom they easily overwhelmed and plundered. Dravidians were also condemned for living in fortified strongholds and hoarding great wealth in gold. For the most part, however, Aryans made war against each other until their seminomadic, pastoral, and nature-worshipping culture merged with or was absorbed into the older Indus civilization and Dravidian cultures. Aryans brought with them a form of social division or classes known as *varnas,* which were originally defined as color and was probably an arrogant expression of their sentiment toward the darker-hued local populations they overran. However, their *varnas* were ineffective in preventing their blending with the population, and color faded as the determining factor in social division.

The outcome of the intermixing of Dravidian and Aryan cultures over several centuries was the caste system and total way of life known as Hinduism.[3] While these ancient Indians were aware of physical differences and quite candid in their vivid depiction of the color, stature, clothing, and habits of others they encountered, they maintained no racial codes or prohibitions about intermarriage or social interaction. Consequently, India became a physically blended but socially and religiously divided society. The rigid caste system that emerged over the centuries following the Aryan migrations divided Indians into fixed hereditary social categories wherein "race, belief, and sometimes even occupation, make no difference."[4] Most of India was swept into Hinduism and its spiritual monism, doctrine of rebirth and karma, and caste system by 600 B.C.E. Various human physical types and hues were found in all the castes, and while some scholars have compared the restrictive rigidity and discriminatory practices of this system to racism, there was no physiological, genetic, or racial rationality associated with caste.[5] An excellent visual portrayal of the diversity of physical types in Indian culture can be readily observed in the abundant artistic works of this culture. Vidya Dehejia's *Indian Art* (1997) has numerous examples of paintings that depict the multiplicity of physical types that constitute traditional Indian culture.

Ancient Egyptians also looked down from the heights of their civilization on the country bumpkins who were outsiders to their cultural achievements. Egypt is important and controversial to some on the question of race. There is really something there for everyone both to claim and to disparage if they wish. The origins of this civilization are so deep in antiquity, and it went on for so long and created so many artifacts and pictographic remains, that many contemporary writers find there whatever they are looking for. Ancient writers had much to say about Egypt as well. In the fifth century B.C.E. Herodotus, in *The Histories,* introduced his long description of Egypt and the Egyptians with the observation: "About Egypt itself I shall have a great deal more to relate because of the number of remarkable things which the country contains, and because of the fact that more monuments which beggar description are to be found there than anywhere else in the world" (p. 115). Were Egyptians darkly hued Africans? Yes, indeed they were. Were Egyptians fairly hued Mediterraneans? Yes again. Were they of mixed hue? Yes. They were all of these at one time or another. As their various imperial ages—Old Kingdom, Middle Kingdom, and New Empire—expanded and contracted, they added or lost control over various populations. Once foreigners, from remote African regions to Fertile Crescent Hittites or Hebrews, learned the language and habits and came under Egyptian authority, either by volition or coercion, they became members of the culture and might have found themselves in almost any occupation, including the highest in the land. The Old Testament story of Joseph, with his coat of many colors, is the tale of a Jewish boy sold into Egyptian slavery by his jealous brothers. Joseph rises to the top of society as the pharoah's confidential adviser. Rich agricultural abundance allowed the creation of a hugely diverse labor force, including priests, administrators, architects, and engineers, who magnificently represented the accomplishments of the various eras of this durable civilization. Ancient civilization and culture were derived from the written word. The authority that stood behind the word usually included coercion, either social or physical. Slaves were buried alive with deceased masters in many cultures. They had no choice. Expulsion from the community was considered in some cultures worse than execution.

Slaves in the ancient world were the captive people of military conquerors. There are references to the existence of slaves in the original Babylonian Code of Hammurabi and in the earliest records of ancient Persia and Egypt. The practice continued throughout the classical period of the Greeks, the Hellenistic age, and the Roman Empire and was continuously present in the African, Mediterranean, Asian, and Eurasian regions from the earliest times through the Middle Ages and into the modern era. Military and political conquest, the coercive force of raw authority, was sometimes augmented by indebtedness, poverty, and starvation as the main reasons for people falling under the control of others. The conditions under which slaves lived and how they were treated socially varied widely, from extremely harsh and degraded in ancient mines to elevated and admired status as artists, poets, and artisans. No population was exempt from the danger of enslavement, and no racial or physical descriptive code prevailed. A contemporary critic of civil rights activism who has looked at slavery in ancient times concludes that "the remarkable fact about slavery in the ancient world is that it had little or nothing to do with race."[6]

The closest any of the ancients came to developing a racial theory about slavery was probably Aristotle's famous rationalization in response to the growing criticism of slavery in the middle of the fourth century B.C.E. In *Politics*, Aristotle criticizes those who "affirm that the rule of a master over slaves is contrary to nature, and that the distinction between slave and freeman exists by law only, and not by nature; and being an interference with nature is therefore unjust" (bk. 1, ch. 2, 1253b, p. 1130). His observations convinced him that the non-Greek primitive people who constituted the bulk of Hellenic slaves were naturally suited for it. In a remarkable statement that would find agreeable repetitions a millennium later, and be repeated for centuries after that, Aristotle declares: "For that some should rule and others be ruled is a thing not only necessary, but expedient; from the hour of their birth, some are marked out for subjection, others for rule" (bk. 1, ch. 4, 1254a, p. 1132). Though there is nothing in Aristotle's view that is explicitly racial, he adopts the familiar nonhistorical view that defends a fixed reality as the product of natural forces beyond control or reason. He does approach racism by recommending that non-Hellenes, "barbarians," are preferable as slaves because it is not part of their nature, as it is with his countrymen, to be free or independent minded (bk. 1, ch. 6, 1255b, pp. 1134–35) Later racists would adopt the same theoretical perspective to defend the actions of authorities on behalf of the expropriations and unifying disciplinary advantages of plantation racial slavery, segregation, colonialism, genocide, and anti-Semitism. Aristotle anticipates the Enlightenment and the static scientism of simple empirically drawn conclusions. Of course, Aristotle meant more to philosophy and science than his traditional patriarchal and Hellenic bias about civilization reveal. Not the least of his importance was the enormous influence he must have had on his student, Alexander, the son of a powerful king, Philip of Macedonia.

The Classical Era in the Western World

To Aristotle and his fellow Greeks, their world was the foundation of an ideal civilization, but in the aftermath of the destructive war between Athens and Sparta, it was vulnerable to the military conquest of outsiders. Macedonia soon expanded its hegemony throughout the Greek world, and

Alexander the Great took the Hellenistic education he had received from his teachers far beyond what anyone could have imagined. Alexander was determined to spread and universalize the culture he revered by every means at hand, military and architectural. The goal he sought, though failed to realize, may not have been a new empire divided into city-states according to the model of his day, the early fourth century B.C.E. One of the great historians of the classical era, W.W. Tarn, wrote in his book *Alexander the Great* that Alexander's "new towns were designed to promote the fusion of Europe and Asia on a basis of Greek culture, they were probably not autonomous Greek cities but a new mixed type" (p. 134). At a town called Susa in 334 B.C.E., Alexander celebrated the conquest of Persia with a great feast, and he, along with eighty of his officers, married daughters of the Persian aristocracy. His troops, some 10,000 men, married their native concubines at the same time. Tarn says, "It was an attempt to promote the fusion of Europe and Asia by intermarriage" (p. 111). A few months later, Alexander had himself deified, held another dinner for 9,000, returned to Babylon, which was to become his new capital, became ill, and on June 13, 323 B.C.E., died at the age of thirty-two after a reign of twelve years and eight months. Most of what he tried to do fell apart soon after his death, and it was reported that many of the marital unions did likewise. Greek culture and the idea of a human universalism continued to spread, however, and its influence has persisted since then. Many other powerful figures would follow with plans to bring all humanity under one vision—Romans, Christians, Moslems, Marxists, and American presidents. The Hellenistic age in the West and the Roman Empire that extended its civilization corresponded to a golden age in China that is sometimes called the classical era.

Hebrews were an important part of this classical era because of their monotheism, an idea whose time was definitely coming in the West. To the Egyptians, Persians, and eventual Roman successors of Alexander's disintegrating empire, the Jews were a tough subculture, a people difficult to control fully. Was there anti-Semitism in this classical world, or racism based on physical characteristics? No. Until the emergence and spread of Christianity no ethnic expression of hostility to Jews is found. Were they identified in any particular way? Yes. From the perspective of the ancient Greeks, Jews were a distinct group noted for their philosophical discourses. A pupil of Aristotle, Theophrastus, describes the Jews: "Throughout this time they discourse together about the Divine, because they are philosophers by nature, and at night they observe the stars, watching them and addressing them in their prayers."[7] Throughout the classical period we discover an ambivalence that is identified as part of the anti-Semitic sentiment by non-Jews toward Jews as members of a community. In the Hellenistic age and later, Jews would rarely hold municipal posts, government or official jobs, "because every such post was connected with the recognition of the city's official cult. They could not be good citizens even if they wished to be, because religion sundered them from the Greeks."[8]

Although Jews lived among many different people in the ancient world and after, they were always suspected of giving their final loyalty to an authority other than that established by the culture or civilization in which they lived. The reason for hostility to Jews was expressed quite openly by the Greeks: "If the Jews are really of our community, let them also honor the gods whom we honor." Or, in another locale, "If the Jews belong to the citizenry, why do they not respect the gods whom the Alexandrians respect?"[9] Conversion, or expressions of fealty to local deities, could mean full acceptance for ancient and medieval Jews. Refusal meant rejection and hostility, the basis for false rumors, gossip, and rampages of violence against them either by the governing authorities, their administrative subdivisions, or vigilante mobs secure in their knowledge that those they attacked were stigmatized by respected and established authority. These attacks have become an important part of the very history of Judaism, from the desecration and rededication of the Temple of Jerusalem (Chanukah), to the murderous plots of venal individuals (Purim). As long as conversion to the prevailing faith was an option, hostility to Jews came from anxiety about religious or broadly based political loyalty, not racism. When submission or responsiveness to authority was built on the emotional social and cultural foundations of language and religious faith, those who cherished their own sacred texts and adhered to the leaders of their own distinct faith were regarded with understandable insecurity by others. There is, moreover, no consistent physical or behavioral description of Jews or dark-skinned Africans or Indians or Asians in the ancient world that is negative or repugnant.

Blackness in many folklores and cultures was associated with evil, mystery, and death. Greco-Roman culture adhered to a black/white color symbolism. Darkness and light were contrasted; one revealed the world, the other concealed it. But sub-Saharan Africans and darkly hued Indians were not described by the ancients in Europe or elsewhere in negative terms or characterized as having negative behavioral traits because of their skin color, hair type, or other physical features, though these were always noted by observers. Africans and Asians were identified as human beings, sometimes admired as warriors and soldiers, and though whiteness was often associated with beauty, they were, nevertheless, sometimes praised for their attractiveness.[10] Herodotus, for example, though he often expressed favorable prejudices toward the Greeks, in *The Histories* reported that the

Ethiopians were "said to be the tallest and best looking people in the world" (p. 182). Aware of the many tribal and barbarian cultures around them, including those far to the north, the ancients were respectful of cultures with qualities that resembled their own, and they never developed racial categories or hierarchies. Their empiricism led many to conclude that dark skin came from exposure to the hot sun in tropical climates. The Harvard scholar Frank Snowden answered the question about racism in antiquity in two of his widely cited and praised books, *Blacks in Antiquity* (1970) and *Before Color Prejudice* (1983): it just wasn't there.

To the Middle Ages

Racism has been connected to the evils of ancient and medieval slavery, the slave trade, and wars of conquest that subjected one population to the will of another. Slavery did vary considerably throughout the ancient and medieval world. Most slaves in the ancient and medieval world were of the same culture or were the same physical types as those who enslaved them. Orlando Patterson, in *Slavery and Social Death* (1982), found that of all the slaveowning societies he studied, more than 75 percent enslaved people just like themselves (p. 176). There were domestic slaves, agricultural slaves, and, in most advanced civilizations, public slaves who belonged to the temples or were under the authority of the administrative bureaucracies. Cynics might describe public slavery as an early version of contemporary American state and local government "workfare" schemes. Treatment of slaves varied enormously from humane standards and protective codes to the most severe brutality, but the practice was indifferent to and unaware of race throughout the ancient and medieval world. The slave trade carried no specific racial consciousness, as the trade took in people of every hue and type in the world. The English word *slave* itself comes from "Slav," which described the trade in people from that part of Central Europe, and which continued oblivious to race throughout the ancient and medieval world. Trade connected traditional China, India, Persia, Africa, and the Mediterranean world and brought exotic goods and unfamiliar people together for several thousand years. Such overland routes as the fabled "Silk Roads" of the first century B.C.E. and harbors wherever ships could venture kept up an uneven rising and falling pattern of commercial activity without consciousness of race.

Warfare and murderous conquest were also quite well known throughout the ancient and medieval eras, and often resulted in the captivity, enslavement, and transportation of populations, but without a racist code. The conqueror invariably adopted an arrogant, self-justifying attitude and sometimes went to the trouble of rationalizing the conquest as virtuous. As in the *Iliad,* heroic battles received heroic explanations. Servants, slaves, and soldiers involuntarily internalized the cultural codes, devoted themselves to those who led them, and came emotionally to accept the labor and losses as they celebrated the victories. Rebellions, uprisings, treason, and desertions took place when the authorities no longer held the emotional loyalty of those around them or, as the Chinese put it, when they had "lost the mandate of heaven." Many banners were unfurled, songs sung, and graves dug, but racial purity was not any part of the explanation for war in the ancient or medieval world.

The two great new influences in the Mediterranean world in the era following the heights and long decline of the Roman Empire were Christianity and Islam. Both carried on the universalized view of humankind from the Hellenistic age and Roman Imperial era, and both borrowed from the administrative and organizational accomplishments of their surroundings. The Moslem world preserved a large part of the scientific, mathematical, and commercial tradition of antiquity. Christianity, once it had become the established faith of the disintegrating empire, kept alive parts of the Roman administrative structure for its organizational form along with the use of Latin. The estate system of a bonded peasantry was merged with the warrior hierarchy of the recently Christianized former tribal preliterate groups to produce a new feudal system that gradually became clearly defined by the ninth century.

Some attempt has been made by sociologists and students of the history of religion to locate the beginnings of modern racism in the monotheism and dichotomous structure of Christianity as it found expression in the Middle Ages. The world of Islam, though similarly monotheistic and no less concerned with notions of good and evil, has not been found to contain the seeds of modern racism. The French sociologist Roger Bastide argued in an essay, "Color, Racism, and Christianity," that Christianity was responsible for bringing the black/white color code into Western consciousness. "White," Bastide claimed, "is used to express the pure, while black expresses the diabolical." Further, he states, "The conflict between Christ and Satan, the spiritual and the carnal, good and evil come finally to be expressed by the conflict between the white and black" (pp. 35–45 in Franklin, ed., *Color and Race*). This division of good and evil was extended to define the European (white) community in contrast to the foreign (nonwhite) outsiders, and became the theoretical basis for the concept of Self/Other that has been favored by some sociologists to describe the foundation for racism when Europeans got around to their overseas meetings with non-Europeans. The theory falls short when it comes to explaining the racination of Irish Christians by English Christians, "white" Jews by "white" Germans, Armenians by Turks, and numerous other cases, but it encompasses most of the age of imperialism.

Whiteness and blackness were around, of course, for a long time, and as images common to many cultures, with lightness holding the advantage over darkness. Robert Miles, an English sociologist, devotes a section of his book *Racism* to the medieval Christian "discourse on the Other as a phenotypic and cultural deviant from a norm which was established by the represented characteristics of European writers. This Other took a plurality of monstrous forms" (pp. 16–17). The depiction of this imagined savage, Other, varied with the imagination of the writer. Most conjured up a hairy, nude, club-toting, and sexually aggressive male, sometimes, but not always, darkly hued. He is not a good Christian. Traditional Japanese culture depicted outsiders almost identically, as did the Chinese, Greeks, and many other civilized (literate) cultures. Prejudices drawn from the dangers that might arise from the unfamiliar always create fearsome images. These images take on antithetical forms from the dominant and customary ones. The evils of the outsider are portrayed in stark contrast to the notions of virtuous behavior of those on the inside. Although prejudices abound, they are not a significant force until they are made into formal codes as law. No medieval Christian canon law or code established color or human type as a basis for discrimination. No papal encyclical of that era declares the existence of race. No monastic order put forward a religious code barring Christian salvation to groups or categories of human beings based on their physical type. It is doubtful if any of the various heresies of the Middle Ages ever advanced any racial notion of salvation or code relating to it in any way. Even though anti-Semitism was a powerful prejudice, and showed itself to be murderous, it was not racist during the Crusades.

The Islamic faith spread quickly throughout the Mediterranean world in the century following the death of its founder, Muhammad, in 632. Its vigor made it the most dynamic influence in the region and would bring it ultimately into conflict with European Christianity, an entity that only defined itself in the eighth century by its resistance to the Islamic worldview.[11] That view also omitted any concept of racial or physical qualification for inclusion and was carried by its faithful to converts throughout the Middle East, Africa, and Asia for centuries. When the Seljuk Turks, followers of the Prophet, captured the city of Jerusalem in 1071, they withdrew the more tolerant practices of their Moslem predecessors toward those Christians who made pilgrimages to this Holy Land of all three prominent faiths of the Mediterranean world. In 1087, encouraged by Pope Victor III, soldiers of Christ and the church from two dynamic Italian trading cities attacked the north African Moslem town of Mahdia. Unlike Venice and Amalfi, Genoa and Pisa had been unwilling to conclude commercial agreements with enemies of their Christian faith. After they massacred the despised "priests of Mahomet," they signed "an advantageous treaty of commerce."[12] The great cathedral of Pisa, constructed soon after this of African stone and marble, magnificently represents both their religious fervor and commercial wealth. Just a few years later, in 1095, Pope Urban II called for a great crusade to secure the beleaguered territories of the Holy Lands. Both Pisa and Genoa joined in with troops and supplies.

With the official sanction given to attack enemies of their faith, the Crusaders prompted a murderous rampage against Jews anywhere in their path, from Rouen in France throughout the entire Rhine Valley, and finally in Prague. One chronicler of the Rouen massacre, Guibert de Nogent, reported: "We desire to go and fight God's enemies in the East; but we have before our eyes certain Jews, a race more inimical to God than any other; this is to start the whole affair backward."[13] Before they left Europe, the Crusaders had sparked the massacre, mostly by mob action, of about 10,000 noncombatant Jews who refused conversion.[14] But this was no racist attack. Many Jews chose baptism and were spared. Some were baptized and later repudiated it. Some were later freed of the coercive baptism by local religious or civil authorities who intervened to protect them in spite of the official church doctrine that sanctioned it.[15] Racism does not accept conversion. It is the physical rejection of the humanity of the despised people. This was a religious slaughter without racial implications, not completely dissimilar to the Albigensian Crusade of 1208, where Christians massacred Christians.

The Moslem world was emphatically multihued. It included, and includes today, people of every description. Their artists reveal people of various hues across the social spectrum from servant and sailor to warrior chieftain and nobleman. Spanish Christian artists depicted the variety of shades of their Moslem counterparts in elaborate, colorful, realistic drawings and miniatures of the thirteenth century. They are shown as gentlemen playing chess, soldiers in combat, and sailors and fishermen.[16] Theirs was the dominant culture throughout the early Middle Ages, but no racism is discernible in the Koran or in any sacred writings, decrees, or practices. Their merchants and scientists were at the forefront of commerce and advanced learning for centuries and never assumed that there was a racially constructed hierarchy of humanity. Social and cultural life were highly patriarchal, but a wide berth was given to secular activity and included pastoral, agricultural, and urban forms of organization. Christian Europe learned about mathematics, navigation, and medicine from their Islamic neighbors; nationalism and racism they developed themselves as the Middle Ages gradually waned.

The Crusades were an important part of the revival of trade and commercial activity in Europe and the Mediterranean that upset the unsteady balance of cultural and power relationships in the world forever. New products were introduced. Crusaders learned about refined sugar, began to supervise its production, and took control over production centers. By the end of the Crusades, Venetian merchants had developed sugar production centers near Tyre, on Crete, and on Cyprus to gratify a growing market's sweet tooth.[17] Trade stimulated the rapid growth of commercial centers, rich city-states, and new banking, commercial, accounting, and insurance practices. Moslem and Jewish merchants and money lenders found more serious competition from ambitious Christians in the growing urban commercial centers of the Mediterranean and Europe. The most important products that came from the increasing prosperity of the towns were the new institutions and new social formations that began to construct new lines of authority. These legally structured practices ultimately undermined the old feudal order and became the foundation for the nation-state as a society and economy legally distinct from all others, and the concept of race, of a people made, by the nation, legally and physically distinct from others within its domains.

Secular Institutions, Laws, and Boundaries

The towns came under the feudal jurisdiction of the seignorial system, but had needs that could not be met by its codes and practices. In the eleventh century, magistrates or "consuls" began to take on more municipal authority. A communal court was formed in 1068 in Lucca, the busy walled market town near Pisa. Milan had elected consuls who met and served annual terms, unlike the lifetime and often inherited offices of the feudal order. Marseilles, Arles, and Nimes followed, with similar parallel developments spreading quickly throughout the busy trading towns of northern France and Flanders. An uprising led by rich merchants formed a civil government known as a commune in Cambrai in 1077, a movement that moved quickly through France with the support of the monarchy and was imitated throughout Europe.[18] Guilds and hanses were autonomous corporations of merchants and manufacturers that were independent of feudal authority. They established their own treasuries, meeting houses called *Gildhales,* and took on public duties that included street maintenance, defense, and the construction of fortifications. Guilds in Flanders initiated complete city autonomy in the eleventh century. The new, nonfeudal burghers, or middle class, acquired legal status as the towns gained simple legal charters. Land itself changed in town. It became ground for building. City-held land became a "free hold" and could be transferred, sold, or mortgaged, or serve as security for debt. A popular German proverb of the period advised that *Die stadtluft macht frei,* or "city air makes one free," since living in town for more than a year ended serfdom. Feudal restrictions on business activity such as market tolls were done away with, and laws quite distinct from church and Roman canon regarding liens, debts, marriage, and business practices changed in the city. New tax systems, courts, and administrative councils became city governments.[19] Race and nation grew from these practical and secular legal beginnings.

Highs and Lows of the Middle Ages

There did not seem to be any losers from the growing prosperity and urbanization trend. Feudal monarchs gained new wealth and increased their status over their aristocracies in England and France. Italian city-states boomed. Genoa backed the successful Byzantine restoration of Constantinople in 1261, and their merchants were, along with those of Venice, dominant there for most of the next 200 years. Genoa extended its influence throughout the area of the Black Sea, the Caspian Sea, northern Persia, southern Russia, and Turkestan.[20] Banking and insurance were officially sanctioned after the Fourth Lateran Council of 1215, when, under the leadership of the most highly esteemed Pope Innocent III, a distinction was made between usury and rent. Within a century, the church of Rome became the most powerful banking center in the world. Magnificent cathedrals are one of the soaring achievements of the religious and worldly harmony and success of this era. This balance is extolled philosophically and theologically in the works of Saint Thomas Aquinas. He maintained that faith and reason constituted two harmonious realms that complemented one another; both were the gifts of God, but reason had its own autonomy. Confident in its faith, prosperous as never before, Europe entered a period described in *The Rise of the West* by William H. McNeill, "when the confluent energies of the Church and of the rising towns provided a basis for eager and systematic appropriation of suitable elements from the high civilizations of Islam and Byzantium, together with adaptation of this inheritance to the special conditions and interests of the West" (p. 547). This great century of the rise of trade and the flowering of medieval high culture had within it, nonetheless, the seeds and potential for great setbacks and conflict, as if to confirm the grim observation of Herodotus: "in this world nobody remains prosperous for long" (p. 15).

Plague, warfare, religious schism, conflict between church and burgher, and the rising power in the East of the Ottoman Turkish Empire represented a drastic setback and disruption of the growth in population, travel, trade, and prosperity that lasted until the first quarter of the fourteenth century in Europe. The Black Death, or bubonic plague, devastated entire cities and returned again and again to decimate the populations of Europe and Asia for over a century. The Hundred Years' War between the rival feudal kingdoms of England and France included destructive, though often romantically depicted, civil wars in both countries. Most historians agree that the emergence of the modern nation-state was delayed in those countries because of that war. The church was divided into rival factions that claimed the papacy, and doubt and insecurity were cast among the faithful everywhere. Barbara Tuchman's *A Distant Mirror* (1978) finds in the terrible losses of the fourteenth and early fifteenth centuries the only era in Western history to compare, albeit without racism, with the human devastation of our own time. The institutions that recovered most quickly were urban and commercial, though their populations had suffered the greatest losses in the time of epidemic disease. The universal authority of the church would never be what it had been under the leadership of Innocent III, though it enjoyed lavish prosperity during the Renaissance and renewed its powerful position until the challenge of the Protestant Reformation. On the northern and western fringes of Europe, adventurous merchants and explorers sought to circumvent Turkish restrictions and monopolies and find their own way to the markets of the East. Recovery in the fifteenth century also brought into existence the beginning of the nation-state and the first distinctive manifestation of its corollary cultural form of identity, racism.

Travelers, Explorers, and Conquerors

European understanding of others outside their trade routes limited Europe to the sketchy accounts of Arab travelers in Africa, epic sagas of Norse voyages, and some good accounts of East Asia. Most Europeans, of course, never left the village or town where they were born. Interest in the larger world was found mainly in the active commercial and maritime centers. The Mongol conquest of China and Central Asia brought to power a more tolerant power that was interested in trade. Their authority assured the safety of travelers under their protection, and a few Europeans made the overland voyage in the prosperous era prior to the Black Death. The best informed and most influential account of Asia from this era is the *Travels* of Marco Polo. His closeness to power as a trusted favorite of the ruling Kublai Kahn gave him an extraordinary vantage point for his careful observations. His detailed descriptions are unadorned with the exaggerated and spurious tales that other popular writers employed. *Travels* was widely copied and was still considered the best account of East Asia in the time of Christopher Columbus, who owned his own printed copy. Prince Henry of Portugal had a manuscript copy; the first printed version was done at Gouda in 1483.[21] Polo described the places he visited and heard about, including the Arab world, Persia, Japan, Sumatra, and East Africa down to Zanzibar. He told of the splendors he had seen, the customs of people, of unusual and unknown products like paper money, coal, and asbestos. He introduced new and exotic foods. Marco Polo expressed an attitude of wonder and a feeling of respect for the unusual qualities of the people and cultures about which he wrote. There is nothing condescending, patronizing, or racially conscious in his writing. He shared the view of his contemporaries that placed his own culture and civilization on a relatively equal plane with those he described. The Other was not inherently inferior or threatening to his European Self. In this regard he was not alone, though his work stood out for its highly regarded credibility. Many travel writers told sensational tales of dog-headed men and other wonders they had seen or heard about, but they, too, along with the more academic geographers and cartographers who followed, had no sense of European superiority as physical or behavioral. Most educated people at the end of the Middle Ages believed that the ancient world, long before their time, had been "more elegant in behavior and expression, more sagacious in the conduct of affairs," than their own.[22]

A century later, another Venetian merchant traveler, Niccolò de Conti, became famous for accounts of a series of voyages that lasted twenty-five years. Conti traveled to the Middle East, where he learned Arabic. He journeyed to Mesopotamia and Persia, where he also studied the languages, and to India, where he married and raised a family of four. He went on to the East Indies, Sumatra, and the Malay Peninsula. On a subsequent voyage he reached Java, his point farthest east, where he stayed nine months. He described the rich fauna of Burma, as well as rhinoceroses, pythons, and elephant hunting. He repeated the medieval myth of Prestor John, the legendary Christian priest and monarch of an Asian or African utopian realm, in his first reports. The story of Prestor John entered racial mythology a century and a half later, along with the concept itself. When Conti told his full story to Poggio Bracciolini, a church official, as penance for his Indian marriage and renunciation of Christianity during his travels, he was more restrained.[23] His fourteenth-century account of East Asia remained the best for many decades through the era of European exploration.

There are many other, less reliable travel accounts and records of pilgrimages during the late Middle Ages that achieved notoriety. They frequently included bizarre accounts of behaviors and peculiar cultural traits, including savagery and cannibalism. Their own prejudices and morality are usually quite obvious, but there is no consciousness or expression of racial categories or hierarchies in the records or tales told by these travelers. Nor are any of them emissaries or representatives of any nation, nor do they identify themselves as having a nation. Race and nation, unlike anti-Semitism, still awaited their formalized entry into human events and discourse.

Jews Before Racism

Jews lived in scattered communities throughout the vastness of the Roman Empire. Suspicion and hostility toward them focused on their unwillingness to accept the authority of the gods of their sovereign, and they were brutalized without mercy by the Crusades. As merchants and moneylenders, they had always lived apart from the feudal system in towns and villages throughout Europe. Their experience and familiarity with trade and the commercial relationships built on trust that many of them maintained from the ancient world helped, along with their Moslem counterparts, in the revival of European medieval prosperity. Many Jews traveled as itinerant merchants, artisans, or moneylenders with the fairs of that era. They maintained the study of ancient texts, and many of them were among the most learned among those non-Jews with whom they lived. Besides the vernacular languages of everyday life, many knew Hebrew and Latin and owned valuable collections of books. They were subject to hostile rumors, prejudice, and suspicion. The credulity of a population for stories of witchcraft was no less vulnerable to tales of ritual murder of Christian children, especially when such a story might cancel a debt or pay back a personal grudge. In an age when the dominant emotional authority centers were religious figures, suspicious of the growing importance of nonfeudal urbanity, it is no surprise to consider that the transference of social or cultural anxiety would be to an alien religious group or faith. Every time a Crusade was launched, Jews were attacked and massacres took place. Plans for the Fourth Crusade and the coronation of Richard I sparked a rumor in England that all Jews were to be killed, and riots spread throughout the countryside.[24] All Jews were officially expelled from England in 1290 during the reign of Edward I. Insofar as the creation of an English Christian national identity was advanced by this act, it can be considered a preracist formation. Jews, however, were not yet a race, England not yet a nation. Those who converted to Christianity were always welcomed in England, the "pure state" of medieval anti-Semitism.[25] Shylock's daughter is fully accepted by the community after her conversion. A school for converts was established in Bristol in 1154, and a royal foundation for converts, a *domus conversorum,* was established in 1234 and continued attracting European émigré members for many years.[26]

The Irish Before Racism

More ominous for the future of English racism was the attempted feudal conquest of Ireland from 1166 to 1318. This was part of the clerical reform movement coming from Rome, which, by then, had gained the support of the Norman monarchy in England. Simony, the sale of church offices, feudal nonclerical control over church positions, clerical marriages, and the keeping of concubines were under attack by Rome, and the Irish church was vulnerable. Worse yet, Ireland had failed to participate in the first and second Crusades, unlike the loyal Norman rulers of England. Cloaked in religious piety, the growing English population also sought to increase its landholdings abroad and to extend the English practices of law and government. The provisions of the Magna Carta were extended to Ireland after 1215, as was the English legal code. The civil and criminal court system and the government departments in Ireland where English feudal lords held estates were modeled from the English practice. The area in Ireland controlled completely by the English had a parliament in which the bishops, abbots, and feudal lords sat in the upper house. Knights from the counties and burgesses from the towns and cities sat in the lower house, as in England. Some long-established and virtually independent English barons in Ireland took up arms with native Irish princes against this expansion of English rule in 1315.[27] The English did succeed in preventing their rival Scottish lords from gaining a foothold in Ireland by defeating the forces of Edward Bruce at Faughart in 1318. Only the coming of the Hundred Years' War and the ensuing civil struggles in England from 1337 to 1453 gave Ireland respite from the more aggressive English campaigns of the future. When the struggle revived under King Henry VIII, England was an emergent nation, not a feudal kingdom, and the Irish became a tumescent race in the eyes of their would-be conquerors.

Renaissance Humanism

It is in the stirrings of modern secular institutions and practices that the double helix of race and nation emerge. The prosperity and beauty of Renaissance city-states depended on the merchants and bankers who fueled it as well as the artists who adorned it and the architects who built it. Religious authorities were partners in the new age, but soon found loyalties shifting away from their influence and control. New social codes of conduct and the increase in individual responsibility drawn from the authority of secular business practices penetrated religious morality and contributed to the Protestant Reformation and the Counter-Reformation within the church.

Beautiful cities were adorned with both the magnificent churches and cathedrals of a prosperous age and the splendid palaces of merchant princes and bankers. The cities were also engaged in tremendous struggles for power among themselves, an ordeal that eventually saw the transfer of European power to nation-states in the sixteenth century. In Machiavelli's Florence, one of the gems of Renaissance brilliance, there was an uneasy balance maintained by Lorenzo the Magnificent between the five major centers of Italian power: the Kingdom of Naples, Rome and the papal state, Venice, Florence, and Milan. Machiavelli was banished from his beloved Florence as control over Italy became an international battle and the city-state was forced to give way in the sixteenth century to the nation-state as the new agency of political power in Europe. In its fascination with humanism and secular art, the Italian Renaissance remained a cultural inspiration for all the ages, but it was an aesthetic vision of life formed prior to the birth of the nation and the concept of race. No racially disparaging art or sculpture is characteristic of this period; indeed, many works depict African royalty or aristocracy as analogous with contemporary Europeans. The Three Wise Men of the East are most often depicted in paintings that include a darkly hued and well-dressed African, known as Balthazar, as part of the adoring Magi in attendance at the birth of Christ. Two good examples of this are by Hans Memling (*Floreins Epiphany*) and Albrecht Dürer (*Adoration of the Magi*). Universal human wonder and recognition of a Messiah precede racial and national categories of power in the great works of this age.

Portugal and Spain Step Out

The advantages of a unified nation over the city-state or traditional feudal kingdom were not yet recognized in the fifteenth century in spite of early signs visible to us now through the brilliant clarity of historical hindsight. When, in 1415, King John I of Portugal took his twenty-one-year-old son Henry along with him on a successful expedition against the overseas Moslem port of Ceuta on the northern tip of Morocco, they hardly could have suspected they were helping to launch the modern world. Before the end of the century, their nation would command a thassalocracy, the greatest maritime and commercial empire in the world. No dynastic or feudal power had ever commanded so far-flung an empire. In Ceuta, which Portugal retained, the impressionable young prince heard wondrous tales of caravan routes from nearby Tunis to the great African city of Timbuktu, of gold and ivory, and stories of the fabled Indies. By keeping the North African city under their rule, they began to define themselves not only as Christians in search of the legendary Prester John, or Crusaders, but as Portuguese conquerors. They were half-English princes, "inspired mainly by crusading ardor to deal a blow at the Infidel."[28] Now they were something else, something new. Only city-states such as Venice or Genoa had great navies before this. The Portuguese had made a unified feudal kingdom with a navy capable of oceanic expeditions, something no one else in the world could claim. Now they had a bridgehead for further African and global conquests that required no pope or feudal land claim to press them forward. Their goals defined their precocious nation-state.

Shortly after the conquest of Ceuta and its reconquest in 1418, Prince Henry established himself at Sagres as governor of the Algarve in the southernmost quarter of Portugal. He created a community of cosmologists, navigation experts, and cartographers to assist in pushing ahead with the explorations that would earn him his nickname, Henry the Navigator, and his kingdom an empire. Over the next twenty years, the Portuguese colonized the island of Madeira, explored the Azores, began an ultimately unsuccessful struggle with Spain for the Canary Islands, and started, in earnest, the exploration down the African coast that would culminate with the voyage of Bartholomeu Dias around the Cape of Good Hope into the Indian Ocean in 1487. Over the course of this remarkable undertaking, motives gradually shifted from traditional to modern. Madeira was found to be suitable for the growing of Malvoisie grapes, brought in from the island of Crete, from which Malmsey wine would guarantee future prosperity. The price of cane sugar was rising. Its cultivation was tried on Madeira, imported there from Sicily, and it was cultivated with slave labor and made into refined sugar in a water mill built there in 1452.[29] From the Rio do Ouro a landing party returned to their Portuguese ship with a small group of captured African native slaves, the beginning of a profitable trading enterprise that increased into the thousands within a few years. When this first group of captives reached Portugal, they were baptized as Christians, provided with some education, and absorbed into the general population. No code or law regarding race was present, but a "chaotic, cutthroat traffic resulted" that was only regularized when Prince Henry constructed a fort, or factory (*feitoria*), at Arguin in 1445, the first European settlement on the coast of west Africa.[30] The Arguin trading station became a model or prototype that was later adopted and modified by the Dutch, French, and English. At Arguin, "European textiles, hardware, hides, looking glass, etc. were bartered for gold dust, Negro slaves, gumlac, civet, and a pepper-like spice called malagueta, or 'grains of paradise.'"[31] While trade increased and drew more adventurers and merchants into the fold, the Portuguese officially maintained their feudal objectives of serving their faith. Now their government also extended its authority over trade in a colonial setting and promoted mercantile relationships in profitable products. Venice and some other ancient and medieval city-states, along with empires both living and dead, had governed overseas territories, but this was something new.

From their travels and experiences, the Portuguese were aware of no particular characteristics or behaviors associated with race in this period. They did observe great distinctions of culture among the Africans they saw and about whom they heard from others that ranged from mythic splendor to base primitivism. As they proceeded down the African coast and into the interior whenever a river passage beckoned, they made no laws or new practices built on any racial theory or concept. Not yet. Civil strife at home and the death of Henry the Navigator at Sagres in November 1460 made for long pauses in their explorations, but they soon passed Cape Verde and entered the Ivory and Gold coasts of southern Guinea, and by 1475 began to reap great profits from west African pepper, ivory, gold, and slaves. War with the Spanish Kingdom of Castile slowed their movement again, but the Treaty of Alcaçovas gave control of all Guinea to Portugal. The disputed Canaries went to the Spaniards.[32] Conflict between two European powers for control of rich overseas colonial properties stretched the feudal order's capabilities, especially after the first voyage of Columbus. Pope Alexander VI stepped in and divided the world in half in a proclamation, or Bull, in 1492 that was agreed to by the rulers of Spain and Portugal only when they signed, with some changes, the Treaty of Tordesillas in 1494. Elmina ("The Mine") was fortified to defend Portuguese Guinea, and interior explorations to the fabled centers of Timbuktu and Sierra Leone were carried out in the 1480s. The Portuguese established a Christian Kingdom of the Congo in what is now northern Angola under the authority of a Portuguese-educated native chief named Cacuta, who was baptized Jao da Silva.

The Portuguese were satisfied to treat these kings of the Congo "as allies and not as vassals; and to convert them and their subjects to Christianity by the dispatch of missionaries to the Congo and by educating selected Congolese youths at the monastery of St. Eloi and elsewhere at Lisbon."[33] The government sent priests and friars to staff the missions, as well as skilled workers and artisans, including bricklayers and masons, blacksmiths, and skilled agricultural laborers. Two German printers emigrated with their press to go to work in the kingdom of the Congo. A group of European women went there to instruct the local women in the domestic arts as then current in Portugal, and a Congolese prince educated in Europe was later formally consecrated bishop of Utica by an uncomfortable pope at the king of Portugal's insistence in 1518.[34] This amazing project broke down under the twin burdens of the growing slave trade and Portugal's vast commitments in other continents after the death of Dom Jao's successor, Dom

Affonso, in 1540. The age of the nation-state and its counterpart in racism made anything like it in the future impossible. In 1500 Portuguese influence had not yet reached its peak. The competition and decline that resulted from the intervention of other powers was still a generation away.

The government imposed no restrictions on Portuguese and African interrelationships in this first century of contact. Conversion to Christianity was expected to grant rough medieval equality, certainly in the eyes of the church, to anyone. The Portuguese have used this early period's muteness on the issue to contend that their empire was free of racism, in spite of its development within a much more complex system of categories, especially in Brazil, later on. Ambitious fifteenth-century adventurers and speculators routinely went upriver to trade, started families, and merged with the local population without any objection from the Crown as long as they paid their taxes. Punishment for tax evasion, a serious offense, by these *tango-maos* or *lancados* was the seldom-enforced death penalty. Beyond the effective jurisdiction of the Portuguese government, these early frontiersmen made their language the standard for the coastal region of Guinea for centuries, and their influence is still present today.[35] After Dias made his successful passage into the Indian Ocean in 1487, the Portuguese entered the rich trading region of East Africa, the Persian Gulf, India, and East Asia and, combined with their Brazilian empire, enjoyed a brief era of early sixteenth-century supremacy, with one historic foot planted in the feudal past and another forcefully stepping into the mercantile future. With no restrictions on the intellectual life of Jews at home or the social life of Portuguese and Africans abroad, they made the most of the labor of a severely limited population. Finally, they were overextended in their ability to administer their vast empire and overpowered by their much larger neighbor and rival.

Spain had just moved seriously into the global arena after the unification of their kingdom following the marital merger of the two rival households of Aragon and Castile in 1469. Ferdinand and Isabella made Spain the largest unified kingdom in Europe after the fall of Granada, the last Moslem stronghold there, in the same year as the famous first voyage of Christopher Columbus, 1492. The year was significant for two other reasons that would contribute to the transformation of this large feudal kingdom into a nation. The victory over Islam coincided with the forced conversion to Christianity or expulsion of the Jews and Moslems from Spain, a cheap internal crusade, one that would lead a few years later to suspicions about the sincerity of these "New Christians." Rumors circulated about secret Jewish religious rituals and observances. By the time of Philip II in the next century, *limpieza de sangre,* or racially tinged religious codes, excluded the converted from government, university, or clerical positions. Purification of the realm in war and by force of royal authority was a step in the direction of establishing the nation as well. One useful definition of nationalism by one of its most respected scholars calls it an "ideological movement aiming to attain or maintain autonomy, unity and identity for a social group which is deemed to constitute a nation."[36] The same might easily be said to define racism and race as well.

The year 1492 also marked the publication of the Spanish grammar of Antonio de Nebrija, the first systematic grammar of a modern European language. Nebrija's Introduction included the statement, "language has always been the companion of empire."[37] Political, religious, and linguistic unity was the foundation for a Spanish feudal national empire built by conquest on the discoveries of a generation of explorers led by the Genoese, Columbus.

Toward Modernity

The last decade of the fifteenth century was still one of discovery for an older European world system. Venetian and Flemish printers had just begun to make classical Greek and Roman literary and historical works more widely available to readers with the use of movable type that revolutionized the expansion of information. Pliny the Elder's *Natural History* was printed and widely read. In it he developed crude categories of human beings, including the dog-headed men story passed on uncritically from Herodotus and kept going by naive travelers. Popular books, travel literature, and scientific discoveries represented an explosion in knowledge unmatched in history until, perhaps, our own electronic age. One of these books was a treatise, *De Arithmetica*, published in 1496 by an Italian named Luca Pacioli, who showed that with the recent adoption of the use of Arabic numbers and the positional decimal system, double-entry bookkeeping was possible. Pacioli's neat division of business transactions into debits and credits was not unknown. It had been in use in Florence since the late thirteenth century and was introduced into Augsbug financial practice by the prominent sixteenth-century banker Joseph Fugger. Now in print, the new method brought speed and efficiency to merchants who wanted to know where they stood, and the practice caught on throughout Europe.[38] Profit and loss were never far from the thinking of royal and clerical authorities, either. The legal geographic and human divisions of nations and races accompanied double-entry bookkeeping and bills of exchange as harbingers of modernity in the early sixteenth century.

Poor Columbus, he never brought back enough gold. It troubled him and the authorities with whom he dealt until the end of his life. He appears to have been quite sincere in his expression of the well-known objectives of serving God and finding gold for the early Spanish Empire. The gold was to be used, he believed, to finance the continued struggle against the Moslem world, a project made more urgent after the fall of Constantinople to the Ottoman Turks in 1453. The search for alternative trade routes to the fabled markets of the Far East stimulated exploratory ventures by the other feudal kingdoms able to do it, including, before the end of the century, a new player, the United Netherlands or Dutch Republic.

The ancient and medieval European and world system was about to be upset in a most dramatic fashion. The old balance or rough equity in development among the great civilizations began to crumble in just a few decades. In 1500 there were no Protestants. There was a unified, powerful church about to construct some of its finest monuments. Heresies were still dealt with effectively, wholesale or retail. There were no bloodied Conquistadors, no transplanted Africans enslaved on plantations in faraway hemispheres by European masters. There was no Bourse or stock exchange that reduced or enlarged human enterprises to the impersonal, the abstract. No feudal kingdom, great or small, had made a national bank, and there were no nations or races. Words such as *country, commonwealth, empire,* or *nation* did not appear in the 1499 edition of the then current standard dictionary, the *Promptorium Parvulorium,* a work that had begun in 1440.[39] Over the course of the next forty years, all these practices and institutions emerged to alter and upset the balance in the course of human history. The Turks joined the other great civilizations and cultures in the world as they gave way to the aggressive advance of the newly forming European national and racial state system.

Chapter 3

The European Discovery of Race and Nation, 1500–1650

The Face of Modernity

Most of the foundations of what is now fashionably called "modernity" can be located in the energetic, conflict-filled era of religious upheaval and cultural dynamism that began in the flowering of the Italian Renaissance after about 1500 and ended with the Thirty Years' War of 1618–48. All the great European nation-states had their origins in this era, and so did the racism that grew up entwined with them. Vast empires built with the blood of conquest and the labor of slaves brought forth unimaginable wealth and unresolved human consequences that remained as permanent troubling legacies. From County Antrim in Ireland to East Timor and Virginia, and wherever aggressive nation-states were formed, conquest and conflict set in motion human dramas that are still being played out. New institutional practices opened up spectacular vistas of opportunity, especially for the ascendant nonfeudal burghers and businessmen who mastered them. A great struggle for cultural authority, global hegemony, and political sovereignty was unleashed that has roiled the history of the next 500 years. The formation of personal and collective identity through cultural, geographic, ideological, religious, or simply political circumstances has made for confusing and inconsistent human groupings. To paraphrase the great bard of this era: some were made what they are, some became what they are, and some have had what they are thrust upon them. Race and nation stand out as the most dynamic examples of this great transformation to modernity.

The discussion to follow seeks to demonstrate the ways that early travel, trade, exploration, and religious zeal gave way to conquest, colonization, massacre, and dehumanization in a process of ruthless amoral competition. As rival cultural and political units formed in conflict with others, they called into existence new institutions and modified old ones. The successful were better able to meet new practical challenges, and for a time defied or upset traditional hegemonic ideologies and practices. Martin Luther's defiance of the church of Rome at Worms in 1521 comes to mind. The new or modified institutions made rules, codes, laws, and practices that set up new or changed hierarchies of power. New incentives and rewards altered relationships to power and authority. "Here I stand," proclaimed Luther the modern man, in defiance of an abstract universal power. It is not the church; it is the individual who is now at the center. Changed identity meant new images of the ideal self and community, about individual and collective images of perfection or purity. The advantages and beauties of new perceptions of virtue generated their opposite in the new understanding of perceived dangers of the vile and evil. A review of conquest and war, new institutions, changes in authority and identity, and collective love and vilification show us the beginning of our modern double helix of race and nation in this stormy era.

The travelers and explorers of the fifteenth century were usually only lightly armed, especially when they did not expect to meet European or Moslem rivals. That continued into the next century as well. It needs to be recalled that the explorers and traders who went into new and strange parts of the world did not take with them a consciousness of an inherent European cultural or racial superiority. In Africa, India, Indonesia, China, Japan, and America they recorded a vast and diverse array of reactions and impressions of peopie and cultures that ranged everywhere from awestruck to disgust. Early merchants often had to submit to dominant local codes and social practices in order to do business at the pleasure of their hosts. As the military and economic presence of Europeans increased abroad during this era, they became more confident and aggressive. The Japanese finally responded to the growing religious and commercial forcefulness of the Europeans by simply shutting them out in the 1630s. Some published collections of travelers' reports were only later edited to undercut the initial positive impressions of local people and emphasize the heroic image of the explorers. One of the most famous of these was an English collection edited by Richard Hakluyt in 1589–90 and expanded a decade later under the title *The Principal Navigations, Voyages, Traffiques and Discoveries of the English Nation.* The travelers included John Hawkins, Francis Drake, Sir Humphrey Gilbert, Ralph Fitch, and Martin Frobisher, and their vivid and detailed observations are of almost the full spectrum of humanity from the polar regions of the Arctic to India, Africa, and the Americas. Some people are depicted as living in a paradisical utopia. Such depictions anticipated the romantic idea of the "noble savage" more than a century before it was popularized by Jean Jacques Rousseau. Other people are described as savage, ugly brutes, some as cruel and fearsome, though the authors never record offenses committed against them. To be sure, many do not fare very well in the eyes of these Europeans; for example, Indian Brahmins are "a kind of crafty people, worse than the Jews."[1] It was only later, however, after conquest and colonization, that these naive prejudices and crude anthropological observations were replaced with more trenchant and consistently negative accounts.

Making the State: Spain and Portugal

Count Tilly, a famous general during the Thirty Years' War, observed that "war makes the state and the state makes war."[2] He was a man with clear insight into his times. While he was reflecting on the impact of the Thirty Years' War, he could just as easily have included the overseas battles and conquests as formative influences in setting human borders and making the new nation-states. At the start of the sixteenth century, the Portuguese planned a second voyage to India. Pero Alvares Cabral, a soldier-nobleman, not a sailor, in command of a larger and stronger fleet, made the first official European landing on the coast of Brazil before turning back to make a successful and profitable commercial voyage to India. The next voyage to India, once again under the command of Vasco da Gama, now with the title Admiral of India, set out in February 1502 with fifteen heavily armed ships, to be joined later by five more under the command of his brother. When he reached the southwestern Indian town of Calicut, he bombarded it, destroyed a fleet sent out to engage him, and, "to have the fear of God put into their hearts," brutalized the inhabitants with "a savagery too horrible to describe."[3] Before he left for home in February 1503, fully loaded with goods for trade, he established military-protected trading bases in two other Indian towns, Cochin and Cananore. This was just the beginning of the use of Portuguese force for the purpose of establishing an Asian maritime and commercial empire.

A war for control of the entire Asian commercial world was made the duty of the most outstanding naval figure of the day, Affonso d'Albuquerque, who followed up da Gama's work by fortifying the trading center at Cochin immediately after his departure. A Portuguese naval victory over a combined Egyptian and Indian fleet off Diu in 1509 under Francisco de Almeida gave them supremacy in the Indian Ocean for almost a century until they were challenged by the Dutch and English. Before he died in 1515, Albuquerque made the island of Goa a headquarters for his successful conquest of the major center for the rich spice trade and gateway to the South China Sea and Indonesia, Malacca, in 1511. His seizure of Hormuz just before his death gave Portugal control of the Persian Gulf. The commercial and military power of the Portuguese in Africa and Asia simultaneously flourished, and, when Portugal was joined with Spain from 1580 to 1640, it became a part of the first truly global empire. Two respected accounts of their treatment of the Muslim inhabitants who resisted their power confirm the use of "great terror" since they "not only sacked, burnt, and destroyed those settlements, but barbarously put all the inhabitants to the sword, without distinction of age or sex."[4]

The Portuguese church had uneven results in its efforts to make new converts among its colonial subjects and those people brought within the sphere of their commercial power. Soon the church began to mimic their more successful commercial counterparts by adopting the recommendation in the 1560s of a Jesuit missionary in Angola, Padre Francisco de Gouveia, S.J., who urged "preaching with the sword and rod of iron."[5] Father de Gouveia argued what became the general view of missionaries and laymen, that Africans were "barbarous savages who could not be converted by the methods of peaceful persuasion. Christianity in Angola," he wrote, "must be imposed by force."[6] It is probably impossible to know the number of Christians who found their faith rather than succumb to the sword or iron of their colonial masters. We will probably also never know the number of those Native Americans who were killed, massacred, or perished as a direct result of the Spanish conquests that immediately followed their exploration.

Before their explorers had finished their work in the Americas, Spanish semifeudal adventurers carried out massacres and depredations against both the most advanced and least sophisticated native people. The rapid and near-total destruction of the Arawakan-speaking Taino people of Hispaniola quickly led to the use of imported African slaves in royal gold mines. By 1516, African slaves were the mainstay of the sugar industry there, and a system of de facto racial slavery was in place. All the eyewitness accounts of the exploits of the *conquistadores* attest to their extreme savagery. Hernando Cortes, a man of refinement and Salamancan renaissance sensitivity, believed that the Aztec cities of Mexico he destroyed were as civilized as those of Spain, and the manners of the Aztec leaders more sophisticated than those of the Spaniards. Their crafts were comparable to the finest in the world: "So realistic in gold and silver that no smith in the world could have made better. Their city was indeed the most beautiful thing in the world."[7] After an initial setback, his smaller force, aided by local native allies, returned to capture and destroy the Aztec capital, Tenochtitlán, in 1521. One scholar estimates that the population of Mexico on the eve of its conquest was 25 million; by 1600, it had been reduced to 1 million: "if the word genocide has ever been applied to a situation with some accuracy, this is here the case."[8] Murder and massacre accounted for large numbers but only a small percentage of the total. Brutality and savage treatment of captives and slaves, especially in the mines, took even more victims. European diseases, in a population without much resistance, probably account for the largest number of fatalities. The harsh treatment came from the frenzy to get rich and the imposition of ruthless work quotas and schedules among enslaved Native Americans. By all accounts, including religious critics and *conquistadores,* there was shocking savagery, with entire village populations burned alive, cut to pieces, and hung up for display.

The Inca culture of Peru was similarly sophisticated and fared as badly a decade later under the command of two soldiers of fortune, Francisco Pizarro and Diego de Almagro, and a priest named Luque who advanced some of the seed money for the adventure. Immense quantities of wealth in bullion and sugar profits accelerated the changes in European business and society that were already under way. Throughout the Caribbean, Central America, and South America the people were devastated. Only the growth of absolutism at home that feared the increasing threat of an overseas powerful feudal aristocracy prompted a bloody and costly intervention by Spain to reign in the *conquistadores* and replace them with royal viceroys after about 1550. All the feudal monarchies took advantage of the wealth brought in by the conquerors or privateers who sailed under their banners and enjoyed the protection of their harbors. The absolutist nation-state gradually supplanted the feudal kingdoms of the sixteenth century as the main outlines of race and nation were being sketched out in slavery and conquest. Tudor England, though much smaller in size than Spain and without any faraway overseas empire in 1500, soon took its place among the leading powers. England carried out its conquest and subordination of a people closer to home than its Iberian counterparts.

Making Race: England and Ireland

The Norman conquerors of England are sometimes credited or blamed for lighting the original fires of European expansionism of the Crusades and the late Middle Ages. From about 1166 to the outbreak of the Hundred Years' War in 1337, Norman heirs to the English throne actively sought to expand their feudal power throughout Great Britain. By 1318, they had kept their rival Scottish barons out of Ireland and were in a favorable position to impose their legal, clerical, and judicial authority further. In some areas of Ireland the Norman English had complete control; in others it was mixed; and some were "beyond the Pale," under Gaelic chiefs.

War with France and internal civil war gave Ireland more than a hundred years of respite while its own language and culture were maintained in support of a subsequent nationalist tradition. The new Tudor king, Henry VII (r. 1485–1509), took a cautious approach toward Ireland; his hold on his own kingdom was not very steady. His marriage united the two houses of York and Lancaster and established an uneasy peace. He acted to suppress the feudal nobility and extend royal authority. He began the construction of a navy, made a successful commercial treaty with the Netherlands, and established claims in the Americas for England by sponsoring the exploratory voyages of the Cabots. He is known as the first mercantilist English king. In short, his reign launched the English nation. English law and parliamentary statutes in Ireland were reinforced wherever possible. Further aggressive action was left to his successors, all of whom vigorously and with much carnage carried out a conquest that lacked none of the ferocity of the Spanish or Portuguese abroad. A temporary English governing authority in Ireland, Thomas Howard, the earl of Surrey, reported to Henry VIII's chief minister, Cardinal Wolsey, in 1521 that Ireland would "never be brought to due obeisance, but only with compulsion and conquest."[9] When asked how that might be accomplished, the earl "indicated that what he had in mind was genocide—nothing less than the total extermination of the Irish race and their replacement by English settlers."[10] It was pointed out that his final solution would require a huge military campaign, one that England did not have and could not afford. Yet.

Henry VIII (r. 1509–47), busy as he was both personally and politically, chose another course with regard to Ireland, the policy known as "surrender and regrant."[11] Under this plan, Irish tribal chieftains or "degenerate English lords" whose land titles became tainted due to questions of loyalty during the War of the Roses could surrender their lands, pledge their loyalty to the Crown, and receive their same lands and titles in return. This policy had mixed success, though it extended and strengthened English legal authority in Ireland. It was left to his successors, particularly Elizabeth I (r. 1558–1603), James I (r. 1603–25), and English Lord Protector Cromwell (in authority 1650–58) to carry out the slaughter, starvation, removal, colonization, and racination of the people of Ireland.

Before the deliberate colonial conquest of Ireland, the views of the English feudal aristocracy toward the Gaelic Irish were similar to those they held toward their own subjects, servants, or most foreigners. The Irish were depicted as social inferiors, vulgar and lacking in the refinements of their betters. Conquest and colonization brought forth a more comprehensive ideology. One unsuccessful English scheme for a colony in Ireland in Ards of County Down was promoted with a great deal of publicity in 1571. This plan, hatched by one of Queen Elizabeth's close advisers, Sir Thomas Smith, was consciously modeled on the colonial aristocratic structures established by the Spanish in Mexico and Peru. The status of the Irish in the colony was to be as clear as day: "Every Irishman shall be forbidden to wear English apparel or weapon upon pain of death. That no Irishman, born of Irish race and brought up Irish, shall purchase land, bear office, be chosen of any jury or admitted witness in any real or personal action, nor be bound apprentice to any science or art that may endamage the Queen's Majesty's subjects hereafter."[12] The plan never was completed owing to a combination of inadequate funding and the murder of Sir Thomas Smith's son by his Irish servants. Plantations were established with mixed results in Leix and Offaly in 1556, in Ulster east of the Bann river beginning in 1565, and in Munster in 1585. Money and thinly stretched military resources continued to stand in the way, though resistance to the English was met with brutal repression. Sir Humphrey Gilbert was appointed military governor in Ulster after some resistance there. For his time, his actions, including the slaughter of men, women, and children and the lining of the walkways of his encampment with the heads of the day's kill for use *ad terrorem,* were considered to be of the utmost cruelty and inhumanity: "indeed the Norman lords were not known to have committed such atrocities in Ireland, and there is no evidence that systematic execution of non-combatants by martial law was practiced in any of the Tudor rebellions in England."[13]

Continued Irish resistance to the English plantation program in the early stages of the Tyrone War (1594–1603) led to the introduction of another conqueror's technique with racial implications, the starvation of an entire people. Edmund Spenser minted an English maxim in his "Breife Note of Ireland," when he advised his queen: "Until Ireland can be famished, it cannot be subdued."[14] This was not a completely original concept, but it became, along with huge increases in muskets, manpower, and money spent, a strategy "prosecuted without remission for three and a half years throughout three-fourths of the country."[15] Harvests were systematically destroyed and stored grain confiscated. Planting was stopped, and people were driven from their homes in winter. The Ulster stronghold was finally defeated, though Celtic resistance continued in Connaught and elsewhere in the country. The Irish again lost out in the course of rebellion and civil war, from 1642 to 1652, when Oliver Cromwell carried out what became the basic policy of English rule over Ireland for the next several centuries: deportation, starvation, military occupation, and the deliberate legal repression of Irish life and culture.

The Dutch Republic Emerges

At the outset of this era there were no Seven United Provinces of the Netherlands, no Dutch Republic, as they were called later. There certainly was no global Dutch maritime empire stretching from Brazil to Indonesia claimed by this tiny state built on a permanent struggle for control of territory with the North Sea. An eighty-year period of war from 1568 to 1648 helped form these Seven United Provinces as much as the Protestant Reformation or their extraordinary trading history in the northwestern corner of Europe. Dutch mercantile accomplishments are an exhilarating story of business and commercial innovations, and their extraordinary artistic legacy is but one example of the wealth and brilliance achieved by their sea power. There was no Dutch navy in 1568 and no grand-scale global explorations, but once the Dutch entered the world of competitive trade, their state was built on war and naval conquest as much or more than any other.

Dutch businessmen alone could not build trade in the valuable Spice Islands of East Asia, argued Jan Pietersz Coen, the founder of a trading company in Batavia, to his governing body, the *Heeren* XVII, the directors of the Dutch East India Company, in 1614. He needed the military backing of his government, and he knew they needed the wealth that trade provided: "We cannot carry on trade," he said, "without war nor war without trade."[16] Dutch leaders understood the need for the use of force and accepted as well the current practice of conquest. To secure a monopoly in the Spice Islands against rival Spanish, Portuguese, English, Chinese, or Indonesian Moslem traders, the Dutch were prepared to accept drastic measures, including the extermination, deportation, and enslavement of the entire population of the Banda Island group in the 1620s. When about 160 Netherlanders were killed in western Surinam in 1651, their military carried out a series of punitive campaigns against an entire people, resulting in the forcible transfer of more than 12,000 from their villages to resettlements in the Dutch colonies of Amboina and Manipa.[17] These attacks and forcible transfers of native populations became the standard in the Dutch colonies of Brazil and New Amsterdam, and for English colonizers in Virginia and New England during the same period. Revenge for Custer's Last Stand two and a half centuries later followed a similar pattern. During this era, the Dutch displaced the Portuguese from their position of supremacy in Asia and made inroads into Brazil, Africa, and especially Indonesia. They were the only Europeans permitted a trading station in Japan when the Tokugawa Shogunate closed down that warlord kingdom to all other outsiders after 1638.

France, Sweden, and Germany

France and Sweden took their places among those forming the new nation-state system in the seventeenth century, and both established overseas territorial claims, though neither built a sustainable colonial empire, and neither is noted for conquests or the development of mythologies or codes of racial practice at the time. Germany's move toward cultural nationalism was well under way at the outset of the Protestant Reformation, but the devastation of the Thirty Years' War was so severe that it stifled the emergence of a strong state for 200 years afterward. Almost completely landlocked and bound to the feudal structures of the Holy Roman Empire, Germany lacked the political unity and the facility to look abroad for conquest. In an age of prosperous expansionist sentiment, where could ambitious, late-medieval Central European burghers turn? The answer was found in a wave of anti-Semitic pogroms that took on a new and ominous turn. Mob attacks, beatings, and expulsions of Jews had sporadically continued throughout Europe in the era following the Crusades. Conversion to Christianity was the only recourse for those who desired full social inclusion. With the rise of a cultural and national self-consciousness, a newfound anti-Semitism emerged. The two old, traditional, hostile motifs—religion and money—were now joined by the idea of the Jew as a member of a foreign people, a harmful alien nation. Texts by clerical and lay authors of this new age of the inexpensive printing press show the merging of all these themes.[18] A wave of pogroms swept through Central Europe in the early 1500s sponsored by the nonclerical town burghers, the precursors of secular nonfeudal governments. In Regensburg, for example, in 1519, the city fathers proclaimed that its Jewish residents had four days' time in which to pack their belongings and leave town, all of them. As an alien people, Jews began to lose the option of conversion. Their property, businesses, synagogues all became subject to expropriation by legal authorities; they were being turned into a race, a people vulnerable to national conquest.

Warfare and the State

Feudal Europe and its agrarian counterparts all over the world were not free of conflict, confiscations, and the brutal destruction of life. After 1500, however, feudal objectives gradually gave way to national goals measured not solely in land or religious obsequies but increasingly in terms of the kind of real wealth that is measured in profits, gold, trade, and commodities of value. Religious authorities lost their supervisory oversight to the prerogatives and strategies of the state. The conquests of feudal adventurers and their armies give way to the authority of royal viceroys or governors and trading companies. National military structures became bound in loyalty to the authority of the nation-state and were paid through the taxes and profits gleaned by that state from successful conquests, expropriations, and trade. War made the state and the state made war.

Warfare in this turbulent era really does need its own book, and of course many books have been written. An outline of the military encounters of this era can provide a perspective here to help reflect on the place of war in the shaping of the concept of the double helix of modernity: race and nation. Feudal conflict over succession rights and religious wars prompted by the Protestant Reformation set the background for the use of massed deadly force; national goals emerged in the course of these conflicts and included colonial and mercantile ambitions. At the beginning, no wars could be considered strictly national, and there were no nations. At the end there were no strictly feudal wars in Europe, only national warfare with dynastic and feudal undertones. Great landlocked powers such as Russia, without navies, moved to the second rank, or found their modernization as nations delayed. Peasants and burghers in the towns were initially protected from, but became increasingly vulnerable to, the horrors of war in that juncture of religious and national zeal that was the Thirty Years' War. Throughout Europe, all the emerging nations, old kingdoms, and regnant Holy Roman Empire fought, prepared to fight, or rested and made new plans or alliances in between fights. Machiavelli's cynical realism may have seemed harsh to some at the opening of the era, but by the end few military or political leaders would have much to say to contradict him. As the Dutch conqueror J.P. Coen wrote to his superiors: "There is nothing in the world that gives one a better right, than power and force added to right."[19] If that is not a modernist statement, what is? Dutch Calvinists moved against Catholic Portuguese trading and colonial bases in Brazil, along the African coast, and throughout Asia during the Thirty Years' War. These Calvinists formed an anti-Portuguese alliance with the African Roman Catholic king of the Congo and the cannibal Queen 'Nzinga of the Jaga that helped give the Dutch control of the Gold, Slave, and Ivory coasts of Guinea and almost succeeded in throwing the Portuguese out of Angola.[20] Dutch failures against the Portuguese led the Dutch to set up their own permanent colonial trading base at the Cape of Good Hope.

Wars were almost constant. The Holy Roman Empire, the last great stronghold of the Middle Ages, was always engaged. The Emperor Charles V (r. 1519–56) had to defend Europe from the expanding power of the Ottoman Turks, defend the Italian kingdoms from an aggressive France, and stop the spread of the newest European danger, Protestantism. When he retired to a monastery, he divided his responsibilities between his brother, Ferdinand I (r. 1556–64), and his son Philip II (r. 1556–98), and neither had much peace. France was engaged in religious warfare or in civil war through the second half of the sixteenth century. The culmination came in the War of the Three Henrys. Finally the Abjuration of Protestantism (he gave it up) by Henry of Navarre, also known as Henry IV, ended the long conflict. Henry IV reigned until his assassination in 1610. Philip II led his nation of Spain into war against France, the rebellious Netherlands, and the Turks. Fed up with their protected privateering of his New World bullion ships and her Protestant queen's noncommittal responses to his proposals of marriage, Philip II launched the disastrous Armada against England in 1588. The death and defeat of the childless king of Portugal in a Moroccan battle prompted Philip II to seize the throne of Portugal in 1580, which Spain held until 1640, though the two empires continued under separate national administrative systems. Only one significant military victory marked the reign of Philip II, the naval defeat by his brother John of Austria, of the Turks at the Battle of Lepanto in 1571. Sweden emerged as a power and intervened to fight in Russia's "Time of Troubles," (1604–13). For Russia this was a series of conflicts over succession in a nation-state recently unified by Ivan IV, known for good reason as Ivan the Terrible (r. 1533–84), the first formally titled czar. The Thirty Years' War involved all the important European powers in a shifting pattern of alliances that began as a war of Catholic against Protestant powers and ended as a war for national self-interest with alliances unrelated to religious faith. War made the nation, and the nation made war.

Most of the worst fighting, and by far the worst losses by noncombatants, was in the Holy Roman Empire of Central Europe, Germany, and Italy. Destruction in Germany was so extensive that most historians speculate that the nation's unification was delayed for the next two centuries because of it. Crops and villages were destroyed, towns severely depopulated, commerce and industry left in ruins. The Holy Roman Empire never recovered, and Spain entered a long gradual decline. Like nothing else, war and colonial conquest both drained and added resources. More of the wealth of the world flowed to a few of these European powers than ever before, and their social structures and institutions were pressed by the urgency of war and the lure of wealth and power to adapt or fade away. These new or transfigured institutions contained the hierarchical forms and practices of authority and identity necessary for both nation and race.

Colonial Conquest and Race

Colonies could not be effectively governed or managed by explorers, feudal adventurers, or soldiers of fortune. Those dashing figures played an important role in setting the original claims and breaking down or eliminating local resistance. They were romanticized and made national heroes because of their service on the overseas commercial and territorial frontiers of the state. Many of them ran into serious problems with the state. Such was the case with Columbus, Cortes, and the original hapless adventurers who founded Jamestown for the Virginia Company in 1607. Profitable or effective colonial trading centers required the different talents of planters, businessmen, and administrators. The Dutch and Portuguese had small populations and few burghers or other workers to spare for these important occupations. Fewer European women could be induced to make the long and dangerous journey away from homes and families to strange and uncertain futures. Coercion was tried by the Portuguese and Dutch but was never adequate. The English used coerced transportation more systematically in the eighteenth and ninteenth centuries to expand or establish colonies in North America and Australia than they did during this period. The Portuguese slave-trading island of São Tomé was forcibly colonized originally by criminals and convicts, white families, and "forcibly baptized Jewish children of both sexes."[21] One result of the chronic need to populate colonial outposts with a loyal intermediary stratum was the apparent lack of opprobrium associated with intermarriage with local women by Portuguese and Dutch settlers, and the consequent development in both colonial worlds of multilevel and complex legal/racial categories. In many instances, the local women faced sharp hostility from their communities for associating with European men. In some remote areas, the Europeans became so highly integrated with the local culture as to merge with it completely. Once the frontier region or trading base was stabilized and the local population destroyed, disbursed, or absorbed, settlement and legal practices that defined marriage, race, and national identity were established.

New Institutions

The plantation was nonfeudal, profit-making land. Its owner or operator held a right to it from the state as a patent, grant, or as part of a company charter. Titles to plantations could be individually or company held, and feudal restrictions on inheritance and division of land such as primogeniture and entail continued to be enforced by royal authorities for several centuries. Unlike feudal land, the owner did not have to provide for his own military protection. That came from the political authority of the state or one of its more localized subdivisions. New lands to be added or disputes among rivals were likewise matters of state. Plantations sought a profit, so they were not organized for complete economic or agricultural self-sufficiency, as were feudal domains. Their ability to engage in commerce and trade depended on the state. They relied on the state and other nonfeudal institutions for their prosperity and expansion. But there was always economic risk, and often internal and external danger.

Banking and insurance had become sophisticated mature institutions in the late Middle Ages. The great expansion in trade would not have been possible without such innovations as bills of exchange, promissory notes, discounting, and advances in bookkeeping, but even the most powerful bankers faced big risks when their royal depositors defaulted. Spain kept its Augsburg and Antwerp banking family, the Fuggers, on the brink of disaster for years until they finally ruined them with royal insolvency. Banks had to become more reliable in the easy transfer and conversion of foreign notes and currencies as trade became more globalized. The Dutch took a big step toward solving the problem by making the bank an extension of the state. The Amsterdam Exchange Bank, chartered in 1609, was closely connected to the government of the United Netherlands, the Dutch Republic. The Bank of England was modeled after its conservative, state-related predecessor and chartered by the government in 1694. The Dutch took the lead in two other formalized business practices that were widely copied: commercial insurance with fixed or set premiums and the establishment of a stock exchange or bourse in 1531. Uniformity of national standards and the secularization of authority reached religious institutions as well.

Throughout Western and Northern Europe the Protestant Reformation, ignited by Luther's famous 95 Theses of 1517, was both a cause and an effect of the movement toward stronger national autonomy. If war helped to make the state, faith in a state whose authority included protection of the religion of the people helped make the nation. Wherever Protestantism took root, it was in defiance of feudal traditions and imperial authorities. In Luther's Wittenburg, John Calvin's Geneva, or Henry VIII's England a new relationship of civil and religious authority was formed to advance their Protestant renegade beliefs and defend themselves from attack. In the Catholic nations of France and Spain the monarchy took on a greater state role in defense of the faith and as a protector of its dynastic claims.

One of the first invocations of the modern concept of race by the government within a specific ruling was the barring by Philip II's Spain in 1556 of "New Christians" from positions in the clergy, the university, or government administration by the doctrine of *limpieza de sangre*. Bloodlines had to be clear of Moslem or Jewish taint without regard to the individual's loyalty, sincerity, or capability. Law, administration, and religion helped forge a Spanish nation on a mythology of blood. Protestant England took a more ruthless turn toward Catholic Ireland in its exclusively Protestant plantation schemes after its separation from Rome. Luther's diatribes against Jews were not philosophical or spiritual, they were visceral explosions of rage: "First their synagogues or churches should be set on fire. . . . Secondly, their homes should likewise be broken down and destroyed."[22] Luther hoped to purify his culture by physically destroying, extirpating what he imagined were impure influences. He and those who shared his powerful sentiments were building an important part of the cultural foundation of a nation long before it became a state. The Portuguese, Jesuit-inspired church militant adopted the physically coercive techniques of the conquering state to make new Christians. One of the founders and long-serving early governors of the Puritan Massachusetts Bay Colony, John Winthrop, announced a plan similar to that of Calvin and Luther when he stated his divine intention: "we must consider that wee shall be as a Citty upon a Hill, the eyes of all people are upon us."23 The state was envisioned as a Christian waiting room and testing arena prior to the attainment of eternal grace.

The Protestant Reformation has long been linked to the new capitalist and secular virtues of the age in which it emerged. Max Weber's classical Protestant Ethic and the Spirit of Capitalism (1920) showed the intimate connection between the highest values and ideals of the new economic practices of capitalism and those of Calvinism. The institutional structures and personal virtues and vices of one resemble the other, or, as in colonial New England or Geneva, they were completely merged into theocratic social and political systems. For prenational explorers and conquerors, finding treasure and promoting the expansion of Christian universalism were the functional ideologies expressed and shared by all. The new nation-state system shifted its expressions of virtuous ideals away from the fading feudal viewpoint and moved toward one that more exactly represented itself and its own new or revised institutions. While they remained on a civilizing mission, the new states added their own imagined secular national virtues to the presumed religious objectives of conversion. Sometimes, people had to be destroyed in order to be saved.

These new sentiments were expressed in a new manner as well. The written vernacular languages of the new national cultures were expressed in books made more readily available to an increasingly literate urbanizing population. The ancient and medieval world cultures, and those that remained true to those traditions, regarded those who were unfamiliar or illiterate in their written languages as uncivilized barbarians. Nations now affirmed in their own vernacular, not the Latin of the Universal Church, the exclusivity and purity of their virtues in contrast to the deficiencies or vices of others. Miguel de Cervantes (1547–1616) gave definition and permanence to the Spanish language. Luther translated the Bible into German for the first time and helped fix a standard language for Germans. French dramatists and essayists, and James I of England's Bible, did the same for the French and English languages. The printing press standardized vernacular language in this era and helped make it, along with the new institutions of trade and commerce, conquest and war, and Protestant Reformation the foundations of a newly self-conscious unit of civilization, the nation-state. The altered forms of discourse, structure, and geographic borders of the new state system changed collective social attitudes indirectly through the establishment of codes and rules, rewards and punishments, and new hierarchies of protective and punitive authority. People's understanding of identity, of who they thought they were, changed accordingly.

The Power of the State

This was an absolutist era, not a democratic one, not even one in which parliamentary bodies had much authority in government or religion. The Dutch Republic was something of an exception as a mercantile oligarchy. The English parliamentary system was more of a Norman feudal remnant than a representative agency that was used by Henry VIII as he moved his state toward royal absolutism. Absolute power held by one, or an oligarchical few, was the political standard of the era. Ruling elites were very small, whether by aristocratic birth or commercial power, and they were often closely linked by marriage and society. There were no open websites or chat rooms, public schools or libraries; the concepts of citizenship and democracy were unknown in practice anywhere. Royalty was highly interconnected by family ties as well as political commonalties. Elizabeth I kept up an extensive correspondence with Ivan the Terrible in which the Russian czar advised the queen about some of the corrupt practices of her English merchants in his country, as he sought her diplomatic aid against his enemies. The vast population in any of these emerging nation-states was the subject of an authority that claimed the right to rule and protect because it was divine, as articulated by James I (r. 1603–25) of England, among others, or because of the demands reality imposed and no other power could satisfy. This latter defense was implied by Machiavelli and defended elaborately by Thomas Hobbes in his masterwork, *Leviathan* (1651).

While they may have had little else in common, Ivan the Terrible and John Calvin shared an easy ability to have dissonant voices silenced. That ability remains one of the efficiencies claimed by absolute authority anywhere at any time. Complex secular legislative procedures were unknown outside canon law, and the legal profession was still in a blessed infancy, though courts had the ability to act swiftly and with few appeals allowed. Henry VII is known for his infamous "Star Chamber," an often cited example of the dangers of the absence of legal due process. Equally reflective of the time, and a step in the direction of the construction of Jews as a race, were the Inquisitional courts of Ferdinand and Isabella of Spain, established under their own national authority in 1480.

Colonial governors and viceroys drew their authority from their heads of state, as did their overseas courts and military or naval tribunals. Where feudalism had almost no civil law regarding persons, private business, contracts, or property, the new states began to develop those new laws, codes, and courts as they were needed. Sometimes they did so slowly and inconsistently. Slavery, for example, was an ancient and medieval practice that was absorbed into the expanding and global mercantile and absolutist European world system without elaborate or even the most simple of legal codes. Such formalized rulings would be added later, especially after 1650. Most of the laws governing trade and navigation between England's North American colonies and the rest of the world were made by England fifty years after the first permanent settlement at Jamestown. Laws establishing the plantation system in Ireland did provide a foundation and serve as a precedent for the sugar plantation system of Barbados (1627) and for the settlement of Virginia and other colonies. Hence a close, indeed almost exactly similar legal situation came to be shared by the Irish and the native North Americans in relation to their common English colonizers.

The plantation was a nonfeudal grant of land by royal authority and under royal protection from the population from whom it was expropriated. It was an agricultural enterprise. Among the Spanish, Dutch, Portuguese, or English the plantation land-title right was primarily economic and derived exclusively from the authority of the state. The absolutist authority of the nation-state expanded its power over every economic realm and institution that added wealth or strategic advantage to the combined interests of emerging business enterprise and state. "L'état c'est moi," declared the royal Catholic king of France, Louis XIV (r. 1643–1715). The same sentiment could as easily have come from royal Protestant England, Calvin's Geneva, or the Portuguese-empowered king of the Congo. Law and authority were top-down phenomena. Those who gained in business or land or power most understandably gave their loyalty to that authority with honest, emotional sincerity. Conquest and war built the same kind of devotion from military and naval forces. Merchants, adventurers, and the queen's privateers were more difficult to control at times, but finally they, too, owed loyalty to their absolutist beneficiary or ended on the gallows or under another authority's protection. Pirates and renegade outlaws were by definition unlikely patriots. Inclusion into a purified religious or cultural community by either a Catholic king's imposed *limpieza de sangre* or a Protestant governor's "city on a hill" strengthened the cultural bond and emotional tie to the authority that created the exclusive community.

Religious, national, and racial identity were made from the top down in this Age of Absolutism. Not all sectors of the population were devoted to the state yet, since they did not feel a beneficial association with it or enjoy security from its protection. The Dutch Republic was more of an administrative structure than anything else, a nearly pure state but not really a nation. At the other end of the spectrum, Germany became a national culture through the shared authority of language and a racialized anti-Semitism without any state apparatus, law, or overseas commercial empire. The German nation became a unified state much later through war and under the leadership of the Iron Chancellor, Otto von Bismarck, in the 1860–90 period. Emotions of inclusion within a purified state or toward idealized national authority figures or structures required a borderline beyond which the impure, the excluded, and the foreign were found. The vilification of alien others defined the behavioral norms and expectations of the pure and the included more than it ever described its object.

The Portuguese Naval Empire

The making of a mythology of exclusion starts with an identification with the authority structure that establishes an advantage for those included. But such a mythology was not yet in place at the time of the initial encounters of travelers and explorers. Goals of displacement, expropriation, or conquest were not the articulated or felt sentiments of explorers and early travelers or their governments toward those they met along their way. The lack of such a mythology also explains the absence of an official policy or ideology on race by the Portuguese. The Portuguese went abroad for primarily exploratory and commercial reasons, not for territorial expansion. The policy of church and Crown was to build a "seaborne empire cast in a military and ecclesiastical mould."[24] The official policy from Lisbon in the old colonial empire was to seek conversion of the faithless, establish commercial relations, and provide military protection for these enterprises. The military and clerical authorities out in the faraway African and Asian settlements sought to remain faithful to the authorities at home, but often had to make decisions and take actions that veered away from those idealized feudal goals. Settler adventurers, ivory, gold, spice, and slave traders departed even further as they adopted local practices that coincided with their own, more material objectives. On-the-spot clerics and entrepreneurs developed practices and habits of thinking or mythologies that worked for them.

Religious conversion by sword and iron, the plantation-driven dramatic increase by 1575 of the slave trade, and the prevalence of malaria and other tropical diseases that discouraged European migration had serious practical consequences. Few European women came out to these unhealthful and disagreeable sites, and new hierarchical categories and mythologies built on the imperial realities of complex European, mulatto, African, and Asian relationships were established. Affonso de Albuquerque, the Portuguese conqueror of Goa in 1510, encouraged his men to marry and bring Christianity to the "white and beautiful" widows and daughters of the Moslem men they had just killed in battle or burned alive afterward. They were discouraged away from the darker-skinned women of Dravidian origin, called "Negresses" by the Portuguese leader.[25] But no formal restriction applied, and many of his men did not share his prejudices and made families without regard to color. Strict color-coded vilification came more than a century later with the expropriation of conquered Brazilian and Angolan lands as plantations and the Portuguese use of their own profitable African slave labor. By then, a complex system of races and restrictive codes was established in their colonies that was different from that of most other Europeans. The Dutch, who also condoned the intermarriage of their burghers with local women because of a comparable chronic shortage of European women in their colonial empire, left behind for their British successors a multitiered legal racial system in South Africa. The Portuguese were both ahead of and behind their European rivals. They got there first, but developed permanent racially exploitative land and labor systems later. Vilification mythologies emerged at the point of conquest or expropriation, not as the official or stated expression of royal authority. White supremacy was not Portuguese Crown or official conqueror policy in India, but all their religious orders out on the imperial frontiers refused admission to Indians and Eurasians by the end of the 1500s just as their Spanish counterparts did in the Americas and the Philippines.

Spain and the Americas

None of these colonial or trading settlements attracted the most secure and comfortable of Europeans. Cervantes could have been describing overseas Portuguese, Dutch, English, or his own countrymen when he referred to Spanish America as "the refuge and haven of all the poor devils of Spain, the sanctuary of the bankrupt, the safeguard of murderers, the way out for gamblers, the promised land for ladies of easy virtue, and a lure and disillusionment for the many, and a personal remedy for the few."[26] Many writers and observers have said the same thing about those who sought a life on the European overseas colonial frontier; few have considered the myths and rationalizations they made as derived at least in part from their own deficient status. Their governments took the lead in setting a standard of Christian purity for inclusion in the aftermath of the expulsion of the Jews and capture of Grenada in 1492. Tainted blood, said official Spain, had the power to corrupt, and medieval mythologies of ritual murder and satanic behavior had a long history. Immediately on the heels of Columbus, who gave mixed bucolic and frightful cannibalistic reports of the people he met in Hispaniola, came the gold seekers and churchmen who created their own dichotomy. Bullion carried the day, though many eloquent pleas were made on behalf of the Native American population by, among others, Peter Martyr and Bartolome de las Casas. The sources and legal definition of imperial wealth changed the status of persons. The original Spanish colonial land-grant system and basis for their plantations, the *encomienda,* differed from the feudal system's greater protection of the rights of serfs and allowed the rewarded conqueror the use of the labor of the indigenous people. The system differed from chattel slavery, however, in that the people could not be bought or sold, and they had to be instructed in Christianity and Spanish civil codes. Atrocious conditions in remote gold and silver mines, murderous assaults, disease, and suicide undermined the limited protection offered the natives.

After several decades of protest and the decimation of millions, Charles V finally acted. In 1542 the New Laws for the Indies were announced by Spain for their American colonies. Native Americans were declared free of slavery and protected as vassals of the Crown, and the *encomienda* was abolished. Settlers protested and disobeyed, and it took more than a century before the land system changed, but the absolutist power of the Crown eventually displaced the semifeudal brutality of the settlers and at least officially mitigated the conditions of the local native people.[27] Slaves, in contrast, were not the vassals of the Crown; they were property. Some free and enslaved Africans had accompanied the earliest explorers. The introduction of more imported African slaves followed almost immediately as personal servants. By 1518, the large number of African slaves brought to labor in the sugar plantations of the Spanish West Indies created a new dilemma. Christians had certain rights. Could Christians be slaves? The answer for the Spanish and Portuguese was a troubled yes. Both Iberian monarchs suffered some guilt over the harsh consequences of the growing trade. Slaves should be brought into the faith; that was the traditional approach to all heathen, but Charles V took a bolder step. In 1557 he ordered the freeing of all African slaves in Spanish America. A year later he retired to the monastery at Saint-Just, and slavery and the slave trade resumed in full force. King Sebastian of Portugal sought ineffectually to impose greater controls over the institution of slavery in Portuguese Brazil in 1570 by requiring more formal registration procedures.[28]

New World Slavery and Racism

The problem was sugar. Gold and silver mines were only one way of bringing wealth back from overseas colonies. By 1526, commercial quantities of slave-produced sugar were shipped by both Spain and Portugal from the West Indies and Brazil. By 1650, English, French, and Dutch plantations were driving the Portuguese out of the rich northern European sugar market. The African slave trade boomed and became a major mercantile industry of its own as tobacco, rice, and indigo were added to the Atlantic trade in the seventeenth century. Vilification and degradation came about at the place where unequal relationships became fixed, on the plantation, or frontier settlement, in the overseas community or monastery, or in the frustrated German nation in search of a state for its cohesive identity. On all these sites, plantation, frontier, colony, or German nation, a population appeared whose subjection, dehumanization, or expropriation helped achieve the conqueror's collective goal. George Mosse has used the term "scavenger ideology" to describe racism, since it appeared to him to have cobbled itself into existence here and there through history.[29] In this absolutist era the authorities in place drew on the power of their religious faith and all its mysteries, the sentiments of an aristocratic class-dominated society, and the sometimes harsh material realities they had to confront to form both new institutions and new ways of viewing themselves and others.

The first clear application of what was later called apartheid was an Ecclesiastical Council enactment in the Portuguese colony of Goa in 1567. Christians of every physical description were forbidden to have social contact with Muslims, Hindus, Buddhists, or other non-Christians, with the lone and important exception that permitted essential business dealings. Jesuits originally had no color bar, but adopted one because of Portuguese pressure to do so at the point of their aggressive imperial contact in Asia and Africa. An Italian Jesuit's relentless urgings convinced the Jesuits to admit Japanese to their order in 1582, and they subsequently accepted Chinese and Koreans, but throughout the Portuguese colonial empire Jesuits maintained a restriction against sub-Saharan Africans and Native Americans. This was a more prohibitive restriction than that of their government, as were the overseas discriminatory admissions practices of the other orders.[30] Why did they accept the Japanese, Chinese, Koreans, and not the Africans, other Asians, or Americans? Barring better evidence, it was probably because of the cultural similarities they found with the accepted groups, and the military and political cohesion in these countries, which they perceived they could not undermine. They were guests in one area, masters in another. English privateers were more indifferent to race than either the Jesuits and other religious orders or their fellow countrymen engaged at the time in the attempted colonization of Ireland.

Captain John Hawkins was, among other things, an English slave trader. He made two successful commercial voyages between the Portuguese African colony of Guinea and the Americas in 1564–65 and 1567–68. None of his journals or narrative accounts treats the Africans he traded in with any negative descriptive sentiment, and his comments on American natives show a consistency in his attitude for both groups: "These people (from the Cape Verde region) are all black and are called Negroes, without any apparel, saving before their privities: of stature goodly men, and well liking by reason of their food, which passeth all other Guineans for kine, goats, pullen, rice, fruits, and fish. . . . These men also are more civil than any other, because of their daily traffic with the Frenchmen, and are of nature very gentle and loving."[31] Sir Francis Drake had served with Hawkins in a voyage to the Indies and was carrying on his own private war against Spain that won him a reputation as one of the greatest romantic sea dogs of the era. In 1573 he raided the Spanish port of Nombre de Dios in Panama and seized a great treasure for himself and his sovereign, Elizabeth I. His success was due in part to the alliance he made with runaway slaves and half-breeds known as *cimarrones,* who lived in the forests of the isthmus. His actions describe what has been called a "streak of English innocence about racial matters," but was more likely a mutually beneficial pact in which the only losers were the common enemy, the Spaniards.[32] At the same time and on the frontiers of plantation Ireland, we observed far different English sentiments toward those resisting their civilizing mission.

Dutch Racism

As the Dutch began to intrude and compete with the Portuguese for some of their Asian and American possessions, they faced similar on-the-spot social and practical overseas issues. From 1617 onward, they encouraged colonization in Asia through the intermarriage of Dutch settlers with Asian and Eurasian women, the descendants of Indo-Portuguese unions. In Angola and Brazil, Dutch burghers likewise married local women with mixed Portuguese and local origins. The results were the greater assimilation of the Dutchmen into the dominant local cultures and the failure to establish a tropical New Netherlands in the Far East, Angola, or Brazil. In their New Amsterdam colony of North America they faced no tropical hazards, but again found their cultural influence eventually overwhelmed by the larger numbers of English settlers. Racial consciousness was present in legislation. In 1617 the *Hereen* XVII ruled that their free burgher colonial settlers could not marry without the consent of the company's local officials, that they could marry only local Asian or Eurasian women who were Christians, and that their children and slaves "in so far as possible" were to be made or raised as Christians. In 1644 the *Heeren* barred dark-skinned Asians and slaves, including the children of Dutch fathers, from entering their European ports. Poor compliance and a complete lack of enforcement of these codes were followed, about thirty years later, by more extensive racially restrictive legislation on employment practices in the colonies as well.[33] The authorities back home just did not understand the necessities of life out in the colonies, or as one proverb put it: "Necessity is the mother of invention and the father of the Eurasian."[34]

Complaints about brutality and abuse of native populations by officialdom back home were disregarded by Dutch colonists on the scene who routinely employed derogatory physical and racial terminology to describe their colonial subordinates or plantation slaves. The overseas Dutch quickly adapted themselves to the harshness and brutality of sugar plantation slavery after their conquest of northeastern Brazil in the late 1630s. They used imported slave labor as well in the absence of colonists in Asia, and in their nutmeg plantations of the Banda Islands after their extermination and removal of the indigenous people. One Pernambuco planter, who had started out with misgivings, could have been defending the plantation system anywhere when he observed: "It is not possible to effect anything in Brazil without slaves ... and ... if anyone feels that this is wrong, it is a futile scruple."[35] It would not be long before quite elaborate explanations would be put forward by slaveowners to explain how positively right it was.

The French in the New World

The French exploratory and colonial enterprises of this era are noteworthy for their differences and similarities with the other powers. Their first great explorer, Jacques Cartier, was looking for a northwest passage to the markets of Asia on the first two of his major voyages to North America in 1534 and 1535. Cautious but friendly encounters were made with the Native Americans on his first trip. By the following year, it was still with friendship and warmth that he engaged the generous people of the settled villages of Stadacona (later Quebec City) and Hochelaga (Montreal). In his last voyage of 1541 he was looking for a treasure-laden city, the legendary kingdom of Saguenay described to him by natives as a northern Peru. His unsuccessful quest was marked by some local hostility but was followed a year later by a French colonizing party to the same region that may have been hoping to establish a sanctuary for Protestants. After one bitter winter, the survivors returned to France, and no serious further Canadian settlements were attempted by them for another sixty years. The next French ventures were also Protestant-led or strongly influenced, but on an island in the warmer waters of the Rio de Janeiro of Portuguese Brazil in 1555, and at the mouth of the St. John's River in Spanish Florida in 1562. Both lasted about three years, until the Portuguese and Spanish threw them out. No plantation system emerged, and in their brief stay they enjoyed very friendly relations with local people, except when they sided with one group in its warfare with another.[36] After a couple of unsuccessful attempts at the opening of the seventeenth century to restart a Canadian settlement, Samuel de Champlain came to dominate the next thirty years of French trade and settlement. He regarded the Native Americans as equals. He sought to extend his religious beliefs among them without coercion. He used analogy and understandable similes in respectful instruction, and helped make a mutually agreeable and valuable trading relationship possible that was built on neither conquest, slavery, nor plantation agriculture. We discover the corollary void of racial epithet, physical brutality, and legal or codified discrimination. The noble Frenchman and *le bon sauvage* broke the rule; they made gain without pain. Unfortunately, Champlain also became engaged in a dispute among rival local tribes, and he and some of his men fired on and killed several Iroquois in June 1609. From then on, the French suffered the animosity of the Iroquois, who ultimately became the allies of the British and together drove the French out of Canada a century and a half later.[37]

National and Racial Culture

The Dutch, English, Portuguese, and Spanish were joined by German principalities of this era in making restrictive laws or codes that went beyond traditional medieval religious or civil practices. The municipality of Frankfurt, for example, forbade Jews from using the public streets without a specific reason, and they were barred from some streets altogether. They could not walk in pairs in public, and a *Kleiderordnung* set a prescribed manner of appearance or dress code for them. They were declared "protégés" or "subjects" of the city and not free burghers as other Germans, the same legal status imposed by Hitler. Official and unofficial expulsions of Jews from towns and cities went on throughout the era.

Martin Luther did not simply write and speak out against Jews, he encouraged restrictive codes and expulsions and was proud of his efforts that helped lead to those ends in Saxony, Brandenburg, and Silesia. His last sermon, four days before he died (February 18, 1546), was a diatribe against the Jews. They should be expelled, he raved, from all of Germany. The common national, cultural, emotional bond for Germans was the love of their language. That sentiment became manifested as hatred of Jews. Jews became alien figures who represented the collective frustration of unrealized German cultural national unity in their failure to build a state.

The last prominent, unofficial expulsion of Jews took place in Frankfurt and Worms in 1616. The Frankfurt Jewish ghetto was besieged by a mob that looted, burned, and beat their way through the neighborhood. They destroyed religious objects as well as any documents or records of debt. The city of Worms experienced the same kind of outbreak a few months later. No action under law was taken because German law faculties found no punishable offenses.[38]

The ravages of the Thirty Years' War had a peculiar and oddly beneficial effect on some of Central Europe's Jews. They became an even more important asset than they had been before. In every large or small disunited Central European principality they were able to assist with banking, commerce, and trade associations that were missing in the hobbled remains of the Holy Roman Empire. There came to be a category known as "Court Jews." As long as Germany remained a disunited collection of semifeudal principalities, a few Jews in each town or principality were able to provide the financial and commercial associations that each court needed with the external economic powers, or with each other. The importance of the Jews throughout Europe gave them enough influence to end their official harassment and expulsions by the mid-eighteenth century. Their efforts at amelioration were aided by the general decline in religious authority and conflict, and the more tolerant atmosphere of the Age of Reason and Enlightenment that followed. In Germany, Jews became the commercial and business intermediaries in the absence of a more unified German nation-state, and what appeared to stand between the Germans and the creation of a national state. Without a German national bank, bourse, credit system, or international diplomatic commercial system, some Jews helped to fill the void and facilitate trade and economic activity. For a few, it was a privileged and advantageous place to be, but for the many, it became a seedbed for catastrophe.

The Kinship of the Irish and the Native American

The English authorities expressed only the most noble of intentions for their colonial projects in Ireland and North America. Civilization in the form of English law and customs, they believed, would help elevate the wild and savage Irish as well as the Native Americans. The two projects were interwoven in their thoughts. Ulster, launched in 1609, two years after the founding of Jamestown, would be, according to Sir Arthur Chichester, King James's lord deputy for Ireland, "as if His Majesty were to begin a new plantation in America, from which it does not greatly differ."[39] The English colonial program was different in an important aspect from that of the other Europeans. They planned to extend settlements into the new lands, as well as search for a northwest passage, find gold, or gain trading opportunities. Their settlers carried semifeudal ambitions to Ireland as Gilbert and Leicester had done before and as they sought to establish plantations in Longford, Leitrim, Wexford, southern Offaly, and Galway between 1616 and 1641. They described the wild and savage Native Americans of Virginia and New England as a similar challenge. They were physically admired by the earliest English; they needed only education, conversion to Christianity, English language, law, and social codes to become fully absorbed into the civilized world of their benefactors. The elder Richard Hakluyt was optimistic about the prospects for converting and uplifting the native population. They were ready, he said, "to submytte them selves to good government, and ready to imbrace the christian faythe."[40]

For several decades, the righteous Puritan leaders of the Massachusetts Bay Colony actively sought to bring civilization to the natives. An early affirmative action plan recruited natives to attend Harvard College from its earliest years. Its charter stated explicitly that its aim was to "conduce to the education of the English and Indian youth of this country in knowledge and godliness." Governor John Winthrop believed other colonial ventures had failed because "their mayne end which was proposed was carnal and not religious." Other colonizers sought "profitt and not the propagation of religion."[41] When Winthrop's virtuous-sounding approach was resisted by Irish or Native American people, who preferred to maintain their own way of life and not adopt the more civilized ways planned for them, the American colonial leaders or English authorities began to describe them in the vilest manner their own ethical and moral code could imagine. It was the language heretofore reserved for the fallen, the sinner, and the depraved among the English and American Puritans themselves, the same terminology flung on delinquent servants and disobedient employees. The English in Ireland and their colonial American counterparts accused both the Irish and the Native Americans of slothful laziness and uncontrollable passions. These savages were inherently drawn to drunken and sexually licentious wildness and physical ferocity. Their rebelliousness proved that the only thing they really understood was the sword. It was not a big step to move from benevolent paternalism to benevolent conquest. In Ireland, Virginia, and Massachusetts the "encroachment and effrontery became unbearable" to the local population, and conflict became inevitable.[42] The Irish fought and resisted the English until they were crushed by Cromwell's forces from 1641 to 1652. In Virginia a massacre of settlers in 1622 led to the takeover of the colony by the Crown. In Massachusetts and Connecticut the Pequot War, which began in 1637, was little more than an extermination campaign against the local population. King Philip's War in colonial New England in

1675 was at least in part the result of a Native American rebellion against their cultural dissolution, quite analogous to Irish armed resistance and similarly ill fated.

Native Americans and the Celtic Irish may have shared some superficial physical commonalties; they both had long hair and wore coarse clothing. A closer, more objective look would reveal enormous dissimilarities. One lived in a late Neolithic hunting and gathering culture with limited tools, agriculture, and few domesticated animals. The other was a Christian neighbor often compared in habits to the Scottish highlanders. The Irish and English had a centuries-old shared relationship. What the Irish and Native Americans of the early seventeenth century truly shared was a common resistance and rebellion against the loss of their property and culture to the same enemy. That resistance to the arrogant authority of English colonial rule earned them a shared opprobrium, a racially mythological kinship with Asians and Africans who resisted comparable Dutch, Spanish, or Portuguese expropriations. They all shared a relationship with Central Europe's Jews, who similarly could not accept a definition of themselves, or new identity, that denied their own human experience and culture. Neither the Irish or the Native Americans, however, could find an adequate protective niche, aside from movement beyond the reach of the new authority, to secure themselves against the overwhelming power of their presumed benefactors. They suffered, as a consequence, overwhelming devastation over the next two centuries. Europe's Jews faced the same kind of devastation three centuries later when German unification, need, and opportunity were present. Industrial technology compressed the devastation of the Jews into nightmarish brevity and efficiency.

Ireland and English North America shared a similar deficiency or lack of consistent laws and codes establishing the emerging plantation system and its racially fixed pattern of ownership and control until about 1660. Virginia had few slaves by 1650, perhaps 300, including at least some Native Americans, lifetime European bondsmen, and Africans. Most laborers were indentured servants of one kind or another. The controversy over enslavement and Christianity (could Christians be slaves?) was not settled until the Virginia House of Burgesses took positive action in 1667. The full codification of racial slavery, the plantation system, and the trade and navigation acts all awaited the more complete establishment of the English mercantile structure that followed the restoration of the monarchy in 1660. The Dutch, Spanish, Portuguese, and English all had come to rely almost exclusively on African slave labor for plantation sugar production by 1650. This was a practice borrowed from Old World and medieval circumstances, now mixed with European overseas conquest and colonialism. The Europeans added their master/servant practices, religious ethics and rationalizations, and national peculiarities to make a foundation before 1650 for the laws and institutions that made their expropriations legitimate.

Faith, Nation, and Race

The civilizing mission and the religious goal of conversion provided initial rationalizations for the conquering intruder. The Swedish armies of King Gustavus Adolphus went into battle during the Thirty Years' War singing Protestant hymns. Portuguese, Spanish, and English conquerors and planters were, they all claimed, offering a hand to their lesser brothers long before President McKinley found his metaphor. Religious righteousness and assertions of cultural purity were one pillar of the myth-making process of vilification and sanctification that brought nation and race into existence in the 16th century. Fascism's similarly distorted claims of purity and historic idealism of the twentieth century generated virtually identical mythologies of their victim's pathology. The second pillar was the different cultural mode of existence that actually did exist. Neither of these two initial pillars was enough to sustain the racism created in this period. Cannibalism or tribal simplicity were not themselves the basis for disparagement or hostility; neither was ancient or medieval slavery. Finely crafted cultures were destroyed by conquerors and colonizers and simpler ones admired, idealized, or overlooked. Jews and Moslems lived on a par by any measurable standard of civilization with their fellow Europeans, who nonetheless constructed malignant self-serving mythologies about them. Native Americans and the Celtic Irish, with little in common, were described as nearly identical by their English conquerors, who soon transferred many of their presumed traits to African slaves. Dutch, Portuguese, and Spanish conquerors and colonizers projected their national behavioral virtues and vices in the identical manner as Germans did internally to form a culture without a state.

One of the most acclaimed studies of the emergence of nations and nationalism is Liah Greenfeld's *Nationalism: Five Roads to Modernity* (1992). The author points out that the words *country, commonwealth, empire,* and *nation* did not exist in formal usage before 1500. She notes the importance of the entry of this new force in history dramatically: "I see modernity as defined by nationalism," and later, "nationality is the constitutive principle of modernity" (pp. 18, 487). I would amplify and agree with her by adding Count Tilly's observation. The modern nation-state was born in war and conquest. It was an autonomous entity that measured its power by the secular standards of wealth and territory protected or taken from other powers and certified by legal treaties or agreements with them. Territories seized from, or expropriations conquered from, those outside the nation-state system were racially dehumanized in the legal terminology of colonialism. Warfare represented either colonial conquest or the seizure of a rival's colonial possessions, or the successful defense of the same from a rival. In one of the first comprehensive modern studies of race, a book by Michael Banton and Jonathan Harwood, *The Race Concept* (1975), the authors note the similar nonexistence of the modern English use of the word *race* until a poem by William Dunbar referred to "bakbyttaris of sindry racis" ("backbiters of sundry races") in 1508. The term was broadly used to assign people to groups, not as a means to differentiate them by skin color, hair, or appearance, until a French physician and traveler did so in an essay in 1684 (Banton and Harwood, p. 13). In her discussion of the second most influential sixteenth-century German national figure next to Luther, Liah Greenfeld in *Nationalism* (1992) describes the great Reformation humanist and poet Ulrich von Hutten as a "precocious racist" (p. 282). The celebration of a perceived uniqueness is a characteristic of national and racial pride that offered the new burgher or business classes and the old aristocracy a new and satisfying collective identity. Each found its voice and its face and moved to develop its internal and external structure in this age.

Toward the Secular State

William Shakespeare used the historical writings of Raphael Holinshed, whose *Chronicles of England, Scotland, and Ireland* (1577) gave the bard plots for several of his plays, all of which were written during the period of England's emergence as a great national power after the defeat of the Spanish Armada in 1588. The Dutch found expression for a similar secular clarity in the paintings of the great artists of this era, for example, in the works of their greatest master, Rembrandt van Rijn (1609–1669). The same kind of literary or cultural expression is part of the flowering of the French classical theater in the works of Molière and Racine, and in the essays of Montaigne. Cervantes and Luther have been noted for their role in establishing a Spanish and German national culture through language. National cultural achievements took several forms. A great monument to Portuguese national brilliance is the magnificent collection of fifteenth- and sixteenth-century ships in miniature in their Maritime Museum alongside the Tagus River in Lisbon. An entire region's mercantile, administrative, and military population began to identify itself as an elite, a status formerly reserved to a tiny segment or to a politically and geographically undifferentiated or religiously defined entity. The commanding power of religious faith and linguistic and cultural unity, when triumphant in war and conquest, endowed the new, nonfeudal political leaders with a new mythological authority. The centralized nation-state became the great engine of modernity, the facilitator of enterprise, creator of currencies, banks, markets, law, and when necessary, for material expropriation and cultural self-definition, racially distinctive identities. The absolutist institutional structures that succeeded in breaking out of the restraints of the old order were going to experience a vast growth in the very class that had helped to finance their success. The business or burgher class flourished within the protective nursery of the absolutist mercantile world they had helped to create. Wealth increased their independence; science and technology altered their vision of race and nation. The end of the Thirty Years' War marked the passing of the old feudal order and the beginning of the new age of the nation-state and the racially defined imperial world system.

Chapter 4

The Colors of Gold: Mercantile Empires, Great Nations, Reason and Racism, 1650–1800

Bullion, Trade, and Law

The modern European world system as it was reconstructed out of the contradictory ashes of the Thirty Years' War was built on worldly wealth and law. Feudal clerical and imperial traditions continued their long withdrawal from the center of power. Clerical leaders and titled aristocrats either made an accommodation with secular business and national political forces or moved to the sidelines of influence. Every area of social importance or economic activity at home in the nation or abroad in the great colonial empires felt the affects of the expanded legal codification and refinement of state control. More of the details of everyday life came within the growing legal authority of the nation-state, either absolutist or constitutional. In the globally triumphant British Empire the fastest-growing profession was the law. Lawyers dominated the Constitutional Convention in Philadelphia in 1787 that established the new government for the United States of America. Mercantilism was the economic and political system of laws, codes, and practices that built the fortunes of the greatest national powers and brought them into armed conflict again and again. Peace treaties became temporal and were legal agreements between and among nations that set their hierarchical relationships. Treaties set up mechanisms for the division and redivision of contested parts of the world. Treaties set borders and defined the authority of nations. The enormous wealth that trade and commerce generated reduced the importance of declining Spanish mineral treasure to a glorious memory. Bullion balances, not mine ownership, became the measure of successful national trade. The Spanish Empire found its specie treasures drained off to pay for the goods it purchased from more adept business rivals in other nations. A peculiar array of old luxuries and spices and new products—rum, tobacco, and slaves are examples—set up complex trading systems and altered social relationships. Business and professional classes were elevated to prominence in every great nation. By the end of the era, they successfully challenged inherited political authority or took its place. A wide gap began to open between the economic and military power of the Western European nations and the rest of the world. Heightened awareness of empirical, worldly reality and the probing of its mysteries displaced theology and yielded new scientific answers and philosophic optimism.

The administrative and structural system known as the state usually preceded the formation of the cohesive nation. Germany stands out as a notable exception; there, a cultural nation was formed first and the state much later. The most successful mercantile nation-states were England, France, and the Dutch Republic. They set the pace or increased their dominion over their rivals. The Portuguese and Spanish empires adopted plantation mercantile systems, but both receded or were driven from their former preeminence by rivals. The new nation, the United States, took on the freshest and most up-to-date system of political and economic organization then current, including the profitable agricultural plantation with its well-established racially codified system of enslaved labor.

The United States was born in a war with England. One result was a transfer of control of the valuable, contested, and strategically important Ohio River Valley that eventually became five new states in the Union. That objective and its achievement was no less important than the idealized political sentiments announced to the world in the Declaration of Independence fifteen months after the fighting started. The legal and institutional structures of mercantile nations took in labor practices as well as property relations. The status of persons became a more elaborate legal concept within the growing authority of the state and included the distinctive concept of race. Citizenship was described by law, its attainment subject to residential time and other requirements. The exclusion of Native Americans and slaves was specified, and states were free to make their own internal laws governing other aspects affecting the legal status of persons, such as the right to vote, hold office, or enter into legal agreements. The expansive nation built interrelated bonds with race that formed cohesive collective identities, internally and externally, publicly and privately.

Law, Myth, and Identity

The idea of the nation was a myth that described broad, collective participation in the benefits of a culturally bonded elite, a socially cohesive and legally or formally defined people. Outsiders were declared by law to be alien, foreign rivals who posed a real or imagined threat. The idea of race emerged simultaneously as a myth that described collective inclusion in the presumed benefits that accrued to a physically and legally bonded elite. Race was socially cohesive and legally defined. The nation-state identified itself by a unified legal code and its subdivisions, one administrative system of secular authority. Race, too, was determined by law, administered and adjudicated by secular authority. The successful nation-state was a mythologized mercantile economic and political unit with component parts: banks, stock exchanges, plantations, products, trading companies, and currencies. It was composed of varied, often competitive, interests with a common need for administrative cohesion. It measured its well-being in hard monetary gains and losses. Not exclusively tied to slavery, racism was a similarly mythologized economic structural foundation of plantation land and labor on which mercantile trade and profits and the rest of the colonial labor system was built.

Thomas Jefferson was mistaken in his belief that racial slavery was a product of British colonial policy and would fade quickly with American independence. His original draft of the Declaration of Independence included among the alleged tyrannical acts of the king the mercantile imposition of the obnoxious slave trade. Jefferson attacked the royally imposed and controlled practices of mercantilism to which he linked slavery, an institution he always disliked. Though he struggled with doubts about its veracity and wondered about long-term environmental influences on behavior, he never expressed criticism or serious doubts about the concept of racial inequality. Though he profited from the ownership of slaves, Jefferson was troubled by the human consequences of the institution: "There must doubtless be an unhappy influence on the manners of our people produced by the existence of slavery amongst us," he wrote in *Notes on the State of Virginia* (p. 162). Slavery flourished in the United States for almost ninety years after the Declaration of Independence asserted the equality of men. It endured in Spanish colonial Cuba until 1884, and in Brazil, following independence from Portugal in 1825, until 1888. Racism outlived European plantation slavery by more than a century, since it is linked to the needs of nations and adapts to the transitory phases of their economic development.

The nation-state defined itself by its legal separation from others, by its formalized conquests, and by military force or the threat of military force. War, or preparation for the next war, continued to preoccupy nations throughout this era. Treaties and the agreements made to interrupt warfare, defined national borders and overseas claims, and confirmed the authority of the state to represent the collective interests of its constituent components. Nations attained a position of status in the hierarchy that resulted from their military competition. Treaties were the secular legal certification of coercion's results. Racism likewise depended on the use or threat of physical coercion to maintain its human hierarchical divisions. The use and threat of physical harm, starvation, or violent death have historically marked racist relationships. Legal codes and scientific rationalizations formalized and confirmed the social stratification of racism. Racism could be considered a primitive form of social warfare in its least disguised and most vulgar manifestation. It is the legal destruction of rights to property, labor, or life itself of one category of people by another. That racism was based on a mythology of superiority of the group with the lawmaking authority should not obscure the mercenary material and political objects of those laws.

Racial laws took many forms. Racial restrictions on employment and education persist through many centuries. Residential restrictions and mobility controls and regulations are also a racially legitimized commonplace. So is the confiscation of property, the use of slave labor, and state-sanctioned acts of genocide. Whenever racial laws were used on the frontier, the plantation, or the concentration camp, wealth and power accrued to the lawmakers and those they represented at the expense of their mythologized degraded human objects. That is why many authors, such as Stanley Elkins, in his book *Slavery: A Problem in American Institutional and Intellectual Life*, are struck by the remarkable similarities between plantation slavery and the concentration camp. Elkins finds that "the concentration camp was not only a perverted slave system; it was also—what is less obvious but even more to the point—a perverted patriarchy" (p. 104).

Paternalism, Patriotism, Racism

The nation-state formed a new mythology of authority, an Oedipal paternal relationship between the people (later the citizenry) and the state. Only the state possessed the naval and military power to protect and extend the joint stock companies, trading monopolies, and other mercantile interests and enterprises. The state used its sovereign right to legitimize confiscations of land and create social relations in law. As its protective enriching power and its ability to provide military security grew, the state took over the paternal mythology previously held by religious or imperial authorities.

Racism was also a mythology of protective and punitive paternalism. The privileged, physical elite, made to feel secure in their property rights by the paternal state, adopted paternal language and personal habits of parental authority toward their presumed racial inferiors and expected reciprocal responses from them. Racial subjects were typically addressed in diminutive language or as children, no matter their age. They were "boy" or "girl" to younger masters, whipped or worse for their own good in the fashion of parental authority. The nation-state envisioned a collective destiny or goal, a common purified ideal. Racism imagined human perfection as a similarly idealized manifestation of one specific image. A hierarchy always existed among nations, though each thought of itself as preeminent in some important way. Racism was always hierarchical too, with those who made the laws and set the codes at the top. The myth of the nation obscured class divisions and inequities and fabricated emotional cohesion. So, too, with racism, which invariably imagined a false paternal aristocracy. Racism conferred an artifice of nobility and privilege by birth. It joined otherwise hostile or dissimilar groups as landlords and tenants, factory owners and workers in imagined hereditary bonds based on physical and culturally related traits. The legally encoded aristocracy of race came with a license to abuse, expropriate property and labor, or destroy another group. The beneficiaries of racial laws carry out their self-serving actions on behalf of the mythological purity of their unity. Racism is many things; it is always an artificial class war. Racism established in the crude and immediate expropriation of wealth from its subjects a new class of infinitely exploitable workers or people. In a simplified Marxian dialectic, the adventurer-capitalist and the racially denigrated plantation worker or miner of the mercantile era were historical class counterparts; one is precapitalist, the other is preproletarian.

Collective psychological expressions of sentiments of love and hate were human responses to inclusion under the authority of the nation-state; what was good or bad for the nation was good or bad for the individual. Racism evoked the same kind of strong psychological reaction, sometimes quite visceral, when its authority was expressed or challenged. Its strictures were held to be a social virtue or necessity. Those who strayed from or defied them disturbed the emotional tranquillity of the rest (of the family), hence emotional reaction, harsh language, sexual taboos and fantasies, and physical violence were always present.

The nation-state was an aggressive economic and political force on behalf of the coalesced culture's wealth-owning groups and interests, including, usually, the monarchy itself. Racism has always secured the transfer of wealth to those same groups or classes. During this period in history the nation-state became, to its own most outstanding observers, the empirically effective, nonmystical structure for the building of wealth and power. Civilization itself, royal and national leaders presumed, was advanced by their national accomplishments. Trading companies and business leaders did not idealize or universalize their accomplishments. They were part of the larger enterprise and glory of their nation. Racial expropriation of land and labor, however, appeared to those who carried it out as natural and within the same framework of advancing civilization as the idea of the nation appeared to its beneficiaries. They were often the same.

The human dynamics of race and nation can be observed in the emotional responses they evoke from those within their authority. The protected beneficiaries of an identity formed by nation or race changed dramatically through modern history. As civic participation expanded through the granting of legal rights or protection, suffrage, and citizenship, nationalism spread. As a popular collective emotional bond, nationalism is usually said to have begun in the Napoleonic aftermath of the French Revolution because of the dramatic, universal extension of citizenship and the raising of massive armies. Racism's emotional power appears strongest at the point of legal expropriation of land, labor, wealth, or life itself. Those furthest removed are often the critics of a racial harshness they do not experience or understand firsthand. The plantation, the mine, and the frontier changed over time. In their own somewhat more bizarre fashion, so did the Native American reservation and Nazi concentration camp. When expropriation was not the foundation of a relationship, and there was no longer a perception of gain, racism dissipated and seemed ephemeral. Foxhole buddies in combat seemed honestly to overcome the emotional constraints of racism with surprising speed. The twists and turns of historical events, perceived gains and losses altered the expressions of nationalism and racism. During the era of unchallenged European national empires and plantations, nations made new, emotionally powerful definitions of themselves in explicit, though not always consistent, detailed legal terminology. Racism, at the same time, was no less an emotional force and became highly defined by law; color was added to racial terminology with similarly inconsistent applications as national terms. A closer look at the laws and institutions that made nations and races in the Age of Reason and Enlightenment reveals the turning of this double helix through another part of modern history.

The British Empire

If a collection of epithets and slang expressions of racial vilification should be assembled in every national language, the English volume would certainly be the fattest because the English colonial empire was eventually the most vast and had under its authority the most diversified assortment of human cultures. When degradation and expropriation are carried forward by a nation, by a whole people against another, it is invariably racist. In this regard, the Celtic Irish and their partially anglicized countrypeople were among the first to experience English national racism. They were joined almost simultaneously by companions in expropriation, the Native Americans and African slaves. Ulster, Virginia, and Barbados were similar English plantation settlements, and all experienced the brutal might of imperial force and racial stigmatization in the early decades of the seventeenth century. "Divine Right" absolutism, civil war, and participation in the Thirty Years' War impeded more systematic English policy development. As soon as they could, the English took action, first military and then legislative, against the Irish. In 1649 Oliver Cromwell took his "new model army" of several thousand and began to earn the sobriquet "Hammer of Ireland" by a brutal assault on the garrison town of Drogheda. By May 1652, after the surrender of Galway, all of Ireland was said to be pacified.

The war against the Irish was itself a form of speculative business enterprise. To raise revenue and troops the English Parliament passed an act in 1642 that promised investor-adventurers repayment with interest in confiscated Irish lands for their services. Parliament also owed regular military officers and soldiers for their services. As soon as the smoke of battle cleared, Parliament passed an Act of Settlement in 1652 that established a formula for confiscating Irish land and distributing it to investors and veterans. Cromwell personally supervised the project, which also hoped to establish a permanent, self-sufficient English Protestant population in a disarmed Ireland. Within a few months, Cromwell exiled some 13,000 defeated Irish soldiers, some to other postings under English or foreign officers, but most to lifetime indentures in plantation servitude in Barbados. Over 20,000 more Irishmen were sold into military service, mostly to the Spanish, by 1654. What turned English policy from its former religious and civilizing mission as a justification for conquest to outright racism was expropriation of land and the forced resettlement of those whose land was taken to reservations west of the Shannon River in Connaught or County Clare. Tens of thousands were told to pack their belongings, take their families, leave their ancestral homes, and go "to Hell or Connaught."[1] Over the course of the hundred years that began with the Act of Settlement, Irish Catholic ownership of good or profitable land in Ireland declined from five of every eight acres to one in sixteen, with the bulk of the good land transferred to Protestant owners.[2] Irish defeat by the English and loss of control over their land brought about recurrences of famine with consequent periods of mass starvation, emigration, and the long-term impoverishment of the Irish people.

Racism was a three-staged process by the English in Ireland and estab-

lished a near-universal pattern elsewhere throughout the empire: first, military conquest in war; second, expropriation and displacement of the population via the Act of Settlement; third, legal racial degradation of the
population. This latter stage was enacted most elaborately by the system of
Penal Laws by the Protestant Ascendancy, as the Protestant English imposed government was called, after the defeat of an Irish-Jacobite struggle
in the collapsing reign of James II.

The Penal Laws, or legislation very similar to them, developed in every
colonial European relationship with native populations not exterminated,
and are an integral part of the making of racism. A specialist on the Penal
Laws observed that they effectively excluded Catholics, though Catholics
were approximately three-quarters of the Irish population, from every position of importance in the country. Catholics were barred from the professions, from government, from ownership of property, from education, "in
the same way as the colour bar has operated to ensure white ascendancy in
African countries in recent times."[3] Edmund Burke called them a "contrivance" in law "for the oppression, impoverishment, and degradation of a
people." Burke, the great conservative, noted the peculiar and illogical way
ordinary Protestants could impose on any Irish Catholic "daily and hourly,
an insulting and vexatious superiority."[4] Without naming it, Burke was
describing one of the hallmarks of racism: its disregard of any social standard for its object other than that which is set for the advantage of those
who make the codes. Catholics could not legally acquire land from Protestants, nor could they buy land, inherit land, or earn income from land. They
were restricted in their leasing rights to thirty-one years and were required
by law to pay rent of no less than two-thirds of the yield from their labor on
the land they rented. The majority of Irish tenants were quickly reduced to
the status of one-year tenants-at-will; those who owned any land were deprived of rights of testament over their estates. Any Protestant had "discovery" rights in charging Catholic evasions of land laws, and rights to that
land should the claims be sustained in Protestant courts. Irish Catholics had
no comparable rights, nor could they receive land as a dowry, since marriage to Protestants was also forbidden. Essentially, the Irish who sought to
remain Irish were deprived of all civil rights or civil liberties.

The English no longer made serious attempts at conversion or assimilation
during this period and later. That was left to the Irish themselves. The satiri-
cally apt description of the best fate for Irish children of this era was Jonathan
Swift's pamphlet "A Modest Proposal" (1729). He urged that they should
become a culinary delicacy for the cultivated palates of the English well-to-do.
This recommendation would solve several problems at once. Instead of
becoming impoverished hungry mouths to feed, Irish infants could be fed to

their wealthy landlords. The Catholic Irish could not own weapons, serve on grand juries, or vote in any election for public office. It was a crime to teach "Papists" to read or write or for them to go abroad for education. In Burke's time the Penal Laws were modified, but they were not repealed until 1829.

Racism and Slavery

Laws that established the concept of race in the English colonies in America went into effect, unsurprisingly, in the same period and for similar reasons. Of course, Native Americans were first dispossessed of any claims they had to valuable land. Removals and reservation policies came later. Their "Hell or Connaught" was massacre, disease, enslavement, and dispacement to the remaining territory beyond the European reach of settlement. Mercantilism was built on laws. As late as 1660, the courts and legislatures of the British West Indies and the mainland colonies had no formalized slave law or racial codes. Court cases were adjudicated individually and inconsistently. In 1656 an African American woman won her freedom from slavery in a Virginia court because she was a Christian. A local council regulation of slavery was adopted on Barbados in 1639 that declared lifetime servitude for all Africans or Indians. They were copying a near-century-old Spanish Caribbean and American practice applied to the African slaves in their mines and on their plantations. Massachusetts (1641) and Connecticut (1650) also adopted the legal concept of lifetime servitude, but without explicit racial details until the end of the century.[5]

Legislation poured forth after the Restoration of Charles II in 1660. Parliament passed the first comprehensive Navigation Acts in 1660 and 1661 to secure greater advantage and control for English shipping interests. At the same time, Virginia established legal lifetime servitude for African slaves on the as yet informal Barbados model. Maryland and Barbados wrote into law the same concept two years later. Virginia stood English common law on its head in 1662 by giving a child its mother's status if the mother was of African descent. The standard English practice in law was that a child inherited its father's status. Two years later, the same legislature prohibited marriage between "ffreeborne English women" and "Negroes." Maryland made all slave descendants, even those of slave fathers and non-slave mothers, slaves for life in its legislation of 1663.[6] Virginia ended the possibility of baptism leading to manumission from slavery when it legalized Christianity for slaves in 1667. One year later, a tax or tithe was imposed on free African American women, though not on any others. The colony did not want freed African Americans. The same racial tax was placed on Native American women after 1688. The great political theorist John Locke included in his careful draft of the Fundamental Constitution of Carolina of 1669 the statement that "every free man" was "to have absolute authority over his negro slaves." Free African Americans and slaves were prohibited by a law in Virginia in 1680 from lifting a hand "against any Christian."[7]

Denial of legal rights went on: no free Native American or African American, though Christian, could own a nonnative or African slave. Enslavement in the American colonies became strictly a racial institution, though it had not begun that way. In 1690 free African Americans were legally expelled from Virginia, though this law was subsequently repealed. Trial by jury was denied by law (1705), along with the right to vote (1723) for free African Americans in Virginia.[8] The other colonies copied or closely replicated the Chesapeake Bay and West Indian plantation slavery and racial laws. In 1705 Massachusetts barred its English residents, later interpreted by courts as "whites," from fornication or marriage with "Negroes, mulattoes and Indians."[9]

All this legislation coincided with the boom of the plantation system in the English colonies and the African slave trade. In 1660 the English government granted a monopoly to the Company of Royal Adventurers. King Charles II had £5,000 of his own invested in this company, which controlled the sale of licenses to English slave traders who sought to do business on the African coast. It took the name Royal Africa Company when it was reorganized in 1672 and held control over a string of fortified slave-trading stations in Gambia, Senegal, Ghana, and Nigeria. The trade quickly outgrew the monopoly, and the company was abolished in 1698. By then, hundreds of trading companies were involved in the business. After 1713 the British won the *Asiento,* the privilege of supplying slaves to the Spanish colonies in America. The trade boomed as England built its global empire. One estimate claims that more than 2 million African slaves were imported to the British colonies alone from 1680 to 1786. The cities of Bristol and Liverpool, and a massive triangle trade that kept an increasing amount of wealth in bullion within the empire, were built on it.[10]

Racial laws and local codes continued to develop even in places without plantations. New Hampshire imposed a curfew on Native, African, and mulatto Americans in 1714, and harsh restrictions were imposed on the same people in Boston in 1723. Their children were required to be bound out in Boston to service at age four to "some English master."[11] Some colonies added their own special nuances on the matter of racial legal inferiority. South Carolina, for example, decided in 1712 that all "Negroes, mulattoes, mustizoes, or Indians" were slaves unless they could prove otherwise.[12] Mercantile legal distinctions sought to enhance both profitability and control for those in charge, either Crown, company, or plantation owner. What worked was kept, what did not work was modified or dropped. Consciousness of color grew awkwardly out of such pragmatism.

Color and Control

Control of the subject population after conquest, or as imported slaves to work colonial plantations, was never far from the thoughts of those in authority. English Poor Laws of the sixteenth and seventeenth centuries had as much to do with social control as with economic or ethical concerns. Deliberate mixing of African slaves by language was often used as a conscious means of weakening their potential collective resistance. English planters in Barbados objected at first to the conversion of their slaves to Christianity in 1680 because they thought it might weaken their control. They protested to clerical and government authorities that they had "no greater security than the diversity of our negroe's languages which would be destroyed by conversion, in that it would be necessary to teach them in English."[13] Education has always been strictly controlled by those who desired to advance a racial or national mythology. Color designation was not a necessary part of racial mythology, but it became one of its mainstays in places where religion, culture, or language were inadequate, or where color simply did the job of cohesive expropriation better than available alternatives. As the North American colonial population grew to include a more diverse European population than the primarily English settlers of the seventeenth century, and as slavery became an exclusively racial institution, the words *white* and *black* came into regular use. Native Americans who, until the mid-1700s, had almost always been described as tawny or copper or bronze in hue, or as Europeans in the wild, were now called "red" or "redmen," or "redskinned" because of the decorative coloration they sometimes applied to their skin.

The Swedish botanist Charles Linnaeus helped standardize the idea of human groups based on color in the second edition of his *General System of Nature* (1740). He described four basic human categories: "European (white, ruddy, muscular), American (reddish, choleric, erect), Asiatic (yellow, melancholic, inflexible), African (black, phlegmatic, indulgent)."[14] By that time, European global conquest also contributed to a color-related sense of superiority in contrast to all others. The color code was an inconsistent but convenient contrivance that certainly had historic precedent in preracist descriptive terminology. But color as race failed to make provision for Irish, Jewish, Armenian, and Hitlerian Slavic racialization, and it confounds any clear understanding of Hutu or Tutsi racial conflicts for national political power among Africans in the late twentieth century. Nonetheless, color served European global conquest and colonialism during more than two centuries because it became part of racial mythology. James Otis, a prominent Massachusetts political leader during the movement toward independence, declared that Americans were not "a compound mongrel mixture"; they were "freeborn British white subjects."[15] Us and them, as Americans liked to say later, as simple as black and white. In other parts of the colonized world, however, it wasn't quite so simple.

Dutch and Portuguese Imperial Racism

The Dutch, for example, whose global seaborne empire eclipsed that of the English for almost half of this era, never had the domestic population to spare or enough European immigration to their colonies for a unitary racial division. They established a more elaborate racial hierarchy, especially when their colonies included West Indian and Brazilian sugar plantations. Their conquest of northeastern Brazil from 1634 to 1638 led to a huge increase in the demand for African slaves, and the Dutch soon overcame their initial scruples and became as harsh and aggressive in pursuit of the trade's profits as any of their rivals. Dutch mercantile law forbade the enslavement of Native Americans, African Hottentots in Africa, and native Javanese. Most of their Indonesian slaves came from the Celebes, Bali, Buton, and Timor. In their spice plantations in and around Batavia (now Jakarta, Indonesia) slaves included Africans as well as Asians. After the removal or extermination of the native population, the Dutch nutmeg-producing plantations in the Banda Islands of East Asia employed slaves drawn from the far reaches of their trading empire, including Chinese convicts. The racial codes and restrictions set by both the government at home and the directors of the East India Company (the *Hereen* XVII), which exercised government authority in the Dutch mercantile empire, acknowledged intermarriage and some of the complexities of its consequences. Dutch "free burghers" were permitted to marry in the colonies, but they could not take their wives back home to the Netherlands in a ban set in 1650 that reaffirmed an earlier restriction and was renewed in 1713. The burghers became an intermediate mercantile social stratum, like Irish Protestants. They were a frontier middle class, though later, after the trading company became a colony, many of their descendants became completely assimilated into the local region's culture.

The same thing happened to Portuguese adventurers on or beyond the frontiers of their African, Asian, and American empire. Mercantile restrictions on Dutch burghers included employment, residence, and behavioral codes. Company officials regarded them with class disdain and spoke of them as drunkards and "the scum of our land."[16] The Dutch sought to emulate the Portuguese in their attempt to establish a managerial colonial population through intermarriage. In some places the Dutch took the place of the Portuguese after driving them out. When the Dutch captured Colombo and Jaffna from the Portuguese in 1658, many of the Dutchmen stayed and married daughters of Indo-Europeans. The conqueror and subsequent governor of Ceylon, Rijkloff van Goens, accepted such intermarriages but ruled that daughters of such liaisons should be married only to Netherlanders "so that our race may degenerate as little as possible."[17] Dutch East India officials had to rely on intermediary groups as managers, overseers, administrators, and soldiers in their far-flung overseas empire. The social consequence was a more complex and multitiered racial system than the English built in Ireland, the West Indies, or North America.

Elaborate racial legislation coincided with mercantile codes as much for the Dutch as they had for the English. From 1644 onward, the *Hereen* XVII barred any slaves or non-Europeans from returning to the Netherlands in commercial vessels from Asia, including the children of burghers who had married abroad. In 1672 Asians could no longer be employed as clerks in Jakarta, and this ban was extended in 1718 to include the children born of "white" parents in Asia because of the possibility of racial taint. It was almost impossible to enforce, but like all of these crude measures, it was the law. At home in Amsterdam there were regular edicts about treating local people fairly and with kindness, but on the colonial front lines vilification and degradation were the commonplace practice and terminology.[18] Hatred-bred suspicion led to continuous racially contrived tension in the Dutch overseas empire, and accounted for at least one massacre: almost the entire Chinese population of Jakarta was killed in 1740 because of Dutch suspicions about a rumored uprising against them.[19]

Social life in the sugar plantation world of Surinam was the same as in the other European West Indian or American colonies. As in the Dutch West Indies and Brazil, white planters were at the top; after them came a class of European clerks, merchants, and overseers. They were followed by a class of "colored freedmen," the children of European fathers and African slave mothers, and a small group of free Africans. African slaves were at the bottom, with the lowest category reserved for "salt water negroes," the most recent arrivals from Africa who were made distinct from the old-timers, who were called "creoles."[20] On both the European frontier of conquest and among the newest arrivals to be employed in profit-driven mercantile plantation enterprises, there was a social nexus where necessity invented unforeseen adjustments in identity and structures of authority. Emotional adjustments took the form of new mythologies. The Portuguese experience in Africa, America, and Asia was similar to both the English and Dutch, but it had some of its own peculiarities.

Frontier Subdivisions

The Portuguese enjoyed a myth that there was never the same kind of racism and color discrimination in their empire as that found in all the others. They credited their religious Catholic universalism and intermarriage with the local women as forces that offset or diminished racial degradation in their empire. They were half-right and half-wrong. To their eternal credit, the authorities at home in Lisbon in both the church and state issued decrees and orders that constantly called for humane treatment and conversion of the local people under their power. Theirs began as a feudal, imperial thassalocracy, a maritime profit-seeking religious crusade, and they never gave up their noble rhetoric even when their religious orders barred Africans from membership and their slave plantations and mines were as racially defined and brutal as any others. Their own trading settlements were relatively small, most often coastal, similar to the Dutch in Africa and Asia and the French river-based trading centers in Canada, and they needed the cooperation and participation of local people. From the start, the Portuguese encouraged the intermarriage of their nationals with them. Backcountry, frontier, and up-river explorations were left to adventurers and some missionaries, who were usually accompanied by mercenary soldiers and friendly locals. Tropical interiors in Africa, Asia, and America were often disease filled and dangerous. Portuguese soldiers of fortune who organized interior expeditions searched for fast profits in slaves to trade, gold, ivory, or spices. They flew their own colors or banners, called *bandeiras,* and in Brazil consequently were known as *bandeirantes.* They were most notorious in Brazil for their murderous depredations against the local people who could offer little resistance. They were usually out of the reach of Portuguese government control in Asia and Africa as well. Tropical disease and the more highly organized and larger populations they sometimes encountered curbed their influence at times or forced them into alliances with local people. There were genocidal atrocities against others. In the mid-1690s large-scale gold deposits were discovered in the rough interior north of Rio de Janeiro, an area known as Minias Gerais. A gold rush and mining boom that included diamond discoveries from the 1720s lasted more than half a century and drove *bandeirantes* farther into the interior, where they continued their prospecting and other forms of ravaging the people and the countryside. Gold and diamonds caused price inflation on everything, and huge profits powered an increased demand for African and Native American slaves. There was a corresponding back-country disregard for "colonial laws which still discriminated against persons of African blood." Brazil soon became widely known as "A Hell for blacks, a purgatory for whites, and a paradise for mulattoes."[21]

Economic development in Portuguese Asian and African colonies was subordinated to the necessities of the slave trade as Africans became the dominant population of Portuguese colonial Brazil. Manumission of slaves was a much more common practice in Brazil than in other colonial or plantation-based economies. Freed slaves and their descendants became an important intermediary group in most sectors of the expansive and still racially conscious society. In Brazil, as almost everywhere else, wealth created a higher status for those who possessed it than those without; the expression "money bleaches" is still used there, both with and without irony.

In Africa and Asia, Portuguese adventurers similarly merged themselves with the local cultural systems for their own advantage. The virtually private principalities they set up were called *prazos*. They schemed, intrigued, and sometimes warred against one another with private armies of free and enslaved Africans or Asians up to 30,000 strong. The *prazos* became so completely autonomous that the Portuguese Crown intervened to reestablish political and racial control. They were turned into "entailed estates" that were granted by the government for three successive generations with yearly quit-rent payments to be made in gold. Racial policy required that such estates be granted only to Portuguese women born of Portuguese parents. These women were required to be married to men of guaranteed full Portuguese ancestry. This was nothing less than a mercantile family land plan for the colonies. Male children could not inherit the estate, only females could, and they also had to marry a guaranteed all-European man. Estate owners were also expected to manage the land in keeping with careful stipulations. Any breach in rules would result in the estate reverting to the Crown. The regulations could not be enforced, however; *prazos* expanded in numbers and size and formed their own intermediary culture as Portuguese power waned in the eighteenth century.[22] Racial policy in the Portuguese empire was only as good as the national political authority behind it. The same was true of all mercantile regulations. Throughout their empire, Portuguese and other Europeans or people of mixed parentage often learned local languages, married or took numerous concubines, and settled in as intermediaries to deal with the native people and other Europeans. A constant tension existed between the frontier, seminomadic, predatory settlers and the attempt to control them by religious and governmental authorities. Jesuits struggled with them on behalf of their missionary goals for

Asians and Native Americans. *Bandeirantes* in Brazil claimed the natives were incapable of the Catholic faith and wanted them for slaves in mines or on plantations. Jesuits were gradually forced out of São Paulo (1640–53), Santos (1640–42), and Maranhão-Para (1661–63) by *bandeirantes,* even though the Jesuits had the official support of the Portuguese government.[23]

Portugal's racial-policy failures and inconsistencies in this era are probably the best explanation for their comparative differences with the other Europeans. Because of their unsuccessful attempts to establish a loyal Indian burgher class in their African trading ports of Mozambique and Angola, it was seriously suggested on at least two occasions, once from 1723 to 1726 and again in 1744, that they import Irish Catholics for that purpose. They were seeking to emulate the relative success that Spain and the Dutch East India Company achieved with an imported Chinese managerial population in the Philippine Islands and the Dutch East Indies.[24] On the west coast of Africa, Portuguese religious authorities welcomed Africans and sons of Portuguese Africans to the priesthood. In east African settlements they rarely did so, and only with the most extreme reluctance. In 1761, the year the Portuguese dictator the Marquis de Pombral pronounced an end of discrimination based on race throughout the empire, a seminary was opened in Mozambique that admitted only Asian Goans or Indo-Portuguese, no Africans. The feared dictator's decree was not promulgated until thirteen years later because of "how deeply the feeling of racial superiority was implanted in the Portuguese colonial authorities."[25] Those authorities were at the point of expropriation and control. Lisbon was far away from a complex and diverse overseas empire and lacked the administrative efficiency of the Dutch East India Company. "What is certain," according to one of the foremost scholars on this issue, "is that racial discrimination in favour of the European-born Portuguese, if not always accepted in theory, was widely and continuously exercised in practice by the great majority of overseas viceroys and governors."[26]

The practices of mercantile reality frequently exceeded its original, protective intentions. Free trade tended to replace protected monopolies. Colonists selectively evaded restrictive trade and navigation laws and substituted similar codes or practices that served themselves. English authorities allowed a policy named by Prime Minister Robert Walpole "Salutary Neglect" when the cost of the rigorous enforcement of navigation laws exceeded its return. The new English king, George III, faced even worse disobedience and disregard for his authority from his North American colonies than his Portuguese counterpart, Pombral. Portugal lost Brazil to independence fifty years after England's loss of her thirteen North American colonies. While Portugal's empire and national power were slipping away in the eighteenth century, the Portuguese were also losing their power to enforce racial codes abroad. In contrast, England, despite the revolt of thirteen American colonies, was moving toward the era of its greatest imperial national and racial hegemony.

Mercantile Warfare

England did not win every European war in this contentious era, only those that counted most. Struggle for control of valuable overseas imperial possessions had been mixed with religious and dynastic motives before the Treaty of Westphalia marked the end of the Thirty Years' War in 1648. Rivalry for overseas power between Portugal and Spain preceded English, French, and Dutch competition. Imperial warfare between Portugal and Spain marked the beginning of national conflict and the decline of church-arbitrated royal disputes. The Dutch displaced the Portuguese in Indonesia in 1641 and established plantations in Brazil.

What seems most notable about conflict among the great imperial powers over the next 150 years is its constancy. Only one time, from 1714 to 1739, might be called a "long peace" in an otherwise unbroken deadly struggle. England, with various and changing alliances, fought somewhat inconclusively against the Dutch Republic and its allies in a series of three wars from 1652 to 1674. The Spanish sugar plantation colony of Jamaica and Dutch New Amsterdam were among the British spoils of that era, along with the occupation of St. Helena in 1659, an important post on the Cape route to India. England's armies and navies fought successfully against the Spanish and French, again with various and changing allies, for the next century. Sometimes called the wars for empire, they were usually named by North American colonists for the reigning English monarch, in contrast to the more formal dynastic designations given to them by the Europeans. They were King William's War (the War of the League of Augsburg), 1689–97, Queen Anne's War (the War of Spanish Succession) 1702–14, and King George's War (the War of Austrian Succession), 1739–48. Americans called the last of these the French and Indian War (the Seven Years War), 1754–1763. Their own victorious battle with England, their War for Independence, brought the new nation, the United States of America, control over the French-ceded Ohio River Valley and launched a century of expansion that included war with Mexico and Spain. In spite of some concessions along the way and the one significant loss of the American colonies, England continued to increase its national mercantile power on every continent and in every ocean. Warfare made the English nation the greatest empire in the world; trade made it the richest. By 1815, an English trading organization chartered early in the 1600s, the East India Company, had its own powerful private army and navy, governed most of India, and was feared from Arabia in the Middle East to Java in the Far East.[27]

Race and Power in the British Empire

Laws defined the British Empire, set relationships, and were the codes by which boundaries and power were measured. Racial laws and codes were internal laws in the colonies throughout the empire. They were also an extension of artificial aristocratic class identity with a national leadership for the same purpose at home: boundary and power. The scale of the British Empire meant that local princes and feudal or semifeudal elites had to maintain local governing authority and share in administrative tasks. The independent United States eventually reconciled itself to a junior partnership with the empire when it promulgated the Monroe Doctrine of 1823. National political and class cohesion were maintained by English racial identity from Dublin to Bombay and throughout the empire as it was built, and was celebrated and scientifically certified a hundred years later. Great novelists such as Daniel Defoe in his *Colonel Jack* or *Robinson Crusoe* expressed the widely held view of the English and most Europeans of the seventeenth and eighteenth century that Africans held them in awe and quite naturally fell under their authority. Enlightened philosophers such as David Hume echoed the opinions of Englishmen who had been to the slave-trading marts of Africa and concluded that the people there were "naturally inferior" due to a total lack of "ingenious manufactures" and "no arts, no sciences."[28]

Wealth poured into England. Bullion became the measure of successful national policy, and colonial mercantile success made contradictory sentiments about the Irish, Africans, or Asians appear false. Coercion was a part of everyday English life and law, with public hangings a fairly common occurrence; floggings, branding, and mutilations were routine expressions of class authority. Racial coercion and physical brutality in the empire were simple extensions of existing domestic practices to foreign or alien subjects and brought about cohesion among diverse imperial authorities among those who shared the same racial identity. In Ireland, colonial America, and India, English subjects enjoyed an advantage because of their racial status that they lacked at home. Colonial conquest was usually physical and required armed force in Ireland, America, Africa, and Asia. Hundreds of specialized tools and gadgets of punishment and coercion were made explicitly for the control of the colonized and the use of the colonizer. Fine human distinctions were put aside, and physical differences, no matter how

slight or contrived, became more important. National loyalty was strengthened among the conquerors and settlers by their inherited apparent physical
bond. A shared racial identity was both socially comforting and militarily
necessary, and it served to create a sharp contrast with those whom they
fought to conquer, displace, or enslave.

The further authorities went from the metropole to the frontiers of the
English empire, the greater the psychological and physical power advantage
they could assume over those under their utilization of that English power.
The imagined vices and virtues of race and nation became idealized in an
expanded hierarchical British Empire. The idealization of race, and the legal
codes and strictures that went along with it, obscured expropriation and
injustice. English deeds might otherwise have appeared contradictory
within the concept of existing English standards. Racism provided the ethical and emotional rationale for injustices in much the same manner as the
imagined virtues of superior class status allowed unearned material benefits
or legal and social privileges to accrue to their possessors.

Fine distinctions of class, race, and nation found a brilliantly high level
of development within England and throughout its empire. Language, law,
clothing habits, education, informal and formal social practices all deliberately made the distinctions that appeared to confirm the empirical reality of
racial and national power. Dissent came from people outside the circle of
those wielding power, such as some religious groups and writers. Doing
what Jonathan Swift did on behalf of the Irish, though without his satire,
Roger Williams, William Penn, and other Quakers wrote and spoke out on
behalf of Native Americans. Aside from these, however, English or American writers on behalf of the Irish, Africans, or Asians were few, and while
there were eventually many critics of slavery and the slave trade, hardly any
voices other than those of its victims condemned restrictive racial laws or
codes. Among American revolutionaries, many shared Jefferson's politically enlightened and legally framed objections to the Crown's mercantile
restrictions and the slave trade, but none of these new nationalists cried out
against the racism that helped define and secure their own social hierarchy.

French Mercantilism

The French and Spanish lost out in the eighteenth-century struggle for
empire to the English, but maintained some of their West Indian sugar
plantations and the imperial, racial divisions that were not very distinct
from those of other European powers. The English took Jamaica from Spain
in 1655, though it was not formally ceded until 1671. Mercantilism was
inherently a competitive international system. Each nation sought to gain

some advantage from its various commercial enterprises that would either divert wealth away from rivals or enhance its own self-sufficiency. Tax revenues from bullion and royal or government participation in the enterprises paid for the construction of navies and the costs of large armies. Once in the game, all the players either adapted to the rules of play or fell behind the competition. The French imposed restrictions and struggled against slave rebellions while they believed they were bringing culture and civilization to backward heathen with the same conviction as their European counterparts. As social tensions increased in the second half of the eighteenth century, the French colonial authorities reversed their earlier *Code Noir,* which granted freed slaves the same political rights as other colonists. After 1766, a new set of rules were applied to *gens de couleur:* they could no longer serve in the militia, hold administrative offices, enter lucrative professions, or use firearms without a special license. A dress code was prescribed to highlight their distinction from Europeans, and they were forbidden to wear sidearms, a traditional mark of class status. After 1779, a troublesome and unenforceable racial curfew was imposed.[29]

The French also faced the continuing problem of an inadequate middle-level administrative and managerial overseas population, and they, too, relied heavily on a population of mixed European, Native American, and African people. Freed slaves and the children of slave masters and slaves became an important intermediary population in their plantation colonies.

In the course of the French Revolution, the slave uprising that embroiled Hispaniola and led to the independence of Haiti brought about some interesting alliances. Slaveowners, no matter their origin or hue, stayed loyal to their property interests and allied themselves with royalists and foreign enemies of the Jacobins in control of the French National Assembly. When these radicals dominated the French government and intervened in Haiti in 1793, they took up the cause of the insurrectionary slaves. Much bloodshed and shifting alliances ensued, but eventually most Europeans left Haiti. The powerful plantation system, once among the most productive and profitable in the West Indies, was replaced, after the death in a French prison of the Haitian leader Toussaint L'Ouverture, by a division of land that collapsed sugar production. The almost complete dearth of investment capital from European and American banks meant a lack of economic development and chronic impoverishment of the population of the new nation.

French mercantilism was famous for some exceptional internal national product developments. The production of French wine, silks, and finely crafted furnishings was deliberately subsidized and encouraged by Jean Baptiste Colbert, a draper turned mercantile economist. Colbert was recommended to King Louis XIV by Cardinal Mazarin to look after the finances of the nation. Before the extravagant waste of his patron forced him into unpopular taxing measures, he was responsible for an enormous array of accomplishments that helped make the nation more economically self-sufficient, scientifically up to date, and militarily strong. He improved the road system of France, promoted the development of a great navy, reduced barriers to internal trade, founded the Academy of Sciences and the Paris Observatory, and helped promote the French Academy. What many love about France and French culture, and many French people believe makes their country unquestionably the best, can be credited to the accomplishments of the great national mercantilist Colbert. War may indeed have made the nations, but it was the wealth of empire and their successful mercantile trade that made and paid for their national cultures.

The French economy and nation depended less on overseas colonies and trading bases than did their rivals. France held no large colonies in the Indian Ocean—only a trading base at Reunion and Mauritius. The French maintained a slave- and gold-trading base in Senegal on the West African coast, and profited from its American, Canadian, and West Indian colonies until they were reduced or lost to their English rivals or sold to the United States by Napoleon. French national sentiment and racial consciousness depended less on eighteenth-century colonial expropriations or conquests than on internal mercantile achievements and nineteenth-century continental and colonial power. Instead of a colonial economy driven by spices, rum, or tobacco trade and built on slave labor, French landowners used (some have said exploited to revolutionary desperation) their own domestic labor force to produce such valuable national products as wine and silk for profitable international trade. France became a strong mercantile power, not because of colonial trade, though the French did enjoy some of that, but because of the highly refined domestic agricultural enterprises that brought the nation profitable trading advantages. French physiocrats of the eighteenth century, led by François Quesnay, were the first modern students of economics and profoundly influenced the work of Adam Smith and the empirical thinking of men such as Thomas Jefferson and Benjamin Franklin.

Empirical Science

The famous French naturalist George Louis Leclerc, the Comte de Buffon (1707–1788) was a contemporary of the great botanist and pioneering taxonomist Carolus (Karl) Linnaeus (1708–1778). Buffon disagreed with Linnaeus about the number of human subdivisions and is considered the first natural scientist to use the word *race*. Buffon described six varieties or races of the human species: the Laplander or Polar, Tatar or Mongolian,

Southern Asiatic, European, Ethiopian, and American. The qualities that divided them were color, stature, physical details, and behavioral traits.[30] Racial science, unlike Newtonian mathematics, has never achieved consensus on its most basic distinctions, but that neither impeded nor discouraged its theoreticians or their followers. There were almost as many different categories or distinctions made among human types as prominent scientists who made them. Not long after Buffon's classification of races, a German physician, Johann Friedrich Blumenbach, published his 1775 doctoral dissertation, *De Generis human varietate nativa* (trans. Thomas Bendysshe, 3rd rev. ed., London, 1795). Blumenbach divided humankind into five distinct races with elaborately detailed diagnostic traits: Caucasian (he was the first to employ this term), Mongolian, Ethiopian, American, and Malay.[31] Like the nation, race had as many scientific definitions as those bold enough to try it. The search for a straightforward universally acceptable definition of the so-called races or of nations parallels the attempt to define pornography; as Supreme Court Justice Potter Stewart famously confessed, he couldn't define it, but he knew it when he saw it.

Denmark, Too

The Danes developed a clear sense of their racial superiority over Greenlanders after they began to colonize the largest island in the world. They followed a Norwegian missionary there after 1721 and used it as a place of deportation for criminals and undesirables who were used as workers in Danish trading stations. Greenland natives were less easily controlled and were vulnerable to European diseases, which reduced their numbers significantly. The Danes operated an Asiatic trading company from 1732 and had a trading station at Tranquebar, which was sold to England in 1845. They maintained a trading base near Calcutta and a West African station called Christiansborg, founded in 1657 and given to England in 1850. Their West Indian colonies were almost completely company-run enterprises that began with the colonization of St. Thomas in 1666. They granted the Brandenburg Company of Prussia a concession to use the island as a slave-trading station, and eventually added St. Croix in 1733 to their Virgin Island group. Convicts, refugees, and African slaves made a plantation system nearly identical to that found throughout the region with corresponding laws and codes.[32] Denmark's modest mercantile power was eclipsed by England in the nineteenth century. Readers of mystery novels can confirm the lingering influence of Danish racism toward Greenlanders in *Smilla's Sense of Snow* (1993) by Peter Hoeg.

Old Empires

Internal warfare, dynastic conflicts, and the remains of feudal divisions were among the factors that impeded overseas imperial mercantile ventures by the other European powers. The stagnant empires elsewhere in the world slipped farther and farther behind the dynamic Europeans and their global armies and navies. Absolutist monarchies in Northern, Central, and Eastern Europe sought to enlarge and consolidate national authority wherever they could. The Holy Roman Empire fought long-running border wars against Ottoman imperial Turkish power and counterinsurgency conflict with various regional or localized national movements. Neither the development of the modern nation-state nor its counterpart in racism were significant characteristics of these powers for another century. The national movements seeking to gain state power within the decaying empires did exhibit all the characteristics of their predecessors. The ethnic conflict of these movements and the binding loyalties toward emerging national authorities found internal expression in the continuing restrictions placed on Jews, Armenians, and others considered as foreigners. Similar outbursts of anti-Semitism and internal domestic racial or religious divisiveness were present in modern mercantile states as well. Anti-Catholic mob violence, for example, in the Gordon riots in England of the 1790s pitted groups of the urban unemployed and poor against one another. Expressions of religious bigotry and antiforeign hostility exhibited much of the same kind of psychological and social frenzy as racism but did not share its legal sanctions or scientific pretensions. Unlike racism, religious or cultural intolerance was almost always condemned with class disdain by the more refined authorities. This was, after all, for the educated and sophisticated few, an age of reason and enlightenment.

Race, Reason, and National Identity

None of the new nations and none of the old empires or feudal kingdoms were popular democracies during this era. The American and French revolutionary upheavals of the last quarter of the eighteenth century signaled the beginning of growing public participation in the state. Until then, the nation, and all public and private institutions, were under a narrowly controlled authority. Nationalism and racism as generalized popular mythologies did not command a broadly based popular appeal or democratic emotional identification until the next century. Their strongest hold on the popular imagination was closest to their empirical reality. The European soldier or bureaucrat in the colony, the merchant and sailor at work in the slave trade, and the plantation owner or frontiersman in the colony found it nearly impossible to imagine his socially structured and racially defined reality in any other way. He was not just in it. He was it. The banker, soldier, planter, and merchant who depended on the state were just as emotionally loyal to the national authority that joined and protected them. When civil liberties were extended to small landowners and some others, they too gave their loyalty to their collective benefactor.

An expanded secular, intellectual world accompanied the material richness of mercantile achievement. Reason, in contrast to feudal tradition and religious revelation, appeared as a significant intellectual and cultural force only after the great religious battles of the Reformation era. One student of this phenomenon, Ernst Cassirer, observed in his famous book *The Philosophy of the Enlightenment,* that reason's "most important function consists in its power to bind and to dissolve. It dissolves everything merely factual, all simple data of experience, and everything believed on the evidence of revelation, tradition, and authority" (p. 13). After it dissolves everything, and here it differs from today's deconstructionists, it builds up from all the "dispersed parts" a "completely new structure, a true whole" (p. 14). Everything was subject to examination and study with this clean-slate approach: government by Locke and Montesquieu, the universe by Newton, the natural sciences by Buffon, and philosophy by Descartes are examples of an enormous flourishing of secular intellectual discoveries and extensions of human knowledge that accompanied the European global expansion of power, commerce, and wealth. The exciting accuracy of their big scientific discoveries caused them to be certified as natural laws. It was an age of laws. Newton's laws and Boyle's law are well known, or should be, to beginning students in science. Most of the prominent intellectual figures of this era came to believe that cold, hard, scientific observation and the power of human reason could unravel the mysteries of the universe. So much was unraveled and discovered in those years that it made for those who participated in it a uniquely optimistic age. Nations were natural things, these enlightened intellectuals believed, and could be studied, dissected, analyzed, and perfected if their inherent laws were revealed. Races, they thought, were natural divisions of humanity, and they, too, could be carefully categorized and studied and their true nature revealed. Among the best of these thinkers are Francis Bacon and John Locke, who posited a sharp empiricism. Just look at what is there; leave your emotional and arbitrary dogma behind, they said. Strip things to their essentials and build from that point. "Knowledge is power," said Bacon. It was a magnificent place to start. When Thomas Jefferson was Benjamin Franklin's replacement as United States ambassador to France, he was asked many things. Jefferson was not only the most esteemed representative of his new nation, he was one of the most enlightened intellectual figures the new nation could have chosen to be its representative. What did he think about the troublesome question of race?

Not everything Jefferson said in private conversation about race is known, but he did leave behind his enormous correspondence and a book aimed at answering many of the queries put to him about his world and the new nation he represented, *Notes on the State of Virginia*. In it he expressed some doubts about reaching firm conclusions about the moral or intellectual capabilities associated with the question of race, but he did accept the premise of its reality. Reaching any kind of conclusion "must be hazarded with great diffidence," he cautioned. He also knew that whatever conclusion he reached might have great consequences, that it could "degrade a whole race of men from the rank in the scale of beings which their Creator may perhaps have given them." And he reminded his readers that his country-men deserve reproach for "a century and a half we have had under our eyes the races of black and of red men, they have never yet been viewed by us as subjects of natural history." With all these cautionary notes and warnings as his preface, he nonetheless concluded: "I advance it therefore as a suspicion only, that the blacks, whether originally a distinct race, or made distinct by time and circumstances, are inferior to the whites in the endowments both of body and mind" (p. 143). He envisioned a time when slavery must end. He speculated about the meaning of freed slaves finding a place within the larger society, and compared it to the emancipation of slaves in the time of the ancient Romans. The difference there was that "the slave, when made free (by the Romans) might mix with, without staining the blood of his master. But with us a second (effort) is necessary, unknown to history. When freed, he is to be removed beyond the reach of mixture" (p. 143).

Race and nation, liberty and slavery were joined in science and law in the foundation of the United States of America. The new Constitution made no provision for race, but protected (through a fugitive-slave provision) and extended the institution of racial slavery (indefinitely) and the racial slave trade (for twenty years), and provided extra political representation to racial slaveowners in government (the three-fifths clause). In the most advanced political cultures in the Western world, racial and national mythologies were legally secure and culturally unchallenged at the end of the eighteenth century. Indeed, they were about to begin their most prosperous era.

Chapter 5

To the Ends of the Earth: Racism and Nationalism Rampant, 1800–1917

Democracy and Racism

The American and French revolutions were an inspiration for popular national uprisings against most of the remaining strictures of royal, aristocratic, and clerical power. Businessmen, farmers, and artisans put aside some of their differences for the common goals of citizenship and free(er) enterprise. The European upheavals of 1830 and 1848 carried those broadly democratic struggles into places of deeply entrenched tradition, to what was left of the Holy Roman Empire and to czarist Romanov Russia in the Decembrist Revolt of 1825. For Spain, such populist impulses linked to nationalism had serious implications. The Spanish Empire in the Americas was almost completely lost in the decades following the Napoleonic Wars as nationalist revolutions hastened Spain's long imperial decline. In the Americas, as elsewhere, coalitions made up of independent planters, businessmen, and ambitious professionals were intent on building secular, independent nation-states based on law. Balance and contractual accountability in an optimistic scientifically enlightened age inspired the rhetoric of these groups. Those whose enterprises and wealth secured the destiny of the state, and paid for it, should run it, they argued. Taxation and representation meant the achievement of liberty and the extirpation of tyranny for those who made and came within the scope of the laws. A cultural bond was forged among ratepayers, and pragmatic unity was built on expanded idealized symbols of observed reality. Race and nation were discovered to be startlingly effective categories for achieving nonclerical and nonaristocratic social cohesion at home and the effective administration of colonies abroad, especially when viewed in contrast to competitive, decaying, imperial alternatives.

In the nineteenth century another turn was reached in the twisting double helix of race and nation as central features of modern public identity. Nationalism brought with it new liberties, a civic bonding that turned former subjects of authority into citizens who became members of a corporate body, the state; they sang "My country 'tis of thee, Sweet land of Liberty. . . ." The new nationalism carried on the empirical and scientific blessings of the Enlightenment and added the politically romantic allure of American and French revolutionaries. For those included in its political embrace, "All men are created equal." Citizens could expect *Liberté, Egalité, Fraternité.* In this new context of nationalism, racism served old imperial purposes by creating a falsely unified aristocracy of blood, politics, and rationalization. In spite of some persistent criticism of its validity, racism was confirmed as scientific and became a physical portrait of natural unity when national conquest or colonial expropriation seemed unavoidable or inevitable. Napoleon turned French nationalism to imperial conquest and the new United States found the term Manifest Destiny to herald the same thing.

Some American, English, and French abolitionists protested war, slavery, and racial brutality as their governments gained influence in the receding colonial empires of Portugal, Spain, and the Netherlands, and added their own new territorial conquests and populations. The success of aggressive nations in making new conquests swept away much of this protest, for example, the indifferent response of the public to Congressman Abraham Lincoln and American essayist and poet Henry David Thoreau's objections to the Mexican War. Moreover, even antiwar protest, like antislavery, did not typically include objections to racial degradation.

Britannia ruled much more than the waves in the nineteenth century and constructed a diverse pragmatic system of political relationships to secure that power. What worked well tended to be used. The English trading companies, then the government itself, incorporated existing elites, feudal and religious local leaders, and often one local tribal group over another, into an imperial relationship of mutual benefit. England, now called "Britain" after the Act of Union of 1707, ruled over this empire as both a nation and a race apart. Race and nation were the emotional, political and cultural bonds found among those new powers with external colonial or subcitizen domestic subjects, and held out a romantic appeal in this expansive and democratic age. Race was democratically inclusive and aristocratically exclusive at the same time. The idealized, virtuous, aggressive nation-state and the concept of racial exclusivity found near-universal popularity in an era of democratic revolutions and European imperialism. They were at the core of the formation of national public identity in the modern world.

Patriotism and Racism

Mercantilism's overtly commercial and crassly honest economic standard of measurement was good enough for the propertied members of the early nation-states, for the French agrarian physiocrats admired by Thomas Jefferson, and for the English and Dutch trading companies and their corporate or royal sponsors or governing bodies. John Locke's premise that government was formed to protect property found little contrary argument for over a hundred years.[1] The mercantile age had not passed when the Founding Founders of the United States did their work. Their desire for economic security and a Calvinistic skepticism about the inclusion of those without a propertied entitlement in the state still placed them in the front ranks of political thought in their time. It only later was found that inclusion of nonpropertied (male) workers within the state as citizens offered many national advantages, not the least of which Napoleon's massive armies forcefully demonstrated in their conquests of Europe. Patriotism became the popular emotional expression of loyalty to the state authority that granted and protected the universal rights of the citizens of the nation. Racism created a similarly pleasurable and childishly simple identification with a physically shared imagined universality and a nationally shared physically identified adversary. In a society that continued to send out frontier settlements, race bound those on the edge and at the highest risk with their creditors. Laws and institutionalized codes and practices secured both citizenship and racial identity.[2]

Nationalism meant adherence to all the laws, respect for all authorities. Both civic inclusion and genuine economic privileges, along with real and imagined social and psychological benefits, accrued to the loyal citizen-racists of the nineteenth century. Patriotism and racism were emotional sanctuaries for a synthetic identification with unevenly distributed profits and arbitrary political and social power. Consciousness of a universal common humanity abroad, or the inequities and injustices of social-class divisions at home, dimmed in direct proportion to the brightness of racial and national sentiment. Race and national mythology provided social and cultural cohesion for every expansive state, at home, abroad, or on the frontiers of European or American settlement everywhere on earth.

In the Age of Innocence

Prejudice, bigotry, and intolerance had nothing to do with the racial and national expression of group identification in this era. Those words were infrequently used. They were almost unknown concepts. The perceived truths about race and nation were confirmed by science and enforced by laws, albeit with inconsistencies made more obvious with the passing of time, and with alterations in law and science. Today the word *bigot* is used to describe the expressions of racial and national identity commonly used by yesterday's presidents, Supreme Court justices, prime ministers, and most scientists, writers, and intellectuals. Until the rapid breakdown of formal colonial and racial structures of the post–World War II era, such words as *bigot* or *prejudice* that depicted racist thinking or behavior negatively were used almost exclusively by their victims or by those who tried to protect them from abuse. The European and American frontier vision imagined nothing of value beyond its own objectives. It saw nothing but its own world. Everything else was nonexistent or was a blank slate awaiting the civilizing hand of the colonizer. Ralph Ellison published his great novel *Invisible Man* in 1952. It is an accurate metaphor for the nationally induced blindness of the racist. From his Oxford chair, the renowned English historian Hugh Trevor-Roper proclaimed, in 1962, the still-lingering colonialist and racial view of Africa, that "perhaps in the future there will be some African history to teach. But at the present there is none; there is only the history of the Europeans in Africa. The rest is darkness . . . and darkness is not the subject of history."[3] His statement accurately reflected a vision of the modern world, of modernity itself, that reached its most triumphant expression before the decay and disillusionment that set in after World War I. That vision was formed on the nineteenth-century frontiers of European and American national and racial expansion and conquest, secured by the wealth and power of empire, and became the focal point of identity for the dominant industrial and commercial class and its institutional leaders, and all those who accepted their authority and shared their aspirations.

Expanding and Closing Frontiers

The continuation of exploration and military conquest took Europeans and Americans to the ends of the earth in the nineteenth and early twentieth centuries. Lewis and Clark traversed the trans-Mississippi Northwest and left behind a remarkable account. The story of Sir Henry Morton Stanley, the Anglo-American journalist, explorer, and empire maker, could have been a better motion picture even without the famous discovery of Dr. David Livingstone, the missing Scottish missionary, on Lake Tanganyika in 1871. Perhaps a new film version can still be made. Stanley was a man of his time. After fighting for both sides in the American Civil War, he went into journalism and successfully covered the campaign of General Sir Charles Napier in Abyssinia (now Ethiopia) for the *New York Herald* in

1868. Lord Napier's reputation was embellished after a victory against the Baluchi people in defense of British imperial power in India when he said, "Never give way to barbarians."[4] Stanley accepted the commission of the *Herald* to go to Africa and search for Livingstone in 1871, then went back there for the paper on a subsequent expedition himself that led to a third and final journey into the Congo River region. With backing from King Leopold II of Belgium, Stanley helped establish the Kingdom of the Congo and played an important role at Otto von Bismarck's Berlin Conference of 1885, which secured the region for his royal benefactor. Leopold personally ruled the so-called Congo Free State until he was forced to turn it over to Belgium in 1908. The Berlin Conference made a number of important decisions about the division and future of West Africa, though not a single African was a participant. Stanley went on to play a role in securing British imperial interests in Uganda and reclaimed his English citizenship. He served in Parliament from 1895 to 1900, and was granted knighthood by Queen Victoria in 1899. Add your own romantic subplot, or find the real one, and with the right cast another imperialist nonfiction adventure is there for the making.

European and American explorers traversed continents, climbed mountains, and charted the oceans and coastlines of the earth. Robert Edwin Peary, with a servant and four Eskimo people, reached the North Pole for the United States in April 1909. Roald Amundsen, a Norwegian, made it to the South Pole at the end of 1911. No earthly obstacle, physical or human, seemed able to withstand the global march of discovery and conquest by these restless and competitive emissaries of nations. The great navies of the world studied the ocean depths, made charts of harbors on every island and coastline, and built far-flung bases and coaling stations to secure national empires and protect commerce. One of the most important and influential books of the end of the century was Alfred Thayer Mahan's *The Influence of Sea Power on History* (1890). The naval arms race that was under way at the time of its publication is often noted as one of the causes of World War I. By the close of this era, only a few desert wastes (with as yet undiscovered oil or mineral wealth) and mountaintops remained temporarily free of exploration by Englishmen and other Europeans.

Invariably, soldiers followed on the heels of the explorers, with the latter in many cases under military authority themselves, as were Peary and Lewis and Clark. The military conquerors were hailed as national celebrities for their victories over nearly defenseless, though often heroic, native people. After the passage of the great Virginia dynasty of slaveowners from the American presidency, and with the exception of the two single terms served by John Adams and John Quincy Adams, the office regularly went to, or was seriously aspired to by, veterans of wars against Native Americans, Mexicans, Spaniards, or Philippine nationalists: Andrew Jackson (1829–37), William Henry Harrison (1841), Zachary Taylor (1849), John C. Fremont (unsuccessful, 1856), and Abraham Lincoln (1861–65). Lincoln was a volunteer, but saw no action, in the Black Hawk War. General George Armstrong Custer was known to have his similar aspirations cut short at the Little Big Horn River in 1876; and Admiral George Dewey, the celebrated victor at Manila Bay, put his hat briefly and awkwardly into the presidential ring in 1900. The "Hero of San Juan Hill," Theodore Roosevelt, gained the vice-presidency and, on the death of William McKinley, the highest office (1901–09). President Jackson carried his indifference to any legal rights for slaves and native people into the White House. He installed Roger Brooke Taney as chief justice of the Supreme Court in 1836. Taney consistently led the Court in rulings in favor of racially based slavery laws, most famously in the *Dred Scott* case (1857) in which he explicitly upheld the constitutional concept of racial exclusion from legal rights. President Jackson's refusal to enforce two major Supreme Court decisions in favor of Native American land rights in Georgia led to the removal of Native Americans in that state and led in other states to an American "Hell or Connaught" of expropriation, transportation, and death. The moderate historian Glyndon G. Van Deusen in his highly praised *The Jacksonian Era, 1828–1848* (1959) sums up the policy of the government of the United States: "Force, terror, and fraud compelled the Indian to the white man's desire" (p. 50). Americans were hardly alone in this kind of enterprise.

Pax Britannia

English parks are filled with statues that commemorate similar military heroes and comparable victories and displacements of native populations in the Middle East, Central Asia, India, Africa, and the Far East. Those who resisted English colonialism in India or Africa met brutal, racially legitimized repression. The century of *Pax Britannia* that began with the final defeat of Napoleon was, ironically, one of almost continuous imperial warfare. From 1817 to 1878, the British military carried out campaigns against the African people of the eastern Cape they called Kaffirs. The British invaded Abyssinia (Ethiopia) in 1867 and Zululand in 1879. A brutal and punitive war was carried out by British forces against the Asante people of the Gold Coast in 1873 and 1874. The British military in India was similarly engaged. There were two campaigns in Burma, 1824 and 1853, and in Afghanistan in 1838–42 and 1878–80. The British conquered the Sind in 1843 and the Punjab in India in two campaigns in 1845–46 and

1848–49. British forces suppressed the Sepoy uprising during 1857–58. Maori fighting in New Zealand went on sporadically from about 1846 to 1870. A rebellion had to be suppressed by force in Canada in 1837, and the British attacked Persia in 1856. Chinese official protest and resistance to the destructive economic and human consequences of the profitable British-controlled opium trade led to three humbling military defeats between 1839 and 1860. By the late 1890s, after defeat by Japan in 1895 and stepped up demands by the European powers for expanded economic, territorial, and political control in China, it truly seemed as if China was being cut up "like a melon." (See *A History of Asia,* vol. 2, by W. Bingham, H. Conroy, F. Ikle [Boston: Allyn and Bacon, 1965], p. 336.) Colonial powers combined to fight alongside one another to relieve their besieged Bejing legations in the Boxer Rebellion, an uprising of frustrated, angry young Chinese in 1900.

At times, the English displaced other Europeans. For example, Boers, the descendants of Africanized Dutch and French settlers, were almost completely unregulated by the fading power of the Dutch West India Company. Also called Afrikaners, they dominated a complex racial and social world of slaves and nonslave Africans, Khoikhois (Hottentots), in the strategically important Cape Colony of South Africa. The English were on the move and on the imperial make in the early years of the nineteenth century. They gradually forced the Boers out of their agricultural coastal settlements and into the interior in what were called *treks.* Trekking was a well-established process of internal frontier movements adopted by Europeans from the seminomadic traditions of local herding and farming people. Soil depletion and younger sons with little or no inheritance expectations continued the practice, abetted now by British pressure. *Trekboers* expropriated land and carried out organized genocidal attacks aimed at exterminating the local people, whom they called "Bushmen." They made servants and slaves of the Khoikhois, or Hottentots, from whom they acquired herding and pastoral techniques. Brazilian *bandeirantes,* American frontiersmen, Argentine *gauchos,* and Australian sheep raisers had much in common with these *Trekboers* of the same period. The Great Trek into the interior that began in 1834 allowed the Afrikaners to continue the practice of slavery after its abolition by the British Empire in 1833, and contributed to a social cohesion among them that enabled them to mount a forceful, though ultimately unsuccessful, defense of their interests against the British in the Boer War of 1899–1902. The complete conquest of the region was sought by the British once gold, diamonds, and other valuable minerals had been discovered in South Africa. Military defeat of strong Ndebele and Zulu people by the Boers enabled them to set up what became the Transvaal and Orange Free State, which they eventually added to their republic of Natalia, and later lost to the British. Boers were recognized as independent by the British in 1854, only to lose South Africa a half century later. British naval authorities secured possession of South Sea islands, reinforced bases throughout the world, and turned the Pacific Ocean into a nineteenth-century English lake. French, German, Belgian, and American military forces took similar action against technologically and industrially weaker European or colonial forces in the second half of the century. They adopted the same racially formulated legal codes and social practices toward those they placed under their national authority as had their Spanish, Dutch, Portuguese, and British counterparts.

"The White Man's Burden"

European colonial expansion, trade, conquest, and conflict accelerated with industrialization throughout the century. The French built the Suez Canal from 1859 to 1869 and operated it jointly after the British bought out the Egyptian share in 1875. The United States took over the failed French canal project in Panama in 1903, created the Republic of Panama to undercut Colombia's claims to it, and brought the remarkable engineering project to a successful conclusion in a decade. Secretary of State John Hay called the Spanish-American War of 1898 a "splendid little war." The Department of the Interior declared the end of an internal frontier of the United States after a review of census data of 1890. The last so-called renegade Native American, the Apache Geronimo, surrendered to military authorities in 1886. The brief war with Spain from April to August 1898 gave the United States an overseas empire in the Philippine Islands, Puerto Rico, and a military protectorate over Cuba. Hay used the military triumph to announce a new, more independent and aggressive American foreign policy in a series of "Open Door" letters to the other great powers (those with navies and colonial possessions) months before the Treaty of Paris transferred the remains of the Spanish empire to the United States. An ugly war of conquest followed immediately against former allies as Philippine nationalists sought unsuccessfully to defend their republic from American colonial control from 1899 to 1902. Military censorship and the racism and jingoism of the press kept most of the information about the indiscriminate slaughter of innocent noncombatants, the use of water torture, and other unpleasantries from the American people.

Aboriginal people were swept out of the way of English settlements in Australia where they were "driven into the wastelands and hunted like kangaroos."[5] Maori resistance in New Zealand was brutally suppressed, though the Maoris eventually escaped genocidal destruction or confinement to reservations. Maoris gained citizen status in the New Zealand Constitution of 1852, but their racial identity and subordination to Europeans continue de facto through social codes and institutional practices to the present time. *Bandeirantes* carried out continued murderous depredations against the native people of the interior of Brazil after Brazil's independence from Portugal in 1825. *Gauchos* in Argentina mimicked them and their North American frontiersman counterparts. Massacres of the innocent by official military forces or unofficial frontier bands were a part of the imperial enterprise of every nation that took it up. At Sand Creek, Colorado, in 1864, U.S. military forces destroyed mainly Native American women and children. Mark Twain sardonically described the U.S. Army massacre of Moro people in the Philippine Island as a "victory." Twain's most savage commentary on imperialism is probably his least-known or least-read book, *King Leopold's Soliloquy*. In this bitter work Twain reported on the near-genocidal extermination of the native population of the Congo River region under the Belgian king's personal authority.

Native Americans in both hemispheres, Maoris, Australian aboriginal people, Africans throughout their continent, Indians, Malays, Asians from Afghanistan to China, all experienced some form of removal, restriction, or internal transfer from their traditional lands. They were all forced to endure military occupation, changes in legal status that were politically and economically disadvantageous, and the application of deadly force to any resistance they attempted. The proclaimed civilizing mission of their conquerors was universally accompanied by expropriation of land, minerals, and, if the indigenous people survived the initial assaults, their labor. Conquerors legally confirmed the exclusivity of their seizures of property in terms enforced by national military authority. Civil authority, when established following the conquest, was enforced by police or military power.

Racial expropriation at bayonet point enhanced national power and prestige. The overseas or frontier conquerors were turned into popular national heroes back home at the metropole. The charismatic victor over the Taiping rebels, Sir Charles "Chinese" Gordon, had his death in Africa at Khartoum in 1885 avenged in 1898 after the battle of Ombdurman in the Sudan. Lord Horatio Herbert Kitchener said he "cleaned" the British flag there "with the blood of 20,000 dervishes."[6] The massacre of Sioux at Wounded Knee, South Dakota, in 1890 had the same kind of vengeful justification, in the words of many of the American troops, for the death of General George Custer and his troops at the Little Big Horn River fifteen years earlier. Rudyard Kipling expressed the popular racial sentiment in American and British magazines when he wrote his well known poem:

Take up the white man's burden—
Send forth the best ye breed—
Go bind your sons to exile
To serve your captive's need;
To wait in heavy harness,
On fluttering folk and wild—
Your new-caught sullen peoples
Half devil and half child.

(Cited in Leon Wolf, *Little Brown Brother*
[Garden City, NY: Doubleday, 1961], p. 190)

Products, Practices, Prestige

The conquests and victories of soldiers made a base for the missionaries, settlers, businessmen, and diplomats who followed them. At times, the civilizing and diplomatic mission on the frontier was left completely to the soldiers. The objectives of overseas colonial conquest varied and changed over time. Trade and the search for trade routes were the older goals set by the Spanish, Dutch, and Portuguese. New profitable products made with slave or cheap local labor by settler groups were quickly added as national imperial objectives. Rum, tobacco, opium, tea, spices, ivory, and slaves became dominant mercantile products. All were marketplace nonnecessities aimed at attracting new customers and diverting bullion from staid commercial relationships and toward the new vendor.

The industrial revolution of the nineteenth century added another dimension to all this. Mass-produced textiles and other factory-made goods needed new customers well beyond the local markets in which they were produced, and the industrial machine needed massive quantities of the kinds of raw materials that were not evenly distributed by nature throughout every nation that wanted them. Prices paid for labor or raw materials in a colony were obviously better for the business interests of the imperial power than they were in the open market. Colonial transactions kept valuable bullion circulating within the national and imperial economy. Customers for mass-produced goods who were also within the colonial system had similarly restricted buying options. Monopolistic trade and company-run colonial mercantile structures gave way by midcentury to formal government-built colonial administrative systems. The size and scope of colonial administration and its burdensome costs became too great for private trading companies. There were also too many companies involved as mercantile monopolistic structures gave way to free trade.

The British were considered more pragmatic colonizers than their precursors, and allowed local administrative policy to vary with local conditions. Racial codes insulating the English were ubiquitous throughout their colonial world, and were common, or became standardized with minor variations, among all the overseas Europeans and Americans in the nineteenth century. More than the British, the French sought to replicate their own centralized system and their culture in language, religion, and food throughout their empire, though they, too, recognized the importance of including local people in administrative and managerial roles. Local rulers frequently became imperial junior partners and in many cases built extravagant fortunes, a practice that continued under corporate sponsorship in the postcolonial era. Cultural divisions among colonized populations were deliberately exploited, with favored groups gaining colonial administrative and managerial status protected by their European overseers. Local minority groups were frequently given privileged positions by their colonizer, since they were often more willing to align themselves with their imperial protectors and benefactors than with those who may have been their former rulers. Ibo people in Nigeria enjoyed this status under the British, and so did the Tutsi population over the more numerous Hutu people in the Congo River region in today's Burundi, Rwanda, and Zaire.

The game got bigger and richer. Texas was annexed by President Polk in 1845; the Southwest was added to the United States after Mexico's defeat a few years later; and Lincoln's secretary of state, William Henry Seward, purchased Alaska from Russia in 1867. In 1877 British Prime Minister Benjamin Disraeli had Queen Victoria named Empress of India. West Africa was divided in Berlin in 1885. Borders were drawn by the European powers throughout the Middle East, Asia, and Africa that had almost nothing to do with local populations. Local or native people were not usually included in the discussions or considered by those who were there except from the administrative perspective of the national imperial authority. Competition for imperial prestige was as overt among the European nations as the arrogance they displayed toward their colonial subjects. France had extensive colonies in North Africa by midcentury and in Southeast Asia somewhat later, colonies they gave up reluctantly a century later with grave national political, racial, and emotional consequences. The stripping of Germany of its overseas empire after World War I became a national humiliation.

The Balance Sheet

The impulse or drive toward empire gained a new momentum by the end of the nineteenth century, at times in contradiction or defiance of practical economic objectives. Critics of imperialism pointed to its enormous public costs, condemned its brutality, and questioned its civilizing mission to little effect. The possibility of undiscovered mineral wealth and new exotic products was alluring. Once diamond and gold discoveries were well known, the British moved quickly to expand their position in South Africa and fought the Boer War. From 1890 to 1900 Great Britain secured the Sudan, Uganda, Nyasaland, Nigeria, Rhodesia, the Transvaal, and the Orange Free State (the last two from the Boers) to become the most powerful nation in Africa. It was argued in diplomatic and naval circles that a sound strategic military position required far-flung imperial outposts to protect trade and, until fuel oil replaced coal in the early 1900s, secure coaling stations. Commodore Dewey attacked the Spanish fleet in the Philippines because of a belief that the United States required a coaling station and a naval base there. Dewey shared the prevailing nationalist view in the United States that competition with rival nations required a more assertive global presence.[7] After Japan's victory over Russia in 1905, and faced with Germany's emergence as a great naval power, Dewey accepted the prevailing view in Washington that Japan and Germany were his nation's most important future rivals.

Imperialism may not have been profitable for nations. Its beneficiaries were private investors, mining companies, railroad builders, exporters of goods, agricultural developers, and career military figures, not the nation-state itself, which bore the burden of military cost and imperial administration. Nevertheless, the political fervor of nationalism combined with racism helped drive imperialism, facilitating, if not its economic, then its domestic, political goals. One scholar, Henri Brunschwig, studying the later stages of the French empire in his book *French Colonialism, 1871–1914: Myths and Realities* (1964), concluded that "the real cause of French colonial expansion was the spread of nationalist fever, as a result of the events which had taken place in 1870 and 1871" (p. 182). The French empire was a "vital element in its national prestige" since 1815, and France "could not endure seeing Leopold II intervene in the Congo or Italy in Tunisia." Brunschwig concludes that "the argument that expansion was profitable was also nothing more than a myth" (p. 183). In a careful examination of the German colonial project, *The German Colonial Empire,* Woodruff D. Smith reached a similar conclusion: "the empire itself was never a practical economic success" and "in most cases of expansion between 1880 and 1900, economic success occurred only by accident and that in other countries, as in Germany, the real meaning of colonialism must be found in its domestic political function" (p. 233). England's frontier in sixteenth-century Ireland and North America was pressed on the Crown by land-hungry individuals. Early empire was most actively sought by feudal adventurers, trading companies, and merchants, who routinely put their own objectives ahead of those of the state, their sometimes uneasy partner. The American historian Frederick Jackson Turner saw in the process of western expansion the formative influence in the shaping of the nation's unique character. The frontier may have been as important to those who stayed behind as those drawn to its allure. Political loyalty goes to those whose visions of the future evoke emotional bonds formed in the images of past accomplishments. Eugene Genovese made a powerful case in a masterful study of the economic aspects of American plantation slavery, *The Political Economy of Slavery* (1965), that came to a similar conclusion that could be applied to the struggle of the Confederacy. Slavery was a decaying, increasingly unprofitable economic system, Genovese argued, but political leadership of the Confederate state was held by the few who commanded the loyalties of the rest and were determined to fight for its preservation. Nationalism and racism built collective emotional visions and political cohesion that seemed to defy economic or practical logic. Karl Marx had plenty of company in underestimating the power of both.

Capitalism and Racism

Racial pride was exclusionary and provided cohesive unity among investment groups that sometimes transcended issues of nationality. These precursors to the multinational corporation were sometimes known as *consortiums,* and they invested in railroad-building ventures aimed at bringing out mineral and forest resources from the interiors of China, Manchuria, and Africa. Multinational investors built American transcontinental railroads and the trans-Siberian line. The nation-state was their bulwark, however, and its diplomatic and military power opened up new investment possibilities. President William Howard Taft could have been describing the duties of the foreign offices of a number of great nations when he said that the United States sought to carry out "Dollar Diplomacy." The government sought to expand American business opportunity by using American national resources. As nations modernized and decreased their remaining feudal and aristocratic inhibitions, they moved quickly to establish their national position in the imperial front ranks. Latecomers had to overcome traditional political divisions, either feudal, as in Germany, Italy, and Japan, or regional, as in the United States. All became more competitive with the established powers and one another, diplomatically and militarily.

The most dynamic expansionist group in most nations were the newest men of business, industry, and banking. Called by some the middle class or bourgeoisie, they soon dominated their states and national cultures in the nineteenth century as never before. They are probably misnamed because they were not inferior to other groups with whom they commingled and inter-married once their economic power was established. In the Middle Ages they were the townsmen, who lived outside the agrarian feudal hierarchy of lord and serf, but not really in between it. In the mercantile age they were neither numerous nor wealthy enough, or fully formed as a class, to dominate the state, except in the Dutch Republic and the fledgling United States of America. Elsewhere they depended more completely on royal authority, patronage, patents, and the navy. Ultimately they prevailed in the nineteenth and twentieth centuries. They preferred to be known as "Captains of Industry" in the United States, instead of the more opprobrious term "Robber Barons," as their critics called them. The arts flattered and exalted their aesthetic outlook, their serene and materialistic sensibilities. Race and nation provided the ideological hegemony for their authority in the same way religious faith had secured their noble baronial and clerical forebears.

In the United States this group included the rough builders in Carl Sandburg's poetic tribute to Chicago, the "Hog Butcher[s], for the world, Stacker[s] of Wheat, Player[s] with railroads." With these leaders of business there were also scientists and engineers, steelmakers, publishers, brokers, and lawyers, who made it possible for shopkeepers, department store owners, independent cattle ranchers and farmers, along with hundreds of thousands of more modest members of the same class, collectively to set the cultural standards for their time. This expansive and expanding class made its vision of the future the vision of the nation and helped inspire the political rhetoric of its leaders. The nation-state was both vehicle and agency of their destiny. That time has not passed, though some business leaders seem to have forgotten how important the nation-state was in helping them establish their great enterprises. While it may be true that in the late twentieth century the consortium approach of multinationalism in business seeks to set new parameters or limits on the role and function of nations, in the nineteenth century the nation-state cleared away obstacles, obtained land for cultivation from indigenous peoples, granted land and people to businessmen for settlement, mining, inexpensive labor, and railroad construction. The early mercantile nation-state was the incubator and nursery for this process, and it protected trade, manufacturing, and banking interests with monopolistic charters.

In the nineteenth century the nation was the sword and shield that made the legal fortress for business power. Colonies, protective tariffs, national banks and currencies invigorated the power of the class proud to be known at the time as capitalist. The nation gave them a world in which they could gain the preeminence formerly reserved to the titled few by birth. Sometimes they fought with one another for control of the direction of that nation, as in the American Civil War. They finally mobilized their massive armies and fought each other for national power in the world as well. The expansion of civil liberties and rights gave them and their allies protection against traditional royal, aristocratic, and clerical prerogatives. Political struggles to secure these rights went on almost everywhere in the Western world, and they continue today. Some have called this the age of democratic revolutions and wondered at the apparent inconsistencies of slavery and imperialism in an age that celebrated liberty, equality, and fraternity.[8] Others have argued that the employment of slaves made the concept of liberty that much clearer to those who denied it to others. Slaveowners most feared the loss of liberty. They knew best what it meant to have or lose.[9]

Citizen Jews

Jews were involuntarily caught up in both the promises and opportunities of political liberty and the racial discrimination that accompanied the quest for national identity. In the transition from feudal anti-Semitism to Enlightenment science, they encountered both national tolerance and cultural racism. Jews lived within the modern state as a people apart. Because they were citizens and enjoyed political liberty, they vigorously entered into professional, business, and public life wherever possible in spite of private social and economic restrictions. One of the great banking figures of the era, Otto Kahn, defined the word "kike" as any Jewish gentleman who has just left the room. The rationalist assumptions of the Enlightenment decreased religious fervor and persecutions, ended witchcraft trials, and moved public policy toward the separation of church and state. Jews played an important role in the business life of Central Europe, which led the Habsburg Emperor Joseph II to proclaim his Toleration Edicts of the 1780s, which extended civic inclusion to Jews. The Bill of Rights of the United States protected religious minorities, through the barring of the state from the establishment of an official religion. The French Revolution's Declaration of the Rights of Man in 1789 and its specific extension to Jews two years later brought Jews civil rights.

These are examples of enlightened, liberal rationalism. The ominous side of it for Jews was the Enlightenment's dislike of all religious mystery, superstition, and faith. The influential philosopher Voltaire repeated commonplace French sentiment when he condemned Judaism and Jews as "the most imbecile people on the face of the earth," as "obtuse, cruel, and absurd," and their history, "disgusting and abominable." He describes *"Juifs"* in the *Dictionnaire Philosophique* in terms familiar to both ancient and modern racial anti-Semitism: "In short, we find in them only an ignorant and barbarous people, who have long united the most sordid avarice with

the most detestable superstitions and most invincible hatred for every people by whom they are tolerated and enriched." He justified the long history
of persecutions and massacres to which Jews had been subjected since Jews
were "the enemies of mankind."[10] Legal inclusion in the nation coincided
with a great flourishing of Jewish culture and the birth of a nationalist
movement in 1896 known as Zionism. Jews were pulled in opposite direc-
tions, both the result of nationalism. Civic inclusion and new opportunities
within a nation encouraged their assimilation and patriotism. Jews modified
their religious and cultural practices to accommodate absorption into the
mainstream. Many others found the concept of a Jewish nation more appealing. Indeed, the early Zionists were drawn from among the most modernized and progressive Jews, with the more religiously orthodox and
conservative opposed to the idea of a separate Jewish nation.

Liberty and Racism

Cohesion at home and abroad was a primary objective of the nation-state.
The powerful new middle class of planters and businessmen needed the
devotion and loyalty of citizens and soldiers as much as they needed each
other. They required a manageable labor force and were highly conscious of
the dangers associated with loss of social and economic stability and control. There had been too many rebellions, strikes, uprisings, even revolutions to allow them to forget the potential hazards of lost hegemony.
Symbols of a citizen-worker loyalty and unity were found in the concepts of
race and nation. Those symbols were formalized in law with the extension
of rights to citizens of the nation. Racial identification with elites was
achieved by the explicit legal denial of these same rights or liberties to an
identifiable subordinate group either at home or abroad. Poor, landless
southerners marched behind their Confederate officers because of a racial
and national identification with them. The unlikely prospect that they or
their offspring might enter the upper levels of society and join the planter
class played the least part in their identity with the authorities they followed. They were already joined by law in nation and race. Freed slaves
and their descendants sought to win inclusion in the liberties offered by the
state by enlisting in all their nation's wars. But the civil credit or liberties
they expected for their services and loyalty as citizens was compared by Dr.
Martin Luther King Jr. in 1963 to a bad check, returned and marked "insufficient funds."

Citizenship rights, granted to some former slaves in the Revolutionary
era, were withdrawn as racial consciousness continued to play its dynamic
part in the unfolding national drama. The Jacksonian era was known as the

"age of the common man" partly because of the expansion of voting rights to male citizens, but it was also a time of terrible losses for Native Americans and the descendants of former slaves in free states. A year after the great national financial panic of 1837, the constitution of one of the most democratic states in a democratic age, the Commonwealth of Pennsylvania, was amended to exclude nonwhites from voting rights. Instead of declining, "the history of the relations between the negro and the white man in Pennsylvania is largely the history of increasing race prejudice," wrote Edward Turner in his 1911 American Historical Association prize–winning *The Negro in Pennsylvania* (p. 143).

Immigrants to the United States, no matter the racial degradation or persecution they experienced elsewhere, in Ireland or Russia for example, quickly adopted the racial and national mythologies of the United States when they perceived their own legal inclusion and the denial of the same to others. Irish and Jewish immigrants sought inclusion as full-fledged American citizens in the nineteenth and twentieth centuries, and most followed the lead of established authorities in those institutions and social classes that set the prevailing codes. Political adhesion carried with it an emotional tie, an association of one's own well-being with that of the national entity. What was good for the nation was good for the citizen. Its enemies or dangers, racial or foreign, were personally internalized as well. Immigrants and native-born citizens alike read the newspapers, listened to the political leaders on the stumps and in the saloons, sent their children to the newly developed public schools, and built their racial and national identities accordingly. Technology and prosperity appeared to confirm their secular faith in these new leaders, and their own religious leaders never seemed to contradict them.

Christianity and Racism

Forrest Wood's monumental survey of the role of religion in response to race, *The Arrogance of Faith: Christianity and Race in America from the Colonial Era to the Twentieth Century* (1990), strongly condemns the role of religious institutions for their support of racism. Wood finds that "Christianity, in the five centuries since its message was first carried to the peoples of the New World—and, in particular, to the natives and the transplanted Africans of English North America and the United States—has been fundamentally racist in its ideology, organization, and practice" (p. xviii). Race and nation were secular expressions of paternalistic authority and quite compatible with similarly structured religious institutions. Religious leaders who enjoyed close social and economically dependent ties with secular leaders lent encouragement to the alleged civilizing mission of the colonialism of the imperial nations. No religious institution could easily afford to put itself in an antagonistic relationship with the nation-state. The Reformation was over. The state had won. Patriotic devotion to the nation by some religious leaders added an evangelical purpose to racial dominion and imperialism. Religion did not create racism. Its institutional dependence on the nation-state made religious authorities racist, though many individual religious figures fought their lonely battles against racial abuses for many decades. Many are still at it. Far more numerous were those who supported, rather than fought, racism, and they always included the leaders of the various Christian churches.

Josiah Strong was the most outspoken and well-known clergyman in the United States to connect Anglo-Saxon racism, nationalist Social Darwinism, and Christianity. Strong was a Topeka, Kansas, Congregationalist minister and became an official of the Congregational Home Missionary Society. He gained national attention from the success of his book *Our Country: Its Possible Future and Its Present Crisis* (1885, rev. 1891), which anticipated and cheered the expansionism (which is what American imperialism is usually called) of a decade later. To Strong, Americans were the leaders of an Anglo-Saxon racial destiny, a "great missionary race." He was convinced that inferior races had to give way to superior races to ensure the continuation of Christian civilization. God had given that mission to Anglo-Saxons, as he pointed out: "thus the aborigines of North America, Australia and New Zealand are now disappearing before the all-conquering Anglo-Saxons. It would seem as if these inferior tribes were only precursors of a superior race, voices in the wilderness crying 'prepare ye the way of the Lord!' "[11] His book was a smashing success. It sold more than 175,000 copies before World War I. Many of the chapters were reprinted and distributed as tracts and pamphlets, or were reproduced in newspapers. His public impact was compared to Harriet Beecher Stowe's *Uncle Tom's Cabin* by the chief librarian of Congress.[12] Two qualities stand out about his imperial sanctimony. First, there is no interest by Strong or in the many who echoed his sentiments in conversion or carrying forward a civilizing mission. Christian religious organizations carried out vast and extremely well-publicized nineteenth-century missionary projects in Asia and Africa. They helped continue the alleged civilizing mission of colonial conquest asserted in earlier centuries. They brought their religious message and good works to those they regarded as unenlightened and unfortunate. Some of the church workers were truly saintly in their dedication and service. Health clinics, schools, and colleges were some of their more successful colonial projects. Strong accepted the more ruthless and well established colonial outlook of conquest as virtuous. Elimination of the weak by the strong was a Darwinian certainty if progress was to be made, and American Christian Anglo-Saxons were the "exponents" of this "pure spiritual Christianity."[13] Anglo-Saxons were at the top, according to Strong, and that race was "more effective here [in the United States] than in the mother country." Among Strong's reasons for this American Anglo-Saxon racial supremacy were the American's "money making power" and "an instinct or genius for colonizing." There would be a fierce Darwinian struggle, according to Strong, "the final competition of races, for which the Anglo-Saxon is being schooled."[14]

Strong was ahead of his times with an eliminationist nationalism and a racial social Darwinism. The second feature of Strong's union of racism, nationalism, and Christianity is the lack of dissent it aroused in the religious community and its enormously popular reception. Willing executioners can always be found wherever national and racial emotions are so clearly joined. When Strong's Christian imperialism was expressed in a softer form as an explanation for taking over the Spanish colony in the Philippines by President William McKinley, there was some scattered political and humanitarian dissent, but McKinley was easily reelected with the hero of the staged battle of San Juan Hill as his outspoken running mate. By the end of the century, political leaders in the great imperial powers all found a similar rhetoric, and made a similar popular appeal that made their colonial rivalry and the naval arms race appear as progressive Darwinian inevitability. The popular press in every imperial power reflected the sentiments of religious and political leaders and helped tighten the bonds of race and nation by the end of the century. Political leaders and a politically enthusiastic scientism joined in to provide a unified racial and national authority in the last decade of the century. Indeed, there was frequent intermixture of the terms as the most erudite French and British scholars often spoke of their countrymen as a race. Scientists continued the confusion by offering as many definitions and categories of race as there were scientists bold enough to make the effort.

Science and Racism

Defining race was an old problem, made new by the termination of slavery in the British Empire and abolitionist attempts to do the same in the United States. Who constituted "the Other," and where did they belong in the human hierarchy? Races were discovered or imagined by empirical scientists in the eighteenth century, though none could agree on the exact number or precise definition of the categories. No clear scientific agreements about behaviors were ever established, though Jefferson and many eighteenth-century observers described what they believed were innate deficiencies among slaves. These descriptions derived from complaints of employers about the laziness and thievery of their unpaid employees. The new federal government of the United States barred freed slaves from participation in the federal militia, and traditional forms of restrictions associated with rank in society or class led to segregated practices in churches and other public places that were upheld in both slave and nonslave states. Formal racial segregation and apartheid were the legal expression and enforcement of these class-originated physical separation and social codes. In the churches and cathedrals, courthouses and public places, the well-to-do sat apart from common folk, with bond servants and slaves separated as well. Feudal codes and derivative social customs were amended to become legal practices. There would be a need for social rationalization as well in a democratic age.

In the two decades prior to the American Civil War several new scientific explanations were offered to confirm what was called the superiority of one racial category in comparison to the others. These new explanations coincided with the political disenfranchisement and racial segregation practices enacted in the colonial world and against former slaves or their offspring in nonslave states. As new liberties were extended to some Americans in the Jacksonian democratic age, others were losing theirs. Expropriation of land and labor became possible to a much larger enfranchised population than ever before. Nation and race meant political inclusion and real material opportunity on frontiers and in the colonies of the great powers to a host of new entrepreneurs. Democratic populism enlarged the social base of what land-and-business-owning elites once built for themselves within the supportive confines of nation and race. Freed former slaves lost or had the political franchise sharply restricted in "free" states that by the 1840s achieved universal "white" manhood suffrage. Native Americans found treaties broken and recently extended civil liberties curtailed. The assimilationist Cherokees lost everything during the 1830s and 1840s. The Maori people, who had accepted British sovereignty in 1840, found themselves displaced and at war a few years later for the same reason. They became obstacles to progress, to civilization itself. Increased demand for liberty and democracy brought more land- and labor-hungry participants to the racial and national table. The concept of progress itself was linked to a national expansion that was always at someone's expense, Mexican, Native American, or African American slave. It was Manifest Destiny. A sympathetic member of the New Zealand Assembly, J.E. FitzGerald, succinctly explained the relationship between expropriation and race: "At the point where his [the Maori's] possession of the land interferes with our industrial and commercial progress, there for the first time we trace antagonism between the two races."[15] It should be little surprise to note that scientists in the democratic era began to establish elaborate racial categories and always found themselves at the top of the scales.

One of the first American scientists to elaborate on and present a systematic explanation for the complexities of racial categories was a Philadelphia physician and professor of anatomy, Dr. Samuel G. Morton (1799–1851). According to Dr. Morton, there were five races: Caucasian, Mongolian, Malay, American, and Negro. Each possessed, he believed, a successively smaller brain, which was the explanation for their alleged different capabilities. Morton claimed the "white race" had "a decided and unquestionable superiority over all the nations of the earth."[16] A Mobile, Alabama, physician and founder of the "American School" of anthropology, Dr. Josiah C. Nott (1804–1873), confined his studies to anatomical racial matters. Nott claimed there was a smaller brain, different-shaped head, and "facial angle" among those called Negroes, resulting in "intellectual powers comparatively defective."[17] A Swedish anatomist and contemporary of the American doctors, Anders Adolf Retzius (1796–1860), helped launch a long-running theory about race based on what he called the Cephalic Index, the percentage ratio of the length to breadth of the human skull. This theory was vigorously taken up by many scientists, who sought to establish the size of cranial capacity as proof of a racial hierarchy with elaborate quantitative and statistical studies of skulls. The problem for these scientists was that every group of humans contained a range of skull sizes that defied simple racial categories. It was impossible to establish a reliable index. Hair, nose shapes, and other physical differences have never been scientifically consistent measurements of race or behavior. Neither has color. By about 1910, studies of immigrants to the United States and their children showed such dramatic environmentally induced changes in stature and size and shape of the head to render the Cephalic Index theory worthless.[18]

European scientists continued their ludicrous, though highly regarded and influential attempts at classification of the races throughout the century. One French naturalist influential in this project was Isodore Geoffroy Saint-Hilaire (1805–1861). For him, there were four principal races: Caucasian, Mongolian, Ethiopian, and Hottentot. All except the last included at least two subdivisions, for a total of thirteen secondary races. An English physician and biologist who became one of his country's most influential Darwinists, Dr. Thomas Henry Huxley (1825–1895), described eleven races in 1865. He amended this five years later to five principal and fourteen secondary races. A French physician, Dr. Paul Topinard (1830–1911), first listed sixteen distinct races, then enlarged his findings in 1885 to include nineteen. Ernst Haeckel (1834–1919), a German protozoologist, disagreed. In 1873 he said twelve races comprised the human species, then revised that in 1879 to thirty-four. The Russian ethnologist Joseph Deniker (1852–1918) broke it down into six primary races and twenty-nine subraces.[19] Clearly, establishing racial categories was an open field, and many contributed their findings. The Harvard sociologist William Z. Ripley (1867–1941) published *The Three Races of Europe* in 1899; it became a standard reference for many decades. Ripley meticulously delineated Celtic, Teutonic, and Mediterranean races, which he said mixed together to form the European people. Giuseppe Sergi (1841–1936), an Italian psychologist, tried a simpler approach based on the shape of the skull. Sergi found two human types: long heads (Eurafrican) and roundheads (Eurasians). There were other, less-well-known scientific speculations and varied attempts to place the races in a Darwinian hierarchy, though there were always problems with that. For example, from a strictly evolutionary point of view, Europeans fell behind Asians and Africans on the issue of body hair. The real intellectual decline of man on the question of race was not taken by the scientists. They were struggling with a nearly impossible question for their time, one that was put before them by social and political necessity, not abstract scientific curiosity. The bigger step down on the matter of race was taken by some serious and highly regarded writers.

Racism *Pur Sang*

The most prominent and influential nineteenth-century author on race was not a scientist at all. He was a French aristocrat, a man of letters, a short-story writer, and diplomat, Joseph Arthur, Comte de Gobineau (1816–1882). He hated democracy and everything it stood for almost as much as he hated Jews. His celebrated work, *The Inequality of Human Races,* was published during 1853–55, then translated and published in English in 1915. An abbreviated translation was published in the United States before the Civil War to bolster the southern defense of slavery. In his book Gobineau trumpeted the cultural virtues of the white race, though in his unscientific prose he sometimes calls that group the "white races." To him, there were but three races, and they were distinguishable by color: black, yellow, and white. His simple categories stuck. Many of his European and American readers must have enjoyed their simplicity, and the association they gained with his aristocratic pomposity. Gobineau declared an "innate inequality in talent and ability to create culture." Only his race was "distinguished by an extraordinary attachment to life." And, "the principal motive [of whites] is honor," something that is unknown to "both the yellow and the black man" (pp. 205–10). Gobineau was pessimistic in the long run about maintaining racial purity, but he was highly influential in the successful legislation to impose new restrictions on American immigration policy after World War I, and his writings were a big hit in Nazi Germany.[20] By the end of the nineteenth century, every great nation came to be represented by an intellectual authority who proclaimed its racial superiority. As national rivalries intensified in the popular mind, so did the connection between racial and national pride. Gobineau found Teutonic linguistic and racial origins in his nation's Celtic past.

Language itself grew in importance as a racial consideration, though few scientists stayed with this theory for long. One of the first serious philologists to connect race with language was the Anglo-French scholar Friedrich Max Muller (1823–1900). He used the term "Aryan race" as derived from language in 1861, but repudiated his own linguistic connection to race in *Biography of Words and the Home of the Aryas,* a book published in 1888. In spite of the paucity of evidence, language and other nonscientific criteria were the foundation of French (Celtic), German (Teutonic and Aryan), English and American (Anglo-Saxon) racial myths as the intensifying national and imperial rivalries grew in the later years of the century. Houston Stewart Chamberlain (1855–1927), the son of an English admiral, became an admirer of Germany and transferred Gobineau's imagined, aristocratic, racial virtues to an imagined Teutonic race. He loved everything German, especially the famous composer Richard Wagner, whose daughter he married. He wrote the enormously popular *Foundations of the Nineteenth Century,* published in German in 1890–91 and translated into English in 1912. He placed every modern cultural or scientific achievement at the feet of his chosen race, and his ideas about "racial purity" and hatred of Jews were adopted and expanded by his better-known disciple, Adolf Hitler.

Anglo-Saxons had plenty of racial advocates as well. Dr. Robert Knox (1791–1862) lectured on anatomy and never presented a complete racial hierarchy, but, like Gobineau, Chamberlain, and so many others, Knox was convinced that everything of value in civilization was attributable to the superior races, and the highest level of those were not Germans but Anglo-Saxons or Scandinavians. His principal work, *The Races of Man,* was published in 1850; in it, he too condemned the Jews and gypsies as *underraces,* a term that found its way into many other languages. A great fan of the Anglo-Saxons was Sir Charles Wentworth Dilke (1843–1911). Dilke took up Darwinian inevitability in his popular *Greater Britain: A Record of Travel in English Speaking Countries* in 1868. To Dilke, the future of civilization and the "freedom of mankind" depended on the conquest of backward "cheaper races" by the English race" (vol. 2, pp. 405–7). One of the most distinguished Englishmen of his age, Lord James Bryce (1838–1922), a temperate statesman, internationally renowned historian, and diplomat, expressed the prevailing racial sentiment of his nation in a famous lecture, subsequently published as *The Relations of the Advanced and Backward Races of Mankind: The Romanes Lecture of 1902*. Bryce held that for the well-being of civilization, "some races should be maintained at the highest level of efficiency" because of "the work they can do for thought and art and letters, for scientific discovery." Diluting the blood of the races, as he called a nonracially defined society, "would be a loss, possibly an irreparable loss, to the world at large" (p. 36). Millions of people believed in this, or in their own national version of it. Too many still do.

Celts? Don't worry about the Celts. Besides Gobineau, they had plenty of prominent advocates. They were the descendants of Gallo-Romans, not Germanic Teutons, according to the great French medieval historian Fustel de Coulanges (1830–1889). Following the humiliating military defeat of the French by the Germans in 1871, and the loss of de Coulanges's professorship at the University of Strasbourg because of it, no racial linkage with the Germans was bearable to him or to most French patriots, so a break with Gobineau's Teutonic connection was made. Racial patriotism came to the rescue. Fustel de Coulanges connected the French people to an ancient Roman heritage in his otherwise masterful *History of the Political Institutions of Ancient France* (6 vols., 1888–92). Other writers followed him to confirm the racial, nationalist mythology. The most strident of the French racial supremacists was Maurice Barres (1862–1923), a novelist whose works were both highly individualistic, as illustrated in his trilogy, *Le Culte de Moi* (1888–91), and patriotic, as the subsequent trilogy, *Le Roman de L'Energie Nationale* (1897–1902). Along with the despised Germans, Barres hated socialism and Jews, and he was enormously popular among playwrights, politicians, and the public. His extremist views and popularity continued into the post–World War I era, and is a troubling legacy in modern France.

In all of Western Europe and the United States sharp intellectual and popularly understood lines were drawn by the final decade of the century that defined colonial relationships, racial ideologies, and national loyalties. As national cultures emerged, racial identity in popular songs, games, theater, and cartoon images displaced regional, local, and other traditional subcultural forms of identification. The benign paternalism expressed toward subject people of former, more aristocratic times gave way to self-righteous hostility and stern guardianship. Political leaders and the popular press reflected a changed mood and a more explicitly national and racial public identification emerged. The overt racial and national stridency and the popular vilification of people thought of as alien were a part of the new imperialism and the intensification of national rivalries with which it was associated.

Racial Anger

The harshness and rigidity of national and racial sentiments expressed by well-educated leaders of the scientific and literary community developed gradually. From the outset of overseas expansion and conquest, Spanish, Portuguese, Dutch, French, English, and American pronouncements about native subjects, colonial settlements, and slaves expressed a humanitarian and civilizing mission. Brutality was understood to be an unfortunate precursor to the uplifting process that would follow. Frontier excesses were justified or overlooked, and colonial leaders, royal imperial figures, and most enlightened intellectuals consistently voiced an aristocratic disdain for brutality. That humane tradition continued into the nineteenth century. Harriet Beecher Stowe opposed slavery in her sensationally popular *Uncle Tom's Cabin,* the way many slaveowners themselves might have done a century earlier. Her racial views were the same as those of most slaveowners. The more they physically resembled their masters or the author, the more intelligent and capable her fictitious slaves appeared; the darker, the duller. Aside from the frontiers and among the rough burghers of the colonial outposts where it remained consistent, the racial attitudes of public leaders and authorities changed from a condescending humanitarian outlook in the early decades of the century to one of stern dominion.

Several important developments seem responsible for this change. Aristocratic and independent clerical influences on governing authorities faded quickly throughout this period in most of the great colonial powers. Andrew Jackson was not the same kind of man as George Washington or Thomas Jefferson. Jackson needed popular votes to be elected in a more democratic age, and he had to obscure any aristocratic pretensions he may have had. Democratic political changes elevated similar blunt social expressions of national or racial sentiment to open public discourse. Powerful leaders could promote the aggressive interests of farmers and businessmen and put aside the nonutilitarian niceties of aristocratic privilege or religious restraint. Napoleon III took a more popular aggressive approach toward the French empire in midcentury. Thomas Carlyle (1795–1881), the renowned philosopher and author, is an example of an intellectual with refined and enlightened views formed in one era who gave expression to the hard delineation and coercive categories of another. Carlyle, a Scotsman, was a close friend of Ralph Waldo Emerson and John Stuart Mill, two men noted for their expansive moral and humanitarian works. Mill ended the friendship after the publication in 1849 of Carlyle's mean-spirited and racially arrogant essay, "Occasional Discourse on the Nigger Question," in *Fraser's Magazine.* Carlyle is well known for a series of lectures published in 1841,

On Heroes, Hero Worship, and the Heroic in History, that was quite congenial to the forceful Jacksonian and Napoleonic (both uncle and nephew) political style.

The civilizing mission dimmed as uprisings and resistance toward colonial and racially oppressive power increased, along with public awareness of this rebelliousness. Nat Turner's slave rebellion in 1831 put an end to criticism of slavery in the Old South. Angry defensiveness in response to abolitionist criticism included strident arguments on behalf of slavery. George Fitzhugh's grim depiction of human nature in his two books, *Sociology for the South: Or, The Failure of Free Society* (1854) and *Cannibals All! Or, Slaves Without Masters* (1857), anticipates Social Darwinism's inevitability of inequality. Criticism of racism was never the primary thrust of the abolitionists. Abraham Lincoln, the Great Emancipator, had no difficulty with that issue. In one of his debates with Stephen A. Douglas in 1858, Lincoln denied any interest in "bringing about in any way the social and political equality of the white and black races." He said he never favored "making voters or jurors of negroes, nor of qualifying them to hold office, nor to intermarry with white people." Since he favored social and political racial separation, he acknowledged that "there must be the position of superior and inferior." So, he concluded, "I as much as any other man am in favor of having the superior position assigned to the white race."[21]

An Algerian insurrection against the French in 1845–46 chilled the previously articulated policy of a humanitarian mutually beneficial colonial association. The Maori Wars of the 1850s, the Sepoy Mutiny of 1857 in India, and the Jamaican Revolt of 1865 "detracted from a socially liberal colonial policy" in England.[22] Resistance to colonial conquest by the Irish, Native Americans, Africans, and Asians was always dealt with harshly and racially on the front lines. When the Herero people of a region in German Southwest Africa (now Namibia) rebelled against German colonial brutality, they were nearly destroyed in a genocidal campaign that was both a portent of the Holocaust in its systematic extermination program and almost identical to murderous racial campaigns against local populations throughout the world. Starvation, slave labor, and military orders to shoot or bayonet any and all Herero people in specified regions led to the reduction in their population of 80,000 in 1904 to 15,000 thousand by 1907. Nazi racial pseudo science that was later used to justify the Holocaust was moved along by a University of Freiburg geneticist who studied in the colony, Eugen Fischer. His book, *The Principles of Human Heredity and Race Hygiene,* was studied by Adolf Hitler while imprisoned in 1923 and deeply influenced the future leader's ideas about inferior races as he expressed them in *Mein Kampf.* Hitler later named Fischer to the post of rector of the

University of Berlin, where he taught the first course for SS doctors in 1934 (*New York Times,* International section, May 31, 1998, p. 3).

A more literate and politically incorporated public, which increasingly identified the purposes and goals of its leaders as its own, welcomed a punitive view of those who stood in the way of their nation's goals. After Custer's defeat by the Sioux at the Little Big Horn in 1876, fewer cries were heard for humane or fair treatment of Native Americans. Some humanitarian writers took up the issue of the mistreatment of Native Americans, though most commonly from the perspective of broken treaties and cruelty, as Helen Hunt Jackson's *Century of Dishonor* (1881). Criticism of racism continued to come mainly from its victims. Both Sioux chiefs, Sitting Bull (d. 1890) and Crazy Horse (d. 1877), were killed while in police or military custody without public concern. Aggressive railroad-building projects, cattle ranching, and expansion of Great Plains agriculture brought forth a strident racial and national justification.

The increase in competition among the great Western powers for colonial territory after 1870 is known as the "New Imperialism." It coincides with a period of sharp economic swings during a time of rapid industrialization. Economic depressions, urban poverty, farm and business bankruptcies were more numerous and severe than ever, and four newly unified nations became more active rivals of the established powers. After its Civil War, the United States slowly began to look beyond self-imposed continental limitations. Germany and Italy, through warfare and political consolidation, were finally unified states, and both had leaders anxious to make up for lost time. Japan's feudal leaders resolutely chose a path toward Western-style modernity after the Meiji Restoration of 1868. As soon as they built their nation-state and a more up-to-date military to go with it, the Japanese went to war against the crumbling Chinese (1895) and Russian (1905) empires for control of Korea. Stepped-up international competition threatened the international balance of power, and a massive naval arms race began after 1890. Economic depression, partly the result of nationalistic tariff barriers to trade, and large-scale unemployment led to political and social conflict that threatened the domestic cohesion and stability of every great power. Great strikes by labor and the rise of socialist and anarchist parties in the industrial nations challenged established property relations and existing political parties. Aristocratic *noblesse oblige* gave way, along with the class that had espoused it, to the hard-headed and strictly business approach of stern guardianship, or to police and military repression. Now conflict loomed ominous: within the nation as strikes and as class divisions became more volatile, and abroad with the possibility of warfare as new alliances were formed around national competition for finite global advantages. The forces turning the double helix of racism and nationalism were intensified and achieved astonishing and unforeseen destructive consequences.

Decaying empires contributed to instability and conflict and uncorked frustrated national passions as the nineteenth century waned. Early in the century, the United States joined with the British under the Monroe Doctrine to assume prominence in the Americas as Spain lost colonial control. Greek independence from Turkey was hailed by the British public as well as by some of its well-known poets in the 1820s. The decay of the power of China in northeast Asia and Turkey and the Austro-Hungarian Empire in the Balkans brought forth aggressive rivalries from among the newest entrants in the great game. Nationalism itself stimulated uprisings difficult for any of the powers to control completely. Serbs, Boers, Irish, and Filipinos were among the patriots who took up arms for national independence in the first decade of the twentieth century. Revolutionary movements threatened economic and class order with upheavals in Russia (1905) and Mexico (1911), and socialist parties increased their legislative representation and popular vote in elections in almost all the great powers. The Socialist Party in the United States reached its peak of electoral influence when it won nearly 10 percent of the presidential vote for its candidate, Eugene V. Debs, in 1912.

By the closing decades of the nineteenth century, the language of national power and racial identity hardened around the prevailing tension and conflict that marked domestic and foreign relations among the competitive powers. The harsh inevitability of conquest, domination, and destruction in the evolutionary natural world revealed by Charles Darwin was crudely transferred to the short-term relationships of human society. Social Darwinism, the conveniently appropriate social theory of the end of the century, put aside humanitarian impulses as unscientific barriers to real human progress. In a jungle-like struggle of classes, nations, and races, it was both natural and proper, the Social Darwinians argued, for the winners not only to dominate their inferior rivals but to destroy them for the long-term good of the human species. Overtly restrictive legal and military action by those who wielded authority no longer had to be cloaked in the refined garb of clerical or aristocratic gentility. Brutal punishments no longer needed to be completely disguised as the unfortunate necessities for the long-term good of their recipients. Blood and iron were running together. War was touted by many Social Darwinian enthusiasts as a natural cleansing process, a rectification of social relationships gone soft or corrupted. President Theodore Roosevelt, among many others, was a proponent of this sort of stuff before the loss of his young son Kermit in World War I. Racism and nationalism congenially accepted violent and deadly measures to achieve their purposes in the heated atmosphere of closing frontiers and competitive burgeoning appetites for national authority and power. Expressions of racial and national hostility toward those deemed inferior or alien gained outward respectability; indeed, they were counted among the attributes of good and loyal citizens in all the great powers.

Restriction and Repression

In the United States the first restriction on immigration was racial, the Oriental Exclusion Act of 1883. It was aimed at stopping Chinese from entering the country once the major transcontinental railroad-building projects were completed. American racial hostility toward Asian immigration, and the formal legalization of segregation in jim crowism, coincided with anti-Chinese racism in Australia, where schoolchildren sang:

> "Rule Britannia, Britannia rule the waves;
> No more Chinamen are allowed in New South Wales."[23]

Reconstruction idealism and political opportunism (former slaves voted Republican overwhelmingly) opened a small window of educational, political, and economic opportunity in the Thirteenth, Fourteenth, and Fifteenth amendments to the Constitution that quickly was closed and turned into legally enforced racial segregation, lynch-law terrorism, and brutal economic expropriation and exploitation in the United States by the 1890s. A series of Supreme Court decisions upheld local racial laws and codes; the best-known, *Plessy* v. *Ferguson* (1896), confirmed a qualified racial citizenship and the racial segregation of public schools. It is estimated that about 100 unpunished, often sanctioned, public racial lynchings a year took place in the United States from 1890 to 1910. Political rights evaporated as the franchise was restricted or lost completely to permissible terrorism and legal contrivances that were obvious to everyone. With nationalism, racism reached a new pinnacle of physical violence, legal and judicial authority, and intellectual credibility in these decades. Practices varied North and South, but overt racial repression and privilege became deliberate public policy. Antiforeign and anti-Catholic nativism coincided with renewed attempts to stop or restrict immigration to the United States in the 1890s. The massacre of Sioux at Wounded Knee, South Dakota, took place December 29, 1890.

The American war with Spain in 1898 was accompanied by sensationalist news coverage and jingoistic propaganda, like so many other military adventures with dubious or publicly unknown objectives. The brutal big and dirty colonial war against the people of the Philippines, the former allies of the United States in the war against Spain, was marked by conventional racial terminology and practices. Debate continues about the exact death toll, but none exists about the savagery and murderous campaigns against entire village and town populations. Theodore Roosevelt, a brash proponent of the racial superiority of so-called Anglo-Saxons and an ardent expansionist, became president in 1901. Roosevelt sent the Great White Fleet on a round-the-world naval military tour to demonstrate the nation's entry into the big game, in case there were any doubts, and launched a big-battleship secret naval building plan in 1903 aimed at making the United States "second to none" in ten years. Booker T. Washington accepted the honor of lunch at the White House with Roosevelt and acquiesced in a racially defined and limited citizenship for former slaves and people who looked like them. Roosevelt reached an honorable compromise with the Japanese in the Root-Takahira Agreement of 1907 about discrimination against Japanese-Americans in California, and left office in 1909 so that he could retire to shoot wild animals in Africa. His successor was his hand-picked former governor-general of the Philippines, William Howard Taft. Woodrow Wilson, president from 1913 to 1921, extended formalized jim crow practices throughout the federal bureaucracy. The landmark film *Birth of a Nation*, by D.W. Griffith, accurately depicted the unity of racial and nation sentiment when it appeared in 1915. At the end of this era, racism and nationalism were comfortably in the saddle.

The Dreyfus affair roiled through the press and public debate in France for most of the last years of the nineteenth century, while France also built a navy, expanded its overseas empire, and nursed its desire for revenge against its 1870 bitter loss to Germany. Captain Alfred Dreyfus, an Alsatian Jew, became a scapegoat for the French military's continuing national embarrassment. The case served as a political diversion from other serious social and economic issues. Dreyfus's alleged espionage, not deficiencies in the French senior military staff, had led in the popular imagination to the betrayal of the nation and the loss to Germany. The timetable and the facts did not matter, especially as they did not add up, but it was a monumental public distraction for several years. The case went on from 1896 until it blew up in the faces of the French royalists, political right, old monarchists, anti-Semites, militarists, and their assorted fellow travelers in the discovery and admission of forged documents in 1898. French anti-Semitism and nationalism were so powerful that Dreyfus stayed in jail until 1906, eight years after the facts that proved his innocence were known. French hatred of Germany went on to World War I. Fortunately, it is gone now.

Great-Power Rivalry Intensifies

The national competition for African and Asian colonies and influence in the Americas became so intense in the 1890s that flare-ups with warlike overtones became more and more frequent. The Americans and British looked at each other's naval guns in a confrontation in Valparaiso, Chile, in 1891. There was newspaper talk in the United States of war with Britain over a Venezuelan boundary dispute with British Guiana after gold discoveries there prompted rival claims. The British statesman and imperialist Joseph Chamberlain, alarmed that there might be conflict between two Anglo-Saxon people, said that such a conflict would be absurd and criminal. Arbitration tribunals or quiet diplomacy settled these and many other disputes short of war. Sometimes troops were dispatched, as in the Mexican Revolution, when one nation's interests, those of the United States, seemed threatened in 1913 by another's, England.

The prestige and importance to nations of their military in this era has encouraged some serious authors to conclude that the military actually began to drive diplomacy. The prerogatives of the admirals and generals became those of the state, and militarism began to characterize relations among the powers. An embarrassing confrontation between England and France known as the Fashoda Incident, a military Punch-and-Judy Show, took place in the southern Sudan in late 1898. The French had to back down because of political problems at home (the Dreyfus affair) and overwhelming British power in Africa. The British were fresh on the heels of one of the most dramatic colonial victories of the century, Lord Kitchener's victory on the plain called Omdurman, near Khartoum, on September 2, 1898. The murderous massacre of prisoners under the authority of Major (later General) Sir John Maxwell was defended by his remark that "a dead fanatic was the only one to extend any sympathy to." Maxwell applied the same principle and the same treatment to Irish nationalists after the Easter Uprising of 1916.[24] Color had nothing to do with race, but race was integral to aggressive and competitive national military policy; ask the Egyptian and Irish victims of Maxwell's soldiers, or the Armenian victims of the Turkish military, or the Sioux at Wounded Knee, or the people of the Philippine Islands.

England was dominant in India, China, and Africa by the close of the century. The American and Japanese governments were as junior imperial partners, and the French hostility to Germany put them in Queen Victoria's lap as well. Anglo-Saxon racial fantasies and real imperial national power put England on top of the world in 1900. Theodore Roosevelt, an ardent racist, anglophile, and outspoken (to his friends) anti-Semite, left the White

House in triumph in 1909.[25] Though the French government finally freed Dreyfus, political leaders continued to exploit a nationalist passion for revenge that was dry tinder to the many sparks that ignited into World War I. Germany was in the midst of an enormous naval-building program and was moving toward greater influence in southeastern Europe and Turkey. Japan humiliated the Russian navy and military in 1905, and both parties were relieved to allow Theodore Roosevelt to intervene and make the Treaty of Portsmouth to end the fighting.

What could possibly go wrong for these successful, aggressive powers, snug in their racial and national supremacy? How wonderful it was to be a citizen and to be able to identify with the technological and industrial world encompassed by the authority of these great nations, and how easy it was, too. None but France and imperial Russia experienced military defeat in the century. England, Germany, the United States, and Japan enjoyed a popular national military hubris, a cultural tradition that welcomed war. French military and political leaders played on a national desire for revenge. Nationalism and racism distorted reality by conferring a false sense of superiority and invincibility among the powers. They were ghost dancing to their own music. There would, of course, soon be a price to pay for this inclusive delusional harmony.

Ties That Bind

Wherever one turned in every nation, the popular culture confirmed the popular self-exalting mythologies. Press, pulpit, and political parties confirmed the verities of nation and race. Marxist radicals applauded the introduction of railroads and industrialism to the colonial world as a step up from feudal and agrarian simplicity. Almost none criticized the expropriation of colonial land or labor and the racial codes that accompanied it. While some trade and industrial unionists regarded racial and cultural divisions of the working class at home or in the colonies as inhibitors of their aims, most of the left rallied around their national leaders and discarded their less passionately held class consciousness. Great intellectual figures and the academic community rallied 'round the flag.

Race and nation were not simple logical formulations; they had achieved so complete a level of cultural integration and psychological power as to define identity itself on all sides. Millions of colonized people saw themselves in the racial image of their imperial authorities and internalized their subordinate role. When World War I called them to the battle lines to kill and to die for their colonizers, there were some who dissented for personal and political reasons. What seems so amazing now is how many citizens, racial subcitizens, and colonial subjects went into the trenches, and how many endured so many years of slaughter with so much loyalty, and for so little in return. Jews, too, embraced their civic duty to their German or French or English and American fatherlands by the tens of thousands when called to arms. As citizens, they loyally fought and died for their respective nations. Race and nation consistently bound (and continue to bind) civic-minded Jews to the states that included (and include) them. Murderous action against the enemies of the nation in wartime aroused too little dissent to make a difference in the outcome. In Russia and along some of the stalemated lines on the Western Front after three inconclusive and horribly bloody years, soldiers became mutinous toward their officers, but virtually none shifted national allegiance. The nation described the enemy, armed its citizens, and ordered them to kill. They obeyed with loyalty and devotion. Among the great Western powers, none was defeated because of a deficiency of patriotism among its people.

When World War I was over, the American president, Woodrow Wilson, urged an expanded version of national identity with the concept of national self-determination. This was the same Wilson who enlarged the scope of racial segregation by extending it to federal agencies that had not yet imposed it in the United States. Racial lines and national lines were probably more academically precise in Wilson's intellect and outlook than in the less idealistic vision of some of the other peacemakers at the Versailles table. To the great nations in the world, making many more weaker nations could hardly impede their objectives. Wilson did not call for creating nations in the colonies of his allies. He accepted the concept of Germany's guilt for the war, and the punishment of that nation included the loss of its imperial possessions, not their independence.

The national half of the double helix showed its enormous power in the opening war for hegemony in the twentieth century. Nationalism was the dominating principle at the peace table, too. The racial half was no less a presence, but showed its comparable and related emotional strength in the brief, peaceful interval that followed and then, most explosively, in the second war. Tightly bound together, the irrationality of race and nation reached a nightmarish pinnacle of industrialized human destruction. In World War I, the national combatants bore the brunt of the slaughter; in World War II, the racialized noncombatants perished as well, and in far greater numbers. Doubts and disillusion began seriously to challenge the prevailing consensus after the first bloodletting, but were insufficient to stop the second.

Chapter 6

No Holds Barred:
Race and Nation, 1918–45

Aftermath of the Great War

The warfare of modernity speeded up all its processes. Technology was forced to find new weapons and production methods with an un-characteristic haste. Scientists and engineers became state assets, and the ivory towers of universities opened up to military and government agencies. The distinctions between public and private institutions diminished as commonly perceived dangers to the nation evoked a collective corporate response. Nationalism is never more strongly felt than in wartime. Commonly shared foreign enemies and sacrifices strengthened existing bonds of loyalty and dependency. In every nation the goals of the war were expressed in idealized national terms: "Revanche," a "World Safe For Democracy," and patriotic expressions of loyalty to king, kaiser, or czar were employed everywhere. The British, French, and other older colonial empires were maintained after World War I, in spite of strong movements toward decolonization. The British and French actually enlarged their colonial influence after the war in the African and Asian colonies taken from Germany and in some contested areas that were placed under their "Mandate," a new term for administrative oversight by which they were given responsibility sanctioned by the League of Nations.

The Great War was fought with racially defined and structured imperial and national military forces. In the period following the war and in the World War II these practices, with added new distinctions, were continued. The emotional and legal importance of racism in the Western nations and Australia was so powerful that it withstood a Japanese attempt to include a resolution against it in the original Covenant of the League of Nations. The part played by the United States in the League indicates the peculiar post-war strength of nationalism in the ironic unfolding of American desires.

President Wilson wanted a League of Nations formed along principles that could limit or prevent the kinds of national practices that he believed had led to war, principles articulated in his Fourteen Points. Because of the tremendous economic and political power of the United States, he could not be refused by nations that were its beneficiaries. Their national interests led them to secretive agreements among themselves and forced compromises on Wilson at Versailles that gave him much less than he wanted. When he returned home, he discovered that the nationalist sentiment in the United States wanted no part in an international body that could impose any limits on the United States. Popular xenophobia and nationalism kept its creator nation out of the League of Nations when the U.S. Senate refused to ratify Wilson's treaty. The United States got the terms it wanted, but did not bind itself to honor them.

The vigor of nationalism itself was stimulated by the war. Colonial populations put forward demands for greater national independence as the price of their wartime sacrifices. The colonies included new military officers, administrators, and professional classes that sought national independence or greater political autonomy within the imperial system. The war may have had its most dramatic consequences in the collapsed Turkish, Austro-Hungarian, Chinese, and Russian dynastic empires. Their future in the world of nations was most volatile and least easy of resolution. The only one of these nations that attained any internal cohesion was Russia through its Bolshevik Revolution, but all the other great nations were opposed to the USSR and took collective and independent military and espionage actions that sought to destroy it. Some national and colonial racial conflicts were old ones that flared anew in war, such as the Easter Uprising in Ireland in 1916 and the bloody aftermath that continued there into the 1920s. As if to press the tarnished concept of nationalism further than ever, new nondemocratic and nonaristocratic political systems, with and without significant ideology, burst forth on the European scene and in Japan. The first serious scientific and intellectual contradictions, or cracks in the wall, of race and nation also appeared in the postwar era. Fascism and militarism carried the double helix of race and nation to its next and most extravagant stage of modern expression in global war and racial genocide. By 1945, in spite of a new critical awareness, most of the people in the world, indeed almost all of them, thought of themselves as racially identified members of a nation or were in search of same. The quest and reverence for national political autonomy in the twentieth century were fired up by the famous guns of August and inspired by racial pride and mythology. That troubled quest and reverence continues.

The old historic problem of every expansionist nation was the establishment of an effective managerial elite on the front lines of empire and the incorporation of that elite's loyalty within the nation. The United States was formed by the successful rebellion of one of those elites. Throughout Latin America in the nineteenth century, nations were formed by civic and military leaders previously established as leaders by the colonial power. In Cuba and the Philippine Islands similar well-educated nationalist leaders directed movements toward national independence at the end of the century. World war expanded the prestige and value of local military and civic leaders throughout the colonial world and placed modern weapons in the hands of soldiers under their military command and administrative leadership. Sidney Osborne, a popular writer who authored several books warning Americans of the future danger of Japan, argued that Britain and France betrayed a "fatal weakness when they made use of their coloured subject races to fight their battles for them in a conflict between two groups of highly civilized white nations."[1] Early Zionism was similarly inspired by the frustrations of talented Jews unwilling to dissolve their cultural identity by assimilation, and in search of the protective legal structure and romantic unity that a nation-state promised. The establishment of an Israeli nation-state must have seemed the lesser of possible evils to the British, in contrast to their colonial system's problems with a rising tide of Middle Eastern nationalism at the end of the war. The Balfour Declaration of November 1917 established a future Jewish homeland in the British section of a partitioned Palestine. It followed an Anglo-French division a year earlier of the entire region, known as the Sykes-Picot agreement. Arthur Balfour, a former Conservative prime minister and postwar foreign secretary, looked out at the unstable troubled postwar world of 1919 and saw only bleak prospects for the British Empire and the sense of an orderly civilization as he understood it.

Instability and Conflict

To those who sought a return to business as usual, there appeared to be serious obstacles wherever they looked. Russia was embroiled in a civil war that jeopardized the railroad and mining investments of banks and investors in all the great capitals. Worse yet, the revolutionary contagion seemed likely to spread as fast and with as deadly a consequence as the influenza epidemic then raging, with protests and militant confrontations in Germany and Hungary and labor unrest almost everywhere. Industrial conflict was widespread in the United States in 1919 and included massive steel and coal industry strikes and a strike by the Boston police. A "Red scare" prompted federal, state, and local attacks on labor organizations, radicals of varied denomination, and deportations, all of which transgressed the Constitution of the United States in their application. The American Socialist Party leader, Eugene V. Debs, campaigned for the presidency in 1920 from his prison cell in the federal penitentiary in Atlanta, Georgia. His crime was sedition. He was a critic of American participation in World War I. New organizations and political groups sprang into existence to meet the challenge of such rebellions. The Foreign Policy Association was an American business-funded reaction to revolutionary and nationalist instability in a world where the United States would have to assume greater responsibility than ever. An American Federal Bureau of Investigation was organized from the wartime antiradical activities unit of the office of the U.S. attorney general, A. Mitchell Palmer. The energetic anti-Red squad leader, J. Edgar Hoover, became the director of the new FBI when it was created in 1921.

Prime Minister Balfour and the British Empire had their hands full. An Irish Republic was proclaimed at the opening of the year 1919; in the same year, Egypt was paralyzed by sabotage and massive popular protests against British rule. Mahatma Gandhi made matters worse as he led massive protests in 1919 against British sedition laws in India. Riots in Trinidad, Jamaica, and British Honduras targeted English colonial officials in the same year. British and Dominion soldiers rioted against delays in demobilization, and in June a detachment of the Staffordshire regiment refused orders to depart for service in India. The summer was marked by police strikes, an upsurge in trade union militancy, and strikes brought on by wartime sacrifices in the United States. An uprising of Kurdish people against the British colonial administration of Iraq broke out at the same time and a year later included Arab uprisings as well. By then, the Irish Republican Army was engaged in a spreading guerrilla campaign. The first use of aerial bombardment of civilians was carried out by the British to put down an uprising in Somaliland in 1920 by followers of the "Mad Mullah." The bombardment was regarded as a model campaign because of its effectiveness and economy. It was so inexpensive that it convinced many military experts that it was the best way to police the empire.[2]

Strikes and sharp political challenges to established authority in France and its colonies, and similar events in the United States, followed the war as well. Benito Mussolini announced the first Italian Fascist Party program in the spring of 1919. Aimed at winning support from leftist groups, the new nationalist party platform included a call for women's suffrage, an eight-hour workday, worker-management joint decision making, and radically progressive taxes, especially on war profits, and confiscation by the state of church property. In the same year, Corporal Adolf Hitler was sent by German Army Intelligence to investigate an intensely anti-Semitic German

Workers' Party. He joined up and soon took it over.[3] Economic dislocations and spreading political crisis engendered a real fear in the major national capitals that things were spinning out of control. The infamous *Protocols of the Elders of Zion* was exposed in the early 1920s as a phony document cooked up by the Russian imperial secret police in 1905. The *Protocols* constructed a diabolical conspiracy based on an imagined Jewish scheme to gain control of the world and the destruction of Christianity by sabotage and subversion. This fantasy became a haven for those with fears of an imagined orderly world slipping away from revered traditional patriarchal Christian authority. Some may have actually believed in the plot; many used it as a deliberate deceit. Henry Ford was its most prominent champion in the United States. His newspaper, the *Dearborn Independent,* warned of the Jewish conspiracy and lauded the work of its most prominent European foe, Adolf Hitler, throughout the 1920s, long after its exposure as a fake. Ford was among the most admired figures of the Jazz Age, after Babe Ruth and a few other celebrities. His public sentiments were openly shared by many other business leaders who joined him in cheering Mussolini's March on Rome and undemocratic seizure of national power in 1922.

The collapsed empires of the Ottoman Turks, Manchu (Ming) Chinese, Romanov Russia, and Habsburg Europe were bristling with ambitious potential leaders frustrated and denied by imperial and aristocratic restrictions and privileges. In all four of these former dynastic empires the twentieth-century expansion of nationalist sentiment included racial or ethnic degradation, displacement, and expropriation of various groups that has not yet reached a stable conclusion. Turks carried out the new century's first genocide as they established a nation-state in the ruins of the Ottoman Empire. Turkish Armenians were sent on a "Trail of Tears" to their "Hell or Connaught" in a series of massacres and deportations that began at the end of the nineteenth century and continued sporadically into the first two decades of the twentieth. Anti-Semitic riots and pogroms in Russia targeted Jews for attack, theft, and the expropriation of their property at the same time. Austrian imperial anti-Semitism, as in Poland and Russia, included inciting or diverting the class resentments of agricultural people toward those many Jews in the professions and business in otherwise nearly stagnant traditional cultures. The great Western nations intervened, chose selected individuals or parties, provided military assistance, or played a direct military role in all four of these fallen empires. Bosnians of all backgrounds, Armenians, Tibetans, Kurdish people, Chechnyans, Hutus, Tutsis, Israelis, and Palestinians are among the many who continue to remind us that nationalism transforms culturally ethnic differences into racist conflicts. Racism is the most enduring remnant of fallen empires, emerging nations, and the unresolved legacy of twentieth-century war.

Quest for Order

President Calvin Coolidge might have been describing almost any nation-state in the modern era when he observed that his primary function was to facilitate business, or, as he put it, "the Business of America is business." The nationalist upheavals and demands of colonized people in the 1920s were met both with military force and with settlements made in businesslike deals and arrangements. The tremendous cost and harm to business of prolonged colonial warfare prompted alternative solutions wherever possible. T.E. Lawrence (of Arabia) advised his Colonial Office that the best course of action in the Arab world was national self-determination within the empire. After a brutal and expensive colonial war, he advised that Iraq, with its enormous oil riches, ought to become Great Britain's first "brown dominion."[4] While his superiors did not always take Lawrence's advice, a series of sensible, businesslike compromises began to unfold that brought some stability to the shaken British Empire. A truce stopped the fighting in Ireland, and a narrow victory in the vote for Home Rule in 1922 led to the establishment of the Irish Republic in 1937. Long-term racially founded bitterness toward England drove the Irish to neutrality in World War II. A territorial compromise was reached in Lausanne, Switzerland, in 1923 between Great Britain and Kemal Ataturk, the popular and aggressive Turkish nationalist leader. Iraq gained its nominal national independence in 1930, and Egypt became an independent nation with the Anglo-Egyptian Treaty of 1936. Abject dependency by Iraq and Egypt on British authorities, whose racial arrogance and practices included the personal humiliation of King Farouk in 1942, spurred many younger officers toward a postwar neutralism. The Indian National Congress, founded as a nationalist movement in 1895, under the great, nonviolent leadership of Mohandas Gandhi, after 1919 carried on a slow, continuous struggle for national independence. Gandhi, along with tens of thousands of Indians, served the British Empire in war. In the Boer War and Zulu rebellion he served in an ambulance unit. Illness kept him from service in World War I, but he became the persistent and unwavering nationalist leader who took the British Empire reluctantly from compromise to compromise and eventually to Indian independence and neutrality in 1947. Winston Churchill caught an echo of Coolidge when he condemned the Gandhi-led Congress as "a political organisation built round a party machine and sustained by manufacturing and financial interests."[5]

The vitality of nationalism and racism was undiminished at the metropole in all the great powers. The great French writer Albert Camus was growing to maturity in colonial Algeria and taking on the identity and

psychological outlook of the settler in spite of himself. Economic nationalist moves in the form of protective tariffs were taken by all the powers in
the 1920s. In the United States the Fordney-McCumber Tariff, passed in
1922, raised rates on imported goods to the highest levels in American
history. Immigration to the United States was now based on national-origin
quotas, thereby excluding or imposing restrictions on all those considered
minorities. The revival of the Ku Klux Klan in the early 1920s was as a
national racial movement hostile to all people of either non-European or
non-Protestant origin. Lynching increased after a wartime lull, along with
attacks on American Jews and Catholics. Hurt by internal financial and
personal scandals among their highest officials, the Klan suffered a sharp
decline after 1924 but achieved one of their chief objectives: new laws
restricting immigration. Americans became more nationally bonded around
their racially segregated northern and southern communities. Film and radio
found that race made a national market in the 1920s. The radio program
"Amos 'n' Andy" enjoyed the largest American mass audience of the time
by offering a congenial, humorous portrait of race that fit right in with
prevailing national, cultural sentiment. Fascination, or amusement close to
obsession, with race was one of the only common cultural bonds that
brought unity to an otherwise diverse nation. Radio broadcasters in search
of cultural topics for a national audience found that race had a universal
grip on popular psychology.

Race transcended region, class, ethnicity, and religion as an American
national emotional force. Anti-Semitism was a parallel obsessive and racially unifying element in the German nation at the same time. Those who
would not live in the neighborhood flocked to Harlem nightclubs because
"they saw Negroes not as people but as symbols of everything America was
not."[6] Race always serves to identify better those who have the power to
impose it than those on whom its strictures are imposed. A racially conscious traveler in the 1920s might have enjoyed the many subtle differences
in the settler capitals of Melbourne, New York, or Capetown, or in the
former slave plantation cultures of Brazil, Virginia, or the West Indies. But
he or she would not have been discomfited or surprised by the racial codes
or legally enforced divisions in any of those places. Our tourist could then
travel from one European or American colony to another and find similarly
consistent racial policies and practices. An Oxford-educated Lebanese
Christian and anglophile, Edward Atiyah, bitterly expressed his disillusionment with the English racism of the 1920s in his book *An Arab Tells His
Own Story: A Study in Loyalties* (1946). A Sudanese friend of Atiyah's
could have been speaking for people throughout the Empire when he complained about the British: "They will never get rid of their racial arrogance;

there is no chance of our ever becoming friends with them. They say they are taking us into partnership, treating us as equals, but it is all words. At heart they remain rulers, fond of domination, resentful of our claims to equality in practice" (p. 175). The brutal British irregulars, the Black and Tans, were used first to suppress rebellions in Ireland and then sent to Palestine for similar service in the 1920s. In all the Western settler nations and in their colonial possessions legal segregation in employment, housing, education, and restrictions on political or civil rights based on race continued unabated after the war. National wage, welfare, housing, and social security benefits of the New Deal were administered with racial differentials and categories in the United States during the Great Depression years. In Brazil, Mexico, and South Africa, racial gradations were more numerous and complex due to the relatively smaller numbers of European women who had moved there and the consequently large intermediary groups that attained higher levels of political, social, and economic status than in the West Indies or the United States. Nevertheless, race mattered as much in forming public identity whether in a majority, minority, or plural circumstance.

Counterdiscourse, Counteraction

Nationalist movements in the British West Indies and elsewhere encouraged Marcus Garvey to break with American leaders of the National Association for the Advancement of Colored People who sought full constitutional equality for all Americans. Garvey was a nationalist in a time of nationalism, but he lacked the business and manufacturing strength, along with the numerical pluralities, that his Asian, African, and Middle Eastern racially colonized counterparts could bring to bear on the struggle for their independence. There was, as well, no distinct claim to a historic geographic space, no homeland to recover from colonialist control. Garvey's United Negro Improvement Association was the largest movement of its kind in the United States and was regarded sympathetically by millions of people. The law finally was used to break Garvey and dissipate his movement. Garvey was convicted of mail fraud, a federal offense, and sent to jail in 1925. President Calvin Coolidge deported him after commuting his sentence two years later. The nationalist movement sputtered along and was rekindled a few decades later in a new time of rising national aspirations.

In all the colonies and former plantations, the experience of war and the growing educated awareness of legal, social, and economic inequities encouraged movements for political independence. In the early part of the century, the Mexican and Russian revolutions were fresh and still untainted by the corrupt and tyrannical images they earned as the years passed. Along with thousands of others, Ho Chi Minh was inspired by Lenin and French communists. Mao Zedong was another student activist mobilized into political action in the postwar struggles of 1919. The great Chinese nationalist leader Sun Yat-sen died in 1925, but he also served as an inspiration to those who suffered from racial and colonial abuses. It was an age in which at least one king gave up his throne to marry, emperors and czars were dethroned, a kaiser retired, and nationalist leaders without aristocratic birthrights became the celebrated focal points of public authority.

Cracks appeared in the ideological walls of race and nation in this era, though they seem to be more important now than they were perceived to be then. Scientific research made important new strides, and racial categories of humanity that had never found a real consensus began to appear more and more dubious. The wartime needs and extreme situations of the battlefields led psychologists to enlarge and refine the innovative field that had heretofore been considered mainly theoretical and speculative. Dr. Sigmund Freud became an international celebrity. His disciples and theories found new audiences that enlarged the intellectual dialogue and literature about the full range of human emotion and behavior, including sentiment about race and nation. Anthropologists discarded popular theories about phrenology and the Cephalic Index as measures of human type or as guides to understanding behavior. Recognition of the importance of nutrition and environmental factors in human capabilities over relatively short periods of measurable time increased and made sharp impressions on behavioral charts and graphs. Discoveries about genetics in the 1920s raised the first hard empirical evidence that undermined theories of human racial subdivision. In 1936, J.C. Huxley and A.C. Haddon published *We Europeans: A Survey of 'Racial' Problems* that argued against the presence of any scientific evidence to support the concept of discreet or distinct human races. The authors called racial biology a pseudo science; they attacked the concept as "a myth, and a dangerous myth at that." Race, they argued was "a cloak for selfish economic aims which in their uncloaked nakedness would look ugly enough" (p. 287). The word *race,* they said, should be dropped from scientific discourse and be replaced by the term *ethnic group* (p. 268).

Revolutionary internationalists, though far from united on the issues, gained followers throughout the colonial world because of their condemnation of racism and the European imperialism with which it was so tightly bound. Marxist theory and literature were, however, most ambiguous on social distinctions other than class. Gender, race, and nation are among the big gaps in the Marxist works about class and capitalism, but postwar socialists began to take up all of them in earnest. Joseph Stalin was not one of these, though he did make a literary and political effort, under Lenin's urging, on the question of national minorities. Stalin's own nationalism may have contributed to unwavering and uncritical Soviet and Communist Party support for movements of national liberation and independence for half a century. Race and nation were both under intellectual attack after World War I, but together they made a remarkable recovery as the unfinished business of one great war among nations led to another.

An intellectual and artistic counterdiscourse had always existed, though largely among the victims of racism. Sometimes, as among many abolitionists, racism was decried for its cruelties and illogic by nonvictims. Music and poetry depicted the absurdities as well as the human resistance to racial strictures throughout modern history. Participation in war and urbanization in a more industrialized world of public education and libraries brought forth new and more numerous voices of intellectual protest and bigger, more receptive audiences to hear them. W.E.B. Du Bois was joined by dozens of other brilliant and unyielding American intellectuals who formed new organizations, published books, and founded journals and newspapers devoted to challenging racism. In every metropole and throughout the colonized world new voices, strengthened by wartime service and scientific findings, brought forth new attacks on legally stipulated racial inferiority. That artistic and intellectual legacy grew and multiplied, while the depredations, force, and consequences of racism climbed to new heights. The music that named the 1920s in the United States the Jazz Age expressed every human emotion and democratic aspiration for the fullness of life denied by racism. Almost everyone who listens to it, even its critics, finds something about human liberty in it.

The rapid growth of communications technology, especially radio and film, took information and cultural data across national and racial boundaries and undermined their credibility. Jesse Owens really did run faster than the competition, and Leni Riefenstal's pro-Nazi propaganda film masterpiece on the 1936 Olympics could not completely ignore the facts. Inexpensive print media, magazines, and mass-produced books were part of a dramatic worldwide educational surge that brought out thousands of talented people whose deeds and desires could not be denied, except by the most extreme contortions of racism and nationalism. Political and labor unity frequently put racism aside, or sought accommodations to diminish its harmful effects on common struggles. Populism among poor southern farmers in the United States is but one prominent example of both the fragility and strength of racism in its authority over an angry and desperate people. Rigorous formal state and local political intervention in the American South with jim crow laws broke up the unified agrarian protest movement, but similar human associations commonly sprouted up. One of the longest running of these in the United States was among New Orleans dockworkers, who formed a permanent biracial Dock and Cotton Council and maintained deliberate work sharing and organizational equality standards aimed at labor solidarity for over fifty years. Their organizational unity was broken only in the 1920s by the use of the open shop and the setbacks suffered by trade unionism at that time, as well as from the constant corrosion of formal and informal racial segregation practices.[7] Like the nation, without a formal structure that includes coercion, racism dissolves. As a part of the apparatus of the modern state, racism is also subject to the instability and cracks in the wall of the nation.

The Great Depression

Postwar turmoil unleashed an array of responses to colonial and national disorders that included everything from Mussolini's fascist takeover of the Italian government and police repression to compromises with colonial nationalist movements. Economic prosperity, or at least its illusory impression, added security and stability to the authority of institutional leaders. The wonders of the new, electrified industrial technology became household objects and appliances and reinforced that authority. Skyscraper architecture, great bridges, and highways were changing the face of modernity under the joint authority of business and government. Henry Ford was a true American hero up to 1929, until the economic crisis that began with the Great Crash and became the Great Depression threw all the great nations into a new crisis. A new state of international conflict tested the cohesive bonds of the nation as never before. Fascism, militarism, and Nazism were together one form of national response to the problem of legitimate authority taken by one group of industrial nations.

Fascism

Fascism never had a consistent or clear-cut ideology. No unified theory or philosophy came forth from its adherents. It was not the same in the various nations that held high its banner, nor was it consistently anti-Semitic, though it was always forthright in its imperial racism. Between 1922 and 1938, fascist or authoritarian, militaristic, national governments displaced or seized power in Italy, Portugal, Germany, Spain, and Japan. (Only when authors refer to Italian Fascism do they use the capital letter, since it was only in Italy that it was the official name of a political party.) If not in ideology, the fascist nations had much else in common. Their nationalism was in essence the official state ideological orthodoxy, replete with legislative codes and enforcement practices. In spite of an elaborate facade of national popularity, and with carefully staged and broadcast propaganda to create its illusion, none of these states dared risk a free or open election. Every fascist state refused to allow a legal political opposition or permit democratic practices such as a free press or independent trade union. Nonetheless, they all enjoyed nearly universal institutional support, especially from the largest banking and business organizations in the nation. The military was or became the most important institution and government agency in every fascist nation. The growth of military power was hardly surprising as fascist leaders presented themselves to their people as saviors of the nation in a time of grave danger. Religious institutions either gave open enthusiastic support to fascism, as in Spain and Portugal, or reached a compromise or accommodation with fascists that included assent or acquiescence. All fascist nations destroyed or sought to crush socialist and democratic leftist organizations that aimed to curb or restrict the power of business. They also smashed independent labor organizations or political movements, though they sometimes, as in Italy and Germany, borrowed some socialist rhetoric to gain popular support in their early days before actually taking power. In every fascist or militarized nation the authority of the state was expanded in areas it already controlled or came to encompass new areas. Police, education, labor, transportation, business, and finance came under increased centralized governmental control, along with new legal restrictions on privacy and personal matters of marriage and mobility. Perhaps the most successful of all the fascist dictators was the former professor of political economy and finance minister Antonio de Oliveira Salazar, who was installed by the Portuguese military to rule with a corporate authoritarian constitution imposed on Portugal in 1933. He stayed close to England during World War II and allowed the use of the Azores as air bases for attacks on Germany. Poor health finally forced him to relinquish authority in 1968 after years of constant efforts to maintain his nation's African empire. He was replaced by the Portuguese military with Marcello Caetano.

One reason that fascism lacks a unified ideology is its deliberate use of national cultural myths, traditions, folkways, and religion to secure its authoritarian grip. Different cultures had different traditions. In Germany, the fascists actually constructed a new mythology from symbols and shards of the cultural past, including an obsession with anti-Semitism, mixed with elements of modernism. Mussolini used the glories of ancient Rome; Franco and Salazar, Catholicism; imperial Japan, the cult of the emperor and the samurai code. In all instances, valued myths and traditions were said to be endangered enough to justify putting aside such democratic niceties as elections and due process in the courts. In every country, some kind of national crisis, real or imagined, was behind the authoritarian takeover. The nation itself became hallowed, to die for; it was above all other claimants to individual affection or loyalty. All these nations either lost their colonial possessions to other powers, as Germany did after World War I, or, as with Spain and Portugal, were gradually losing them, or they were legally prevented from realizing their heightened colonial ambitions, as in Japan or Italy. The need for imperial conquest or power were intensely felt and openly expressed objectives of fascist nations. Deficiencies of vital natural resources for industrialization were especially important in Germany, Japan, and Italy. They all lacked oil, for example, and had to shop for it in the colonies or markets of rival nations.

Other nations that experienced similar colonial rebelliousness, trade union militancy, and democratic leftist political opposition generated internal fascist movements.[8] The corporate fascist state had the power to sweep away internal obstacles to its aggressively capitalist goals. Mussolini and Hitler earned praise throughout the business world for their transportation achievements, both real and imaginary, their no-nonsense anticommunism, and their murderous and repressive labor policies. In spite of other national differences, fascism was most emphatically and universally a secular ideology made to stand up to communism and decolonization. It was an emotionally driven expression of pure and unconstrained modern nationalism. Fascism's expressed willingness to break existing laws, or to make new laws, was appealing as well as dangerous.

The Use of Force

Wilsonian adherence to the idea of national self-determination sustained a hands-off policy toward fascist government takeovers that was not consistent with interventions elsewhere, as, for example, the Great Power participation in the Russian Civil War of 1918–22. All the former belligerents of World War I put aside their differences and, joined by Japan, sent aid and military forces to Russia to fight against Lenin's revolutionary government. Nor did the principle of national self-determination extend to the protection of colonial populations. The League of Nations was powerless to assist colonized people who sought national independence. England, France, and the United States, for example, freely used military forces to stifle or destroy nationalist movements under their authority. The League was similarly helpless when it came to the protection of national populations from arbitrary internal seizures of power and the destruction of democratic forms of government. Mussolini, Salazar, Hitler, and Franco took power without a murmur from the world organization or significant protest by future military rivals. The world was less safe and less democratic a generation after the Treaty of Versailles than it was prior to Wilson's visionary plan for the future. As renegade powers, the fascist nations enjoyed a peculiarly free pass from their potential opponents. Recognition was not withheld, and full economic participation in capitalist markets was granted fascists. This was in contrast to the restrictions and obstacles put in the way of the Soviet Union, a permanent problem for the corporate business world.

Finally, it was the success of their foreign policy that got the fascists into trouble. The frontier era was over. There were no new continents for these frustrated, well armed conquerors to invade. Every place was spoken for by somebody else. Japan invaded Manchuria and turned it into a colony called Manchukuo in 1931 with very little objection from the League. In this part of the world, Japan's closest competitor was Russia. How much further they were prepared to go and how much further their traditional rivals and friends were prepared to allow them to go was settled in the Pacific War of 1941–45. How far they went as a nation, and the place of race in that journey, is part of the story of the war. For now, Germany's parallel national and racial journey of conquest warrants special attention.

As discussed in Chapter 3, from the time of the legal identification of the modern nation-state and the emergence at the same time of the concept of race (both about A.D. 1500), a relationship between the two in conquest, expropriation, and cohesion was established. Germany, Japan, and Italy were among the national latecomers in the quest for colonial and global power, a competitive reality among Western nations for most of those five centuries. All three newcomers drew on deep homogeneous cultural well-springs of literature, art, music, and folklore to establish the modern state. All were unified national cultures long before they were modern states. German military power and scientific technology brought the nation to the front ranks by 1914. Serious students of physics, chemistry, or military strategy anywhere in the world were advised to study the German language for many decades thereafter because of that nation's impressive and leading position in those fields. Until they were unable to function after 1933, about one-third of the disproportionately large number of German Nobel prize-winners in physics were emancipated Jews in a flourishing national culture. German music, poetry, and philosophy were an eighteenth- and nineteenth-century gift of that culture's genius to all of human civilization.

Germany

What the German nation carried out in conquest, war, and racial identification and devastation from 1933 to 1945 had all been done before, though never with the same industrial and technological ferocity, and never with the same internally focused efficiency. The wartime destruction of European Jews seems so singular a historic event in part because its nightmarish irrationality appears at first to have no precedent, nor did it seem, in spite of revelations about secretly hidden Nazi gold in Swiss banks, to bring the German nation any significant material benefit. Germany's primary racial target, the Jews, were not found on its colonial frontiers. There were no colonial frontiers. Jews in Germany did not inhabit a society or subculture whose development was more or less advanced than the dominant one in which they lived. When anti-Semitism became the racial focal point of the authoritarian military state, it drew on a popular sentiment as old as the nation. The expressed hatred of Jews had been a formative part of traditional German national identity since the time of Martin Luther. Social-class divisions brought forth this anti-Semitic sentiment in varied forms. Sophisticated and well-educated German people, as their counterparts everywhere, eschewed vulgarity. Working-class people and the lower middle class are more blunt in the ways they express themselves. The use of language is usually consistent with the harshness of the perceived reality. Hitler's appeal to the broad mass of German people took a populist form; it was stark and unequivocal. Before Hitler, it was not the custom for German political leaders to give plain voice to deep-rooted emotions. Jews were also highly integrated into German cultural and institutional life, as much or more so there than anywhere in Europe. Jews played a disproportionately large role in German professions, business, and banking. Some of the force of anti-Semitism was deflected class resentment. By making the Jew a hated class scapegoat, a false German national-racial unity dissolved or obscured real class and political divisions. With all external avenues to conquest blocked by the Treaty of Versailles, and all overseas colonial possessions taken away, the only place to turn for conquest, if Germany was to be a great national power again, was internally. Jews became Germany's Irish, Native American, African, Asian, or aboriginal victims in expropriation and death with blowtorch intensity.

Over the centuries of anti-Semitism, Jews were racially stigmatized outside the conventional colonial notions of inferiority and superiority. Their racial evil or danger to civilization was reconfigured from religious and secular mythology and expressed in demonic terminology and physical repugnance. Japan, lacking a similar tradition, rather more awkwardly racially demonized its European and American adversaries in a comparable manner during World War II. Jews, because they bore so close a physical resemblance to their conqueror and destroyer, were forced to wear distinctive markings. Here is racism without a race, final evidence of its complete irrationality. Color did not work at all, and phenotype was unreliable, though grotesque and physically exaggerated depictions of Jews were used and were consistent with all prior racist mythologies.

Racial mythologies seize on one or more distorted physical features, which are assigned as characteristic of the group. The same is done with behavioral characteristics. The brevity and intensity of German racial and national fusion in the age of the Nazi Party, and its leader, Adolf Hitler, give it the appearance of uniqueness. What Germany did had been done before by other expanding nations, but other nations had done it to people overseas, to foreigners, or to those without fair or sympathetic witnesses. It was done by Portugal, Spain, the Dutch, Great Britain, the United States, France, and other nations without the efficiency of mass communications, industrialized technological speed, and popular enthusiasm. The racism of the other Great Powers was not intimately tied to their conflicts with one another, as it was with Germany. German racism did not become an issue of significant international political commentary during Hitler's first six years. During that period, Jews were completely stripped of all civil and human rights in Germany without significant international complaint. When the other powers took up arms against Germany, Italy, and Japan, the racial or colonial degradation of conquered people by the Axis nations played no part in that decision. Between 1933 and 1945, Germany carried out the full program of nationalism and racism in pursuit of preeminence in the modern world. What was the full program?

After the Nazi Party came to power in 1933, the civil rights of Jews were gradually taken away. Germans, too, lost civil rights under the emergency measures that secured the dictatorship for Hitler after the Reichstag fire. For Jews, everything that had to do with citizenship and its protection was lost. More than 400 separate laws or decrees were passed or promulgated that effectively turned German Jews into a subject people, a conquered or alien population within the state.[9] Race itself was determined by law. As in Brazil, the United States, Australia, or any colonial settlement, law finally determined race, since, as we have seen, there was never one clear scientific definition or accepted rule on the matter. Whenever there were racial laws or codes, there had to be a legal line, or boundary, that set the human groups or individuals apart. These laws have varied from one drop of blood, or any biological linkage, to one or more grandparents or great-grandparents to establish racial kinship. Laws were established for intermediate or so-called mixed groups as well. Germany faced the matter squarely and with thoroughness in 1935. After several meetings and conferences with legal and so-called racial experts, the Ministry of the Interior came up with a definition of a Jew and, no less important, of those persons with a mixed heritage who should be considered as Jews, a category known as *Mischlinge.* A category (1) Jew, according to the government definition, had three or more full Jewish grandparents; next (2) came a *mischlinge,* first degree; and finally (3) *mischlinge,* second degree. Full (1) Jews were also those with two full Jewish grandparents who belonged to a synagogue or Jewish organization when the law was promulgated on September 15, 1935, or who joined or were married to a Jew after that date, or were born out of wedlock after July 31, 1936, as the result of extramarital relations with a Jew. One-eighth or less, one Jewish great-grandparent or great-great grandparent, allowed the subject to be considered German. In common usage, and what came to be a matter of life or death, Jews were considered to be anyone with one Jewish grandparent, a *mischlinge,* second degree (3).[10]

Jewish property was confiscated by law. Bank accounts were seized. Businesses were taken over; transactions or contracts with Jews no longer were valid or legitimate. Schools and universities imposed restrictions on or were shut to Jews. Employment was restricted and professions and occupations denied to Jews. Many who could afford it or could not accept living in this collapsing civil situation left. Among hundreds of distinguished figures, Albert Einstein and Sigmund Freud left their homes and country. Transportation was carried out once again "to Hell or Connaught." Before the start of warfare, expulsion, deportation, and removal of Jews was the official policy of Nazi Germany. The goal, they said again and again, was to cleanse Germany, to make the nation free of Jews. There was to be a trail of tears for millions of Jews.

In wartime, when conquest made Germany the master of Europe, slavery and destruction replaced expulsion. Jews had no wartime Connaught. There was no wilderness, no reservation for them outside or beyond German military power. Their ultimate destination became military transportation and extermination. Because military gunfire accounted for so large a part of the murderous German racial campaign, there were a great number of willing police and military executioners. Innocent civilian populations have known the gunfire of willing executioners in racial and colonial settings for centuries. There is not much evidence of military mass refusals and desertions from such frontier duty until very recent history. Among German soldiers, participation in mass executions was acceptable duty. When offered the option to stay behind or seek other assignments, very few opted out of the killing details.[11] Good soldiers were also good citizens and patriots who loved their nation, and as they were prepared to give their own lives for it, they took other lives without regret or restraint. Race and nation set moral and emotional guidlines for those whose identity they shaped.

A definitive genocidal decision may or may not have been reached at one or another meeting of Nazi leaders, at Wansee (January 1942), for example, or long before that. The Wansee meeting stands out to some students of the subject because several new, large-scale extermination projects were authorized there; however, prior to this meeting the process of extermination was already well under way and quite well known to British intelligence. Ridding the nation of Jews was always among the most popular items on the Nazi agenda. From Luther's sixteenth-century diatribes to Hitler's *Mein Kampf* (1927), nothing destructive of Jews was precluded. Racism never needed a conspiratorial plan or specific fateful decision to carry out its work; it required an expansive nation mobilized in conquest or expropriation. Murderous extermination, deliberate starvation, and racial slavery were not German inventions. Nazi expropriation of Jewish labor included slavery and murderous exploitation as official German policy prior to the war. In Germany, slave labor was used to advantage, though not necessarily with economic efficiency, by virtually every major industry. Stratification of Jewish labor was employed in factories, ghettoes, labor and death camps. Jewish religious and secular officials, workers, inmates, and individuals faced horrifying social and personal choices that created hierarchies of temporary relief while abetting the destructive process. Random acts of collective or individual violence and terror against Jews went unpunished. There were virtually no legal prosecutions against mob or individual attacks against Jews in Germany or in nations under German occupation. Inside the nation, there was near-complete unity among social, economic, political, and cultural institutions. Authoritarian states took over all aspects of national life. Stalin's multinational reach also went into every corner of social and economic activity. But the Soviet Union was an ideological imperium, not a modern nation-state, and while its terror was no less vast, its goals and victims were different from those of Germany. When the objectives were nationalistic and racist, as in Germany, the society experienced a cultural unity in conquest and purity of identification that was enormously popular as well as murderous.

Once the war was under way, front-line military decisions consistent with the expressed goals and ideology of the German state could hardly be expected to raise objections from Nazi leaders in Berlin. Indeed, smart and ambitious military leaders could be expected to look for ways to please their superiors. Poland's Jewish population was the largest in Europe; as a percentage of the total nation, it was the largest in the world. As the German military rolled eastward, decisions had to be made about the captive and subject population. More than six years of officially sanctioned virulent anti-Jewish language and law preceded the war. Nazi Germany placed no restrictions on institutional actions or practices that were harmful or destructive of Jewish life. Medical experiments and research in disease control and for military purposes took thousands of Jewish lives in controlled laboratory settings that a few years later were considered by many critics to be horrific when carried out on dogs, monkeys, or rats. No German doctors or research scientists were reprimanded for their murderous brutalities or other inhumane actions by their civil authorities or professional associations.

The apparently earnest original postwar denial of awareness by so many Germans of the torture and mass murder of its nation's victims has been somewhat puzzling. Certainly good citizens in an authoritarian state were told only what they "need to know," the standard military concept of information distribution. Nonetheless, medical or scientific murder, mass shootings, gassings, and extermination programs were certainly known by those multitudes who loyally took part in them and sought to please their superiors by doing their jobs well. The disciplinary blinders of an authoritarian society at war restricted their vision to just those horrors and injustices directly in front of them. By accepting a narrow authoritarian vision, they gave their passive assent to everything else that took place. Most Germans were probably largely ignorant of the total picture but were perfectly comfortable with the multitude of small outrages, including murder—if murder can ever be thought of that way—that were inescapable from their knowledge or sight, and right in front of them. Racism desensitizes its practitioners to their own religious, moral, ethical, or civil standards in the same way that nationalism insulates and separates one people from another, both legally and psychologically. When racism and nationalism were unified in conquest, there were no limits to what was humanly possible. All conventional human restraints were effectively negated. Conscience was a rare prize for those few who risked their lives in dissent. Euphemisms and coded language were also common practice in military communications and were used deliberately to disguise reality. The absurd denials and pretensions of latter-day fascist apologists are based on the controls imposed on information by an authoritarian state that was dominated in wartime by ideological and military leaders. The massive destruction of the people of the Philippines by military forces of the United States early in the century was similarly obscured by censors and denied by authorities and their defenders. Archival evidence now confirms that British officials knew from their famous code breakers at Bletchley all about German genocidal police massacres of Jews by late summer 1941. The decoded messages described German mass shootings of Jews as "cleansing actions," and one document noted on September, 12, 1941: "The fact that the police are killing all [!] Jews that fall into their hands should by now be sufficiently well appreciated. It is not therefore proposed to continue reporting these butcheries [to Churchill] specially, unless so requested."[12] Ordinary British or American citizens certainly did not know what their governments knew about the German genocidal program. The prime minister was no longer going to be told what was routine stuff to British intelligence officers three months before the attack on Pearl Harbor and the intervention of the United States in World War II.

One of the German objectives on the eastern front was to obtain *lebensraum* ("living space") for an expanded nation. The Slavic east was to become a frontier region for the subsequent settlement and expansion of a greater Germany. Jews and other *untermenschen* ("inferior humans") on the eastern front were disposed of by the military in an ideologically and historically consistent manner as other expansive, national, military conquerors had done on their frontiers. Jews, and others caught in the maws of a German frontier, racial, military juggernaut, now joined the Irish, Native Americans, Africans, Asians, Maoris, and aboriginal Australians. In Poland, Croatia, the Baltic countries, Austria, and elsewhere, the invading or welcomed Germans found anti-Semitism, the destruction of Jewish life and the seizure of Jewish property, to be politically congenial as well as consistent with German national goals. Expropriation of Jewish life and property was as politically helpful to Germany and its collaborators and friends in occupied nations as the racial laws were in Germany, or the racial laws were in colonial America that united the landless poor with the wealthy planters. Without anti-Semitic friends and collaborators, Jewish life was not easily destroyed in German-occupied nations. Tragically, for the Jews of those nations, Hitler enjoyed the racial cooperation of thousands of non-German willing executioners in such countries as Austria, France, Poland, the Baltic countries, and Croatia. He, and Germany, were also enabled in the pursuit of their racial program by the indifference to it of millions of people and most nations throughout the world.

An imagined and legally contrived Aryan or German race created and was the simultaneous product of astonishing national unity. Racism served the German nation-state as it had served Portugal, Spain, the Dutch Republic, England, France, Belgium, the United States, and even tiny Denmark. Nationalism, too, even in the absence of conquest, created a desirable though false aristocratic bond, a transcendent political and cultural unity. One prominent author on the subject of nationalism, Anthony D. Smith, could as easily have been describing racism when he observed: "To identify with the nation is to identify with more than a cause or a collectivity. It is to be offered personal renewal and dignity in and through national regeneration. It is to become part of a political 'super family' that will restore to each of its constituent families their birthright and their former noble status, where now each is deprived and held in contempt."[13] Michael Hughes, a superb student of German nationalism, reveals the identical parallel with racism when he reflects on it as "sentiment and action" in *Nationalism and Society: Germany, 1800–1945* (1988): "Nationalism must contain an element of aspiration. Like Peter Pan it never grows up: if it does it disappears. Nationalism involves dissatisfaction with the existing situation and the desire to change it by the achievement of national goals. It envisions an attainable ideal centered on the nation, seeking, for example, to achieve 'national self-determination,' whatever that is, to make the nation and the state coterminous, to achieve a tangible demonstration of the supposed innate superiority of the nation or to exclude foreign influences from the nation" (p. 17).

It is hard to imagine that a continuing and comforting residue of that intensely appealing and unifying sentiment does not still exist in Germany as it does elsewhere, though no one can be expected to admit to membership in a community now deemed one of evil madness. Hitler really did have willing executioners. It was the patriotic thing to do. It served the nation. It was the law. It felt right.

Japan

Japan, with the exception of its indigenous Ainu people of the northern islands, and Italy found their so-called inferior races abroad in conquest, not at home. In Korea, Manchuria, Malaysia, Indonesia, Southeast Asia, Libya, and Ethiopia, local populations felt the stigma and loss of racialization and expropriation. The Japanese themselves experienced the racism of modernity firsthand. They objected to the slights and racial restrictions suffered by their people who traveled or settled abroad. After their victory over Russia, they still experienced, through their people who settled in California, racial insults and abuses from American school authorities that required the intervention of Secretary of State Elihu Root and President Theodore Roosevelt to straighten out. Japan's Twenty-One Demands, put forward as a price for neutrality in World War I, went nowhere, along with their attempt to get the League of Nations to adopt a simple declaration of "racial equality" in its Covenant. In the heightened nationalism of the 1920s, Japan was forced to accept the humiliation of naval-force limitations set by the Washington Naval Conference in 1928. Japan's leaders thought of their country in the image of great nations, as they understood them. The Japanese were careful students of modernity and had not been defeated in war. By accepting military restrictions, Japan would be forced to accept a permanent secondary rank among nations. Japan also lacked important mineral and energy resources, sought new markets for its expanding productivity, and expected a front-row seat among the great nations. If they were in the Great Game, they did not expect to be consigned to the margins or made losers. For the Japanese to go abroad as conquerors in a conquered world, their neighborhood was the Asia of European colonialism. In Korea, Formosa, and Manchuria, they established their imperial authority at the beginning of the century. During a generation of overseas power, they discovered or created their racial identity as a superior people, a race apart. When they went to war, they "routinely referred to themselves as the leading race *(shido minzoku)* of the world."[14]

The Japanese initially presented themselves to the people of the Philippines, Malaysia, Southeast Asia, Singapore, and Indonesia as liberators from European colonialism. The people of the former European and American Pacific Rim colonies were fellow Asians who, from Japan's perspective, were in a Great East Asian Co-Prosperity Sphere. The plan soon revealed itself as no more and no less than conventional imperialism. The Japanese military displaced French, Dutch, English, and American administrators and replaced them with their own. Most often, local well-to-do collaborators, administrators, civil servants, and police continued as before, only now under Japanese authority. Their Japanese conquerors soon imitated the racism of the Europeans by constructing a myth about their own lightness of complexion as indicative of their racial purity and superiority. Whiteness and lightness of complexion were part of Japanese cultural traditions of purity and gentility, though the historic Buddha was portrayed as black skinned. People who labored in the sun were tanned, in contrast to the fair complexions of the sheltered Japanese nobility, who also were abetted by powder and other cosmetics. Japanese racism, like the rest of their modernization, was relatively new and less long-standing than it was to their European counterparts. What mattered to the traditional Japanese was purity of spirit. Their racism was a natural, national contrivance of conquest, and was part of the modernity package they so vigorously adopted. They were in an awkward alliance with a German nation that lumped the Japanese with other *untermenschen.* Disdain for each other was mutual among the Axis powers. The Japanese ignored Italy. Japanese officers were delighted with a captured wartime copy of Charlie Chaplin's satiric film depiction of Hitler in *The Great Dictator.*[15] While they attacked the "white supremacy" doctrines of the Western imperial nations, the Japanese as imperialists soon appropriated whiteness, or indulged during the war in "Caucasianization" of themselves.[16]

Japanese popular culture during the war continued a racial theme of imperial conquest that began with the wood-block prints in the news reports of the Sino-Japanese War at the end of the nineteenth century. Those old, prephotojournalism images depicted Japanese officers and soldiers as tall and fair-complexioned with long, rectangular, Westernized faces and clothing. The Chinese were portrayed as short, darker, yellow-skinned, and round-faced. The Chinese were made to appear to Japanese audiences as the Japanese themselves were simultaneously being stereotyped as a "Yellow Peril" in the Western press. During World War II, the same racial distortion was repeated by the Japanese with the conquered people of South and Southeast Asia and Pacific Islanders. They appeared in cartoons as dark-skinned with exaggerated features, in contrast to the Japanese who were always taller and lighter and endowed with finer features.[17] On their overseas frontiers, the intensity of nationalism drove the Japanese military to shocking, murderous rampages not unlike their German counterparts and allies.

In December 1937 the Japanese intensified their attack on China and overran the Nationalist capital in what became known as the "Rape of Nanking." During a period of about two months, the Japanese military carried out rampages of looting, rape, and massacre that some estimates contend left 300,000 dead. Iris Chang's book, *The Rape of Nanking: The Forgotten Holocaust of World War Two (1997),* is an attempt to bring to light details that confirm an event many Japanese officials claim never happened. Her work was aided ironically by the discovery of the meticulous 1,200-page diary of the atrocities kept by a Nazi official and businessman, John Rabe, who lived and worked in China from 1908 to 1938 and was in Nanking (now Nanjing) throughout the rampage. Rabe, who tried to protect as many people as he could, was so appalled at what he witnessed that he wrote to Hitler to protest![18]

During the war, Americans were demonized and vulgarized in the popular Japanese press, though a comprehensive racialization of them or the English did not materialize. Except for prisoners of war, Japanese authority was not extended to English or American national territory or persons during the conflict. Nor did the English or Americans racialize Germany or Italy, as they did Japan. European nations fought with each other and took things from each other for almost 500 years; they drew their racial images exclusively among those they conquered or destroyed who were outside the royal and aristocratic family lines their racism allowed them to imagine they shared. The Japanese had the same problem. They could not completely racially denigrate those they so actively emulated and sought to better. Europeans, Americans, and Japanese fought each other on the same terms for the same things. They were modern nation-states.

Italy

The other Western nations sneered in diplomatic circles or in their newspapers at Mussolini's awkward and difficult conquest of Ethiopia in 1935 because they all believed they would have done it with far less trouble. They paid scant attention to the passionate warnings and eloquent pleas for aid they received from Haile Selassie, the emperor of Ethiopia. Twice in the League of Nations, Selassie appealed to the organization to do what it was set up to do or reap a worse whirlwind than that which prompted its creation. Nothing was done. Racism was not the only reason for the League's inaction. The economic depression and hatred of a communist or socialist threat to power led many European and American leaders toward a sympathetic interest in fascist solutions and permitted Hitler and Mussolini's unchecked intervention on its behalf in 1936 in Spain. In 1938 in Munich, Mussolini brokered the destruction of another creation of the Treaty of Versailles: Czechoslovakia. In spite of the pleas of the Soviet delegate in the League, Maxim Litvinov, for collective action to fight against them, the British and French capitulated to Hitler's demands and abandoned the Czech Republic. In doing so, they treated the democratically elected Czech president, Eduard Benes, a socialist, as they had the Ethiopian emperor; they ignored them both equally. As long as their own imperial interests were not threatened, the British led the other powers in putting aside League legalities violated by Italy in Ethiopia or by Germany in the occupation of the Rhineland. Human rights or racial abuses evoked no significant public commentary. In which of these glass houses could, or would, stones be thrown?

War

While the Japanese nation quickly learned and soon mastered the racial and national lessons of modernism, the Western Allied Powers appeared to have learned nothing new about them in their struggle for contested global influence. Racism was not solely a device used consciously to divide and exploit labor at home or abroad. Although it served that purpose, it was also a deeply rooted part of national identity, and it crossed class lines. During the war, it proved itself harmful to the English and the United States as they prepared for and then made war against Japan. Racism toward the Japanese was similarly not just a wartime device used to degrade the enemy or a contrivance to allow for the destruction of civilians without remorse, though it certainly had those effects. Nor was it simple propaganda aimed at inciting public hatred on behalf of a greater willingness to make sacrifices in war, though there was plenty of mass media racism and nationalism used by all sides before and during World War II. Racism was real enough at the decision-making centers of national power to cost the English and Americans enormous strategic setbacks and material losses and the lives of thousands of soldiers and sailors. English and American racial contempt for the skills and technical abilities of the Japanese led to a severe underestimation and lack of preparation for conflict with them.

General Robert Brooke-Popham, commander in chief of all UK forces in the Far East, revealed near-universal British and American racial contempt of the Japanese when he described them from firsthand observation during a December 1940 tour of Hong Kong as "various sub-human specimens dressed in dirty grey uniform." He reported to General Hastings Ismay in London, "I cannot believe they would form an intelligent fighting force."[19] His comments were typical of German and American leaders as well. During the war and until the very end, Japanese technical prowess was never accurately estimated or understood because of racially induced ignorance and stupidity. As the war progressed, more and more American and British experts increased their firsthand appreciation and respect for Japanese abilities, but racism never lost its detrimental influence. To explain early Japanese wartime victories and dogged defensive determination, the Japanese became either fanatic supermen or devious cheats in the minds of their Western enemies, not their human equals.

Singapore was lost two months after the attack on Pearl Harbor. Because of their racial underestimation of the Japanese, the British surrendered 100,000 troops to 34,000 brilliantly commanded Japanese in Singapore. The Americans lost the Philippine Islands to the Japanese two months later. When the Japanese pilots wiped out his air power on the ground in the Philippines, General Douglas MacArthur, like the British in Hong Kong, believed that Germans or European mercenaries were flying the planes. The pilots, he thought, were just too good to be Japanese. Throughout the Far East, the British and Americans shared a racially induced arrogant lack of concern and preparation that they covered in defeat with a racial myth, that of Japanese treachery, the sneak attack. Two days after Pearl Harbor, Japanese bomber pilots "with astonishing ease" sank the two English battleships *The Prince of Wales* and *Repulse,* which had been dispatched to Singapore as a show of strength to deter any such thoughts of a Japanese attack on the British colony.[20] The powerful self-delusion of racism continued unabated throughout the war. Physiological and behavioral traits, including inner ear-problems that were said to impede balance and myopic eyesight, were assigned quite seriously to the Japanese by knowledgeable authorities.

There may be nothing so powerful in history as a well-funded myth that is appropriate to its time. Government-sponsored films, news releases, and radio broadcasts in Japan, Germany, England, and the United States put forth even more outlandish racial and national nonsense. Truth, or at least more accurate information about the war, was as carefully censored and controlled as propaganda was deliberate. Nationalism was the driving, destructive force in World War I, where most casualties were suffered by the armed forces of the contending powers. From 1939 to 1945, nationalism was joined by racism to shift the worst destructiveness of war to racialized noncombatant civilians.

The bombardment of cities and civilians was not racially restricted or determined by any of the powers. Germany bombed and was bombed by England. The United States participated with England in the fire bombing of Dresden, and accomplished the same kind of near-total devastation of the city of Tokyo in July 1945, just a few weeks before the destruction of Hiroshima and Nagasaki. Racism did not stand alone as the cause of wartime civilian massacre. Bombardment from the air will not topple the government of a dictatorship. Bombing a democratic nation seems only to toughen the will of its people to resist the attacker; Hitler's air raids proved to be England's finest hour. Destruction of resources and warmaking capability might have been better achieved with more extensive attacks on mines, rail lines, and productive facilities. Mass civilian killing of the enemy or alien nation was the incorporation of racism's emotional indifference to the humanity of the Other into nationalism when the perceived modern enemy was a nation, not a race. Destruction of the enemy's cities, like the universalism of racism, aided the national unity of the destroyer more than it helped achieve its stated goals. As the Germans sought to destroy the Jews of the Europe they conquered, the English, French, and Americans borrowed a page from their racinated handbook to destroy noncombatant Germans and historically racinated Japanese. The worst suffering and destruction of civilian populations in World War II took place after the military outcome was no longer in doubt. The unconstitutional incarceration of Japanese Americans was aided by racial suspicion and myth, but other Americans could and would be similarly stigmatized as aliens and have their constitutional rights waived by nationalist fears in the Cold War.

Racism was not based on color or biology or behavior; it was based on national conquest, expropriation, and the building of political unity and cohesion. The Japanese carried out some horrific civilian massacres, medical and scientific experiments, and a near-total disregard for the human rights of tens of millions of Asian people under or within the grasp of Japan's authority with awkwardly adopted racial and national myths. Japan suffered atomic bomb attacks unique in history, though it is doubtful that any other modern nation, including Japan, would have hesitated to use such a weapon on any opponent, though that may never be known or proven. Jews were the only group depicted solely as a race but attacked and destroyed as both a nation and a race. The Japanese were portrayed as a nation and a race, but their destruction was mitigated by their surrender. Jewish surrender only hastened Jewish destruction. Racism ultimately weakened Germany's national war effort and power, the final irony of the irrationality of racism and nationalism.

Winners and Losers

World War II was won through the successful British and American mobilization of their combined global resources. These were greater than any combination of their adversaries, and included the fighting determination of the Soviet Union. These resources were human, industrial, and material, and they meant making compromises or reaching accommodation with racial codes and colonial practices. Compromises in the United States and Great Britain began before the outbreak of war. The New Deal secured the loyalty of the industrial labor force in the United States, and a Fair Employment Practices Commission was set up in 1940 to forestall a racial breach and cancel a protest march on Washington. Employment to all, including women, in formerly restricted industries was opened up for the war effort. Great Britain and the United States maintained their influence and resources in the Middle East, Africa, and India, and kept China and Russia with them in the fighting against Japan and Germany. Combined human and material resources defeated white-hot racism and nationalism in World War II. In the United States the War Labor Board acted to abolish the classifications "colored laborer" and "white laborer" and replaced them simply with the term "laborer." The board made a sweeping ideological argument against racial discrimination that could be considered as much a part of the foundation of the postwar era as it was a reason for the victory of the Allied Powers when it stated: "Whether as vigorous fighting men or for production of food and munitions, America needs the Negro; the Negro needs the equal opportunity to work and fight. The Negro is necessary for winning the war, and, at the same time, is a test of our sincerity in the cause for which we are fighting."[21] Neither Germany nor Japan had the political flexibility or the opportunity to turn the resources won by their conquests to their warmaking advantage, nor did they have anything to offer those they conquered, as their racism and nationalism were so implacable as to limit their options. Anti-Semitism and a *faux* Asian identification were not enough. The United States and Great Britain were bringing formerly racially segregated units and colonial forces into the front lines of the fighting. The Commonwealth supplied Australians, New Zealanders, South Africans, and a surprisingly large number of Maori and aboriginal fighters, along with West Indians, Indians, and Africans. Can anyone imagine Jewish military units fighting for Germany?

In the 1996 Broadway drama *Taking Sides,* the great German orchestral conductor Wilhelm Furtwangler is interrogated by an American officer who is part of a de-Nazification program in postwar Germany. Two unasked and unanswered questions from their exchange are useful in understanding the state of racism and nationalism at the end of the war. Furtwangler, the audience is told, helped many Jews escape death and found small symbolic ways to assert his independence from Nazi authorities. He protests innocence of true Nazism, which to him meant the acceptance of the national and racial orthodoxy. As a German, however, he claims he could not have abandoned his nation for a career elsewhere, so he stayed at the helm of his world-renowned orchestra as an artist pure and simple. His only public protest was against the prohibition by the Nazi government of the performance of the modern music of Paul Hindemith in 1934. Furtwangler was not asked by his imagined American interrogator how the orchestra sounded with the Jewish players removed, nor whether the deletion of the works of Felix Mendelssohn made the repertoire weaker. Furtwangler and Germany accepted their loss and were the worse for it forever. Great Britain and the United States, reluctantly perhaps, used everyone and everything they could lay their hands on to win the war and paid a price in opening up new historical currents that changed racism and nationalism forever.

Chapter 7

Cold War Watershed, 1946–90

Consequences of World War II

Hitler gave racism a bad name. Its essentials were laid bare, undisguised, and it was left with no place to hide. Its victims were not preliterate faraway people this time. Its murderous proclivities were on nightmarish display at the very center of European culture. Where was the civilizing mission? Gone. Expropriation and deadly nationalist delusion were the only remains of racism as Nazism. What about the question of European racial superiority? That was gone too, at least from the standpoint of those who made sacrifices to destroy it in a bloody conflict initiated by Hitlerian Germany. Too many non-Europeans played decisive wartime roles as antifascist allies in the face of battle and on the assembly lines. Frontier distinctions evaporated as resources and people everywhere were devoted to common goals. After the war, in spite of its defeat, Japan quickly proved itself in every way to be a match for its European and American modern world rivals. The benevolent paternalism that had often shrouded racism was similarly discredited in the aftermath of the war. Coercion was all that was left, as demonstrated all too frequently by governments, mob actions, or individuals, as in South Africa, the United States, Europe, and the Middle East. Science jumped ship as well, with but a few vestigial racist remnants marginally hanging on to political, corporate, or individual subsidies. Colonialism, the historic originator of racism, was in disarray in the Far East as the Japanese were driven from Dutch, French, English, and American Asian possessions. Stalin and the patriotic Red Army drove the Germans out of their brief imperium in Eastern Europe as Tito did on a smaller scale to the German force in the Balkans. The British and French colonial systems were on the verge of collapse. What had not been negotiated away in exchange for wartime aid or neutrality, or lost in war, was in a state of protest or open rebellion.

The historic force of nationalism seemed blunted by the internationalism or regional coalitions that stopped its most extreme manifestations in German, Japanese, and Italian form. A United Nations organization was aimed at continuing that cooperation at the instigation of the United States before the end of the war. Globalism as a vision for the future security of humanity in the ideological conflict of the ensuing Cold War, and the economic integration of power blocs, also appeared to raise questions about traditional nationalism, its autonomy and prerogatives. Regional organizations and alliances such as NATO, the OAS, SEATO, and the Warsaw Pact were formed, which seemed to diminish the traditional autonomy of the nation-state. Nonetheless, and in spite of all the damage, race and nation managed to survive World War II. While each appeared weakened in some respects by Hitler and war, in other respects each found renewal in the postwar era and managed, phoenix-like, to thrive again.

Leadership in war and its aftermath was, unsurprisingly, in national hands. Throughout human history, there was never a time when national leaders, not dynastic or hereditary royal or aristocratic figures, dominated public life so completely. From the fall or abdication of the czars, Chinese emperors, Turkish sultans, German kaisers, Holy Roman emperors, and the fading political importance of dukes and princes, there was never a time when control of government institutions fell so completely to leaders with no birthright. The Japanese emperor was maintained by the gracious goodwill and self-interest of bourgeois national leaders who, in the course of just a few weeks, had blown away three of his cities and probably more than 300,000 of his people. Stalin stood astride most of the states formed after World War I from the wrecked Austro-Hungarian Empire. The nonfeudal, nonroyal, nonaristocratic leaders of nations were the leaders of the world in 1945. They captured the imagination and held the loyalty of most of the world's people. Good nations and good leaders, so the victors proclaimed, had defeated bad counterparts. Postwar trials of war criminals in Germany and Japan helped sustain the claims of the winners. Stalin was famously portrayed in American wartime newsreels as "kindly Uncle Joe," though anyone with any interest knew there was another, far less savory side to the general secretary. The names of those leaders and their intimate association with their nations evoked a peculiarly clean and simple world system as the war came to an end: the Big Three, as the media called them—FDR, Churchill, and Stalin—were joined in international recognition by China's Chiang Kai-shek, Yugoslavia's Marshall Tito, and Charles de Gaulle of France. Even such fascist survivors as Franco in Spain and Salazar in Portugal were part of the club of acknowledged and credible leadership. Juan Peron was one of the first postwar admirers of Hitler and Mussolini to be elected to power, and he led or played an important part in Argentina's political life for more than a generation, until his death in 1974.

For almost fifty years, individual leaders of nations continued to hold the spotlight of international attention. This group encompassed Chairman Mao, all of the American presidents until Nixon's resignation, Sukarno and then Suharto, Gandhi(s), Nehru, Nasser, Allende, Castro, and even those as notoriously petty, tyrannical, and corrupt as Marcos, Amin, Pinochet, and Somoza. The nations that seemed to make a difference were celebrated through their leaders, democratically elected or not. To the quality of leadership was ascribed the well-being of populations; bad leaders made things hard on their people, according to the so-called good leaders, whether the people had no choice or deliberately chose the ones they had. Nationalism as the emotional expression of collective public political identity was still awkwardly in the saddle, sometimes propped up and sometimes in places that never previously dreamed of being thought of as nations at all.

The United Nations

The new agency intended to maintain the global stability formed by the Allied Powers in their wartime victory was one that was consistent with the Open Door Policy of its chief proponent, the United States, the most prominent among the victors, and the nation least damaged internally by the ravages of the war. Unlike Germany, Japan, and Italy, the other latecomers to the imperial or global table of markets, resources, and labor, the United States favored after 1898, with but a few exceptions, the reduction of restrictions and cost penalties to its national business in the colonial possessions of its rivals. The United States had eschewed traditional colonialism and preferred to avoid the burden of colonial maintenance and administration. Diplomacy, ingenuously called "Dollar Diplomacy" during the administration of President William H. Taft, and a world made "Safe for Democracy" by President Woodrow Wilson, consistently sought greater global access for American national interests to the raw materials, markets, investment opportunities, and labor resources held under rival national colonial authority. Business and investment interests in the United States sought new competitive opportunities, not colonial exclusivity. By the end of this era, a Communist Party–led China that was willing to open its doors was regarded as less of a national rival to the United States than the intensely nationalistic governments of Iran or Iraq, which followed independent paths that were seen as barriers. Wartime leadership and postwar colonial instability allowed the United States to move closer than ever toward achieving its Open Door.

A United Nations organization, with the United States at the financial and industrial center of power, was FDR's achievement at Yalta, a concession from Stalin. At Bretton Woods, New Hampshire, six months before the Yalta meeting, the United States led its dependent and vulnerable allies in the creation of an International Monetary Fund and an International Bank for Reconstruction and Development. Great Britain, with Churchill as its wartime and, after a five-year Labour Party hiatus, brief postwar leader, sought the maintenance and security of its empire and was less enthusiastic about a United Nations, but in no position to object. An effective world organization devoted to universal human objectives seemed to so many people, in the ashes of another war, to be an idea whose time was long overdue. Critics of nationalism blamed it for the horrors of war and lamented the absence of an international agency that might restrict its roguish tendencies. In their prewar correspondence, Sigmund Freud complained to Albert Einstein that "the League of Nations has no power of its own."[1] Something had to be done, something new was clearly needed.

The United Nations, formed in San Francisco in May 1945, experienced many of the same frustrations as its predecessor. Unlike the League, however, it eventually included all the nations of the world, and that was no small accomplishment. The very design of the United Nations, however, was in keeping with the concept of national sovereignty and the protection of the independent political autonomy of its members. The nationalism of the Western nation-states in modernity became the governing political standard for all the world's people. Instead of a reduction in the narrowly focused cultural or linguistic loyalties spawned by nations, there would be an unfolding of almost endless claims and conflicts as new states were established. Within a few years of its founding by about forty nations, the world organization was made up of almost 200, some on islands with little more than 100,000 people. Decolonization brought forth the greatest number of new nations, a birthing process that was never easy, even when the colonial power did not put up resistance, as was true, for example, with the United States in the Philippine Islands. The legacy of racial identity was intimately tied to struggles for national independence in most former colonies. In all of Africa, India, the Middle East, and Asia, the drawing of national boundaries, the struggle for political power and the withdrawal of European power were fraught with conflicts, many of which remained unresolved more than fifty years later. The abrupt and largely unforeseen disintegration of the Soviet Union and Yugoslavia are only the most recent examples of the continuing energy of national and ethnic identification, though they may not have been the only forces spinning these ideological assemblages apart. Formed to prevent warlike excesses and other human or globally dangerous catastrophes, the United Nations struggled gamely with an oxymoronical destiny; the nation-state is an unstable entity in constant conflict with any and all other nation-states. Unity would put them all out of business. By definition, they are each against all. Internally, a similar instability emerges from class, ethnic, and racial conflict within the nation. Great nations are not unhappy with lots of smaller or weaker nations in the world.

For the United States, the formation of many such smaller nations must have seemed a more attractive alternative in 1945 than continuance of traditional colonial formations of power. Though even colonialism, of France in Indochina, for example, was preferable to revolutionary nationalism and a closing out of the American business and banking community to markets, resources, and labor. Cold War leadership also cast the United States in the role of principal opponent to any and all socialist- or communist-led national governments, including those that enjoyed popular support and were democratically elected, as in Guyana, Guatemala, Iran, and Chile. Hence, the United States found itself in the peculiar position of both supporting and opposing national self-determination and decolonization. The same dilemma confronted the United States on the matter of race, a legally structured national social division that could no longer be sustained on its former basis. The nation could neither continue to maintain its racial practices as they were nor continue to maintain its social structure and identity without them. The tribulations of the civil rights struggle and the Vietnam War were part of the enormous price paid for that duality. Effective international conflict resolution remained an elusive goal as well. The word *superpower* described nations that could not be governed by, or would not submit to, international law or the authority of any other nation. The formation of the United Nations had other unanticipated implications for the United States and the legacy of racism.

New York, the new home of the United Nations, is only a little more than 200 miles from the nation's capital, Washington, D.C. Diplomats travel freely between the two great cities, the postwar poles of financial and political power. Hotel and travel accommodations, rest stops, restaurants, and gas stations continued legally sanctioned racial restrictions in both cities and in between the two. Diplomats fresh from the racial experiences of colonialism in India, the Philippines, Indonesia, and most African nations could feel its lively presence in "the land of the free and the home of the brave" whenever they shed the protective surroundings of the UN organization. The same diplomats and representatives of former colonies quickly combined their political numbers to seek relief from the racial discrimination they had experienced and the genocidal dangers it had so recently displayed. One of the earliest resolutions of the UN General Assembly, put forward on December 11, 1946, condemned genocide, and made it a crime under international law. Genocide was defined as any of the five following actions taken with the intent to destroy in whole or part "a national, ethnic, racial, or religious group": (1) killing members of the group, (2) causing serious bodily or mental harm to members of the group, (3) deliberately creating conditions calculated to harm or destroy physically members of the group, (4) creating conditions intended to prevent or reduce births within the group, and (5) transferring by force children of one group to another group. The resolution was finally ratified in 1951, but without the vote of the United States.[2] The UN diplomats from former colonies rarely represented the most angry or radical factions of their populations. They usually sought an economic and political accommodation with the Great Powers wherever they could find it in their national interest. Racism, however, could not be so easily accommodated, even by diplomats. Like nationalism, racism's human borders were always irrational, no matter how clearly drawn or implacable they appeared. The failure to resolve the division of Germany and the Cold War conflict between the United States and the Soviet Union further underscored the political liability of American racism in the United Nations and within the nation itself. Germany, the defeated citadel of racially destructive nationalism, had to be quickly de-Nazified and reindustrialized by the United States in order to become an ally in the new conflict. The Soviet Union, the great ally of the United States in the battle against Nazi Germany, blasted racial segregation in the United States as the hypocritical Achilles heel of democratic pretension.

The terminology of the new conflict was harsh. Churchill coined the term "iron fence," then, in February 1946, more lastingly, "iron curtain" to delineate the Western European nations, including fascist Spain and Portugal, from those under the authoritarian control or military occupation of the Soviet Union. President Harry S Truman called on Americans to join him in defense of this "Free World" from the dangers posed by the USSR and, after 1949, from "Red" China. The terms lasted throughout the tense period, with President Ronald Reagan adding the opprobrium "Evil Empire" to describe a far milder and de-Stalinized Soviet foe. Subcitizenship in racially restrictive social, economic, and political American practices could no longer be sustained by federal or state authorities without serious domestic and international consequences. The United States had moved from the wings of the world's stage to its center. The flaws in its democratic claims to world leadership were vulnerable to the exposure of the bright spotlight of world attention, especially by former colonies with bitter racial legacies of their own. In the United States equal protection by law as required by the Constitution was inconsistently interpreted by the states. They were able to use the legal cover of "separate but equal" doctrine and the judicial tradition of allowing broad deferral to the states in the interpretation of Bill of Rights issues.

Racism had flourished legally on both federal and state levels through all of American history, not simply as a matter of personal bias or as a non-functional social hangover from the era of plantation slavery, but as an integral part of the national social hierarchical order. It had the force of law in the North and South, in every federal agency, and was nearly universal in public and private employment, housing, and education. Racial restrictions on marriage by state law and federal and state prerequisites for the naturalization of immigrants existed from the earliest days of the Republic. From 1790 to 1870, citizenship could be achieved only by an immigrant who was a "white person." When other categories were included, petitions were received by federal courts to decide the race of the applicant. In the fifty-two prerequisite cases determined from 1878 to 1952, all but one were from those who sought a "white identity."[3] Explicit racial restrictions on naturalization came to an end only in 1952. As Portugal, Spain, and England had once been globally dominant national powers, and Germany, Japan, and Italy had sought similar preeminence, the Cold War era witnessed the passing of this dubious mantle to the United States. Racism became both a national vulnerability and a mainstay of social cohesion in the United States during the Cold War.

Jim Crow Attacked

Aside from the victims of racial abuse and discrimination and a few of their religious or intellectual defenders, the only sharp criticism of racism came from within the radical left. The American Communist Party, an unequivocally renegade, though legal, organization, did some of its most important and difficult work in the battle for equal rights. In a nationally publicized case, Communist Party lawyers defended the Scottsboro Boys from jim-crow justice in depression-era Alabama; its organizers were active in rent strikes in Harlem and among tenant farmers in the rural South and in every large-scale nonracist union organizing drive of the depression and war years. Outstanding research and books by Mark Naison, *Communists in Harlem during the Depression* (1983), and Robin Kelly, *Hammer and Hoe: Alabama Communists During the Great Depression* (1990), attest to the vanguard position and selfless courage of this part of the American radical tradition. Though the Communist Party analysis of racism was formed as part of its global strategy of decolonization and national self-determination, its brave legal actions and mobilization efforts exposed the soft underbelly of America's democratic idealism. One of the great novelists of the era, John Steinbeck, opened his story of a union-organizing campaign among migrant agricultural workers, *In Dubious Battle* (1938), with the observation that "it's hard to be a Negro in the land of the free and the home of the brave." The Communist Party, though small, was influential and probably one of the least nationalistic of political groups or parties active in the United States, a position that made it vulnerable to charges of disloyalty then and of subversion during the era of the Cold War. Its weakest position was its awkward and slavish devotion to the Soviet Union; its strongest was its unambiguous battle against racial injustice. Both contributed to its unpatriotic image and reality.

The most unyielding critics of American racism, communists or not, were typically the least nationalistic. Many who were able to do so chose to live abroad or divided their residential lives. The novelist Richard Wright, for example, after a brief association with the American Communist Party, left it and his homeland to live in France. James Baldwin divided his time between his New York birthplace and Paris, and many talented jazz musicians did the same. His unwillingness to accept conscription into the military during the Vietnam War marked the heavyweight champion Muhammad Ali as unpatriotic and barred him from working at his trade while at his prime for three and a half years. He would enter the ring and fight an opponent in professional sport, but refused to kill or die for his country when, as he said, "no Vietcong ever called me nigger." Malcolm X, Martin Luther King Jr., various leaders and members of the Black Panther Party, and countless other uncompromising and nonnationalist foes of racism were killed, jailed, or brutalized. In most of these cases law enforcement and government officials were participants in the isolation and stigmatization of antiracist activists. Controversy will probably linger for a long time about the extent to which figures in authority shielded, protected, or otherwise contributed to the hostile atmosphere that invited or countenanced freelance racist violence in defense of the nation.

One of the most outstanding American intellectual figures of the century, W.E.B. Du Bois, named race as the issue of the age in *Souls of Black Folk* (1903) and, like Wright, was drawn to the nonpatriotic Communist Party before he was finally driven abroad in the nationalistic hysteria of the 1950s. The renowned actor and singer Paul Robeson was broken, blacklisted, and hounded into obscurity by his nation for his similarly uncompromising opposition to its racism. The racial test in the Cold War was the national test. Thurgood Marshall eventually passed and went to the Supreme Court. Du Bois and Robeson flunked out. Wright, Baldwin, and countless others dropped out or sought refuge or escape elsewhere. Ali eventually returned to the ring, sustained by the courts as a conscientious objector. The dead stayed dead and were not replaced.

The nation as an entity had met the challenges of depression and war.

Now it had to meet its own racial legacy. The works of federal judge and legal scholar A. Leon Higginbotham Jr. show the centrality of law in the structure and maintenance of racism throughout American history. Higginbotham emphatically confirms C. Van Woodward's trenchant comment in *The Strange Career of Jim Crow* (1974): "I am convinced that law has a special importance in the history of segregation, more importance than some sociologists would allow, and that the emphasis on legal history is justified" (p. xiii). The importance of law and the authority of the state are inseparable from race and racism. Higginbotham's most recent book, *Shades of Freedom: Racial Politics and Presumptions of the American Legal Process* (1996), deals with the modern postslavery period, with a powerful indictment of the nation and its courts in setting up the formal structures that enforced racism after the legal destruction of the institution of slavery in the decades that followed the Civil War. In one of the first significant post–World War II actions, the Supreme Court signaled a change in 1946 when it ruled in *Morgan* v. *Virginia,* 328 U.S. 373, that state statutes that required separate seating of passengers by race placed an undue burden on interstate commerce and could not legally be imposed. By Executive Order in 1948, President Truman ordered the racial desegregation of the armed forces of the United States. The Truman action permitted slow compliance but was nonetheless an important federal step in the alteration of the nation's formalized racism. So was the Supreme Court ruling in *Henderson* v. *United States,* 339 U.S. 816, two years later, which barred segregation by race in railroad dining cars.

The dramatic action of the Court in 1954 that challenged the autonomy of the states was its decision in the landmark *Brown* v. *School Board of Topeka, Kansas,* 347 U.S. 483. Kansas was not a former slave state, but its racially segregated public schools, and those made that way by statute elsewhere in the country, were found to be in violation of the Constitution of the United States. The successful attorney for the National Association for the Advancement of Colored People (NACCP) in *Brown,* Thurgood Marshall, had worked covertly with the FBI and shared information about the influence of communists in his organization. Marshall and the NAACP chief, Roy Wilkins, received secret briefings from agents of the bureau. Their sordid story is well documented in Kenneth O'Reilly's 1994 *Black Americans: The FBI Files* (pp. 22–37). Having passed his national loyalty test, Thurgood Marshall was one of the most successful constitutional lawyers in American history before he went on to become a distinguished member of the U.S. Supreme Court. After 1954, former decisions of the Court that allowed "separate but equal" public facilities were reversed or thrown out. The total mobilization legacy of World War II and the Cold

War induced a national political interest in the termination of overt legal complicity in racism's coercive establishment, not in its destruction. A less activist federal government; the gradual shift of power in areas of social policy toward the states, first through revenue sharing and noncategorical block grants of the Nixon-Ford-Carter era and then in the "New Federalism" of the Reagan-Bush-Clinton years; and an enlarged and much stronger private sector of social and economic power allowed racial division and inequality an extended and vigorous national life after the brief civil rights activism of 1954–65.

The federal government completed its legal racial-code cleansing operation when Congress passed, and President Johnson signed into law, federal protection of voting rights (1964) and civil rights (1965 and 1968). Reminiscent of New Deal programs on behalf of labor and universal social solidarity on the eve of World War II, these two federal initiatives to eradicate formal racial segregation preceded the nation's massive military intervention into its longest, most unsuccessful war. A disproportionate share of the fighting and American death rate in Vietnam from 1965 to 1974 was carried by those who had just gained federal protection of their civil and voting rights. Antipoverty federal aid went as well to communities whose sons bore the brunt of the fighting. Eighteen-year-olds won the national franchise in a lost war. Just as the newly won achievements of labor and social welfare went flat or began a period of reversal after the passing danger of World War II and the Korean War, the War on Poverty and measures aimed at the protection of the rights of all citizens came to a halt or were reversed as the mobilization to fight the Vietnam War faded. Harvard sociologist Daniel Patrick Moynihan earned national attention that turned his career toward politics at the outset of the Nixon administration by advocating a federal policy of "benign neglect" on the question of race. Everything that needed to be done was done, he and others argued. Indeed, the cultivation of racial resentment, tagged as a "white backlash" by media pundits, was used by the Republican Party to induce a voter rebellion against New Deal and Great Society Democrats among the "silent majority" of Americans who favored Nixon.

Racism Rebounds

The ending of deliberate racial discrimination by federal and state authorities from 1946 to 1968 did not mean the end of federal policies that supported or perpetuated racism. As ever, race and nation took new turns and found fresh opportunities as circumstances altered. Suburbanization was underwritten by federal tax laws that exempted mortgage interest payments and local taxes from income. Suburbs had no economic base. They were residential enclaves dependent principally on politically disconnected nearby urban, commercial, or industrial and manufacturing centers. Earlier American history indicates that as transportation expanded, so did the political jurisdiction of the city or town where its workforce lived. This was not to be the case in the age of the automobile. Urban renters enjoyed no residential tax exemptions comparable to suburbanites, but many of them faced rigid racial barriers if they chose to join the flight to the new suburbs. The Supreme Court permitted suburban builders and mortgage bankers to set racial restrictions in their sales and financial policies. Virtually all of the federally aided public housing that had been constructed during the depression and wartime emergency was racially segregated by federal, state, and local authorities. Within twenty-five years, racial segregation would remain, though those occupying public housing would change as a result of social and economic shifts. By 1990, what remained of public housing was racially homogeneous and disparaged along with welfare as a form of public dependency. Suburbs were massively constructed and made racially exclusionary, not by statute, but by legal acquiescence and public subsidy. Racist buyers and sellers were unimpeded by law during the twenty-year postwar building boom. Their loan agreements were federally insured.

In 1948 the Court found in *Shelley* v. *Kramer,* 334 U.S. 1, that racial covenants (agreements restricting title transfers) in mortgage agreements were not legally enforceable. They were permissible, however, as "gentlemen's [*sic*] agreements" and similar to a handshake. Restrictive racial or religious covenants were not unconstitutional. Though unenforceable, they were not illegal and could not be prohibited by law. Millions of racially restricted suburban homes were built and sold during a twenty-year boom of Federal Housing Administration (FHA) and Veterans Administration (VA) taxpayer-insured mortgages. The new suburbs were emphatically racial in identity. They were advertised that way. Euphemisms such as "good schools" were used with a wink and a nod in places that were still cutting down trees and putting up school buildings. Zoning control, an innovation of the 1920s, gave local suburban governments primary control of land-use decision making. Brand new suburban communities such as Levittown, Long Island, and thousands of similar large and small residential developments were racially restricted by builders, restrictive covenants, and zoning codes. The local savings-and-loan banks that provided the mortgages that made suburban expansion possible were backed, and, until the Reagan presidency, restricted from reckless investment policies by the federal government. VA and FHA mortgages were federally insured as well. Bank redlining, a form of racially coded investment zoning, was a wholesale application of similar legal concepts that protected private property rights, and this practice was also unimpeded throughout this same era. Urban development projects in cities throughout the nation were most affected by redlining. Renewal projects in big cities often meant removals or obvious racial displacement. City and suburb became statistically more racially segregated than ever in the era of civil rights legislation and judicial activism.

The roads, highways, bridges, and tunnels that connected suburban communities to urban workplace centers were also federally underwritten, while public mass transit suffered disinvestment, deterioration, and decline.[4] The National Defense Education Act disproportionately aided suburban school construction because urban centers required less new physical plant construction, which part of the act provided. Everyone in politics and government soon learns that once something is done, it is hard to change. Innovation, if it is going to take place at all, must take place at the beginning of a project.

The American suburbs built after World War II were made racially differentiated residential communities in a nation that was neither ignorant or naive about these matters. When he was nominated to be chief justice of the U.S. Supreme Court in 1981, the fact that William Rehnquist had purchased a home that made him a party to a racially restrictive covenant while he was an associate member of the Court made no significant difference to the Senate confirmation committee. The federal government may have appeared to have had clean hands in the Cold War era, but it was a complicit partner in policies that secured racism in the nation for more than another generation. When it truly desired something, the nation employed incentives and subsidies to get it. Oil-depletion allowances, crop subsidies, research grants, and tax exemptions were available for those things deemed good for the public or necessary for the nation. Racially segregated suburbs enjoyed such federal largesse; desegregation never did.

The Force of Law

All that remained of federal antiracist policy in the United States within a few years of the Nixon administration were the controversial and contentious battlegrounds of federal court-ordered school desegregation plans (for example, "busing"), and similarly coercive employment and political goals known respectively as affirmative action and the creation of minority political districts. The irrational legal fiction of race was maintained under the apparently worthy rubric of corrective remediation of former harm; a slightly bitter medication to cure a lingering malady. Now the entire population was racinated. What is a "minority" voting district? Affirmative action offices and officers in the private and public sector, along with federal judges, set up categories around gender, race, language, ethnicity to include everyone. Segregated school systems were targeted by courts for coercive remedial action. South Boston High School (known in its racially distinctive community as "Southie") was among those singled out for court-ordered racial change. A traditional residential racial pattern reflected in the public school came under the guns of the court. No incentives, tax breaks, or extra educational funding were offered to ease the transition. Similarly divisive dramas were played out throughout the nation. Racial conflict around public policy and the courts ensued. In Boston and most other municipalities, racial consciousness found a new area for combat. The federal government was now depicted as adversarial and coercive. To many residents, less government seemed better than this kind of intrusion.

Affirmative action had similar consequences. Presumptions of advantage or favoritism were statistically attributed to some groups, while little or no attention was given to the more overwhelming attributions to others as a consequence of wealth, class, or other important social distinction. Numeric goals and hiring or admissions guidlines, not "quotas," as affirmative action defenders frequently reminded critics, were set during a time, beginning about 1973, when the economic pie and traditional careers offered less and less to most students and employees and more to those in charge. Courts played both sides of the issue, finding for and against affirmative action in education (*Bakke, Weber,* etc.) and employment and deliberately created minority political districts, polarizing debate for over twenty years. Courts were likewise inconsistent with more and then less activism on school-ordered desegregation plans, college admission policies, dormitory and housing arrangements. Affirmative racial measures sometimes were damaged by their own contradictory premises. New groups of students, previously excluded because of race from campus life, found social solace or refuge from chilly cross-racial relationships in segregated living arrangements. When race was perceived as one new criterion for admission, those turned away included it in forming defensive reactions to the bitterness of rejection. Schools regarded social segregation as understandable and either barred its practice or allowed it. Institutional ghettoization, "glass ceiling" employment barriers, and economic, scarcity-driven racial resentment undermined the expressed goals of affirmative action, the last standing remnant of civil rights activism carried forward by the Nixon administration and its successors. After twenty-five fitful years, voters in California rejected affirmative action when they had the opportunity to do so in 1996, in a referendum vote on Proposition 209.

The diminishing of the public sector of American life since about 1973 in favor of private alternatives in such areas as health, education, transportation, and housing corresponds to the popular perception of government as out of step with prevailing racial sentiment. Justice and the administration of government have become more directly privatized as campaign-finance dependency and well-heeled legal defenses strip away the veneer of equity and democracy in the making and judging of law. Prescription drugs to alleviate the blues are available to those with the private wealth or insurance coverage to pay for them. For the rest, illegal drugs do the same thing but criminalize their users and have helped make the United States the leader in incarceration statistics in the industrialized world. While the power of the state has declined in matters related to private property, it has increased in matters of personal privacy. President Bill Clinton was not the only American to experience the force of law in his personal affairs. Race itself has been partially criminalized by presumptions and enforcement practices of police authorities, and the restoration of capital punishment in the United States has been criticized by the UN Commission on Human Rights as "unfair, arbitrary, and racist" (*New York Times,* April 7, 1998, p. A17).

Court decisions in the United States put racial- and gender-specific cases on discrimination through kaleidoscopic interpretations. Inconsistency in interpretation and application was often accompanied by inaction. Generally speaking, women, a nonracial group, were the only Americans to make important and noteworthy statistical economic and political gains from affirmative action policy. Racism historically required managerial intermediaries, work and slave drivers, religious leaders, and those who could broker or seek political accommodation with authorities. Affirmative action brought administrative and managerial positions to women and excluded groups in new or poorly represented employment fields. The deliberate racial appointments of Supreme Court Justices Thurgood Marshall and Clarence Thomas were consistent with the carefully controlled racial managerial policies followed by nations throughout their colonial empires. Old frontier, colonial, and plantation practices found new domestic applicability. Inclusion on courts, in middle management, and in elective office of those previously excluded reaffirmed and renewed the traditional loyalties to authorities formed by privileged house servants, the mediating effectiveness of religious leaders, and the commercial and social necessities of small business and professional elites. Affirmative action policies shifted the loyalty and dependency of its beneficiaries toward the nation-state, which during the same period was diminishing or dismantling more universal economic supports, employment opportunities, and protective political and legal measures.

Public and private funding to institutions encouraged or punished compliance with racial innovations inconsistently. Ford Foundation support for
school decentralization in the late 1960s in New York City helped spark a
destructive community confrontation and strike by teacher unionists. The
Ocean Hill–Brownsville conflict left a poor school system no better off and
a strong teacher union less powerful and more divided when the foundation
folded its tent and quietly crept away a few years later. A new voter category was discovered by the American media in the early 1990s: "the angry
white male." New Deal and Eisenhower era–inspired universal social and
economic programs were gradually retired or allowed to languish for lack
of revenues. The public sector, built large in the economic hard times of
depression and war, was made deliberately smaller in the far less menacing
boom times of the Reagan-Bush-Clinton era. Racism was alive and well in
the nation, but the federal government turned over most of its repressive
institutional enforcement to state and private hands.

South Africa and Israel: The Appeal of Nation and Race

Few American business or government leaders expressed opposition to the
formal establishment in 1948 of national racial laws, elaborate definitions
of race, and strict racial segregation put forth under the apartheid program
of the National Party in the Republic of South Africa. The passing of the
Cold War threat to the American Open Door in South Africa after 1990
finally permitted the collapse of the South African racially defined settler
government and the ascendancy of the popular Nelson Mandela to government power. With no Soviet Union to offer alliance or aid, Mandela, like
Cheddi Jagan in Guyana and Michael Manley in Jamaica, would have to
seek economic and political accommodation with the United States and its
multinational structural institutions. The State of Israel, founded on thin and
contested historical ice, has relied on economic and political support from
the United States since 1948. The local population of Palestinians suffered
racial displacement, legal expropriation, and political subordination without
significant American objection for over forty years. Until the end of the
Cold War, American government, corporate, and labor leaders were among
the most persistent defenders of the racially exclusive and repressive South
African and Israeli regimes. Leadership in the United Nations in the era of
the Cold War had made deliberate racism a federal embarrassment inside
the United States. It was difficult to be too hard a critic of Israel in spite of
its racial abuses as a settler nation on Palestinian Arab soil. Widespread
international compassion for its Holocaust survivors and refugees gave the
new state latitude denied the Republic of South Africa. Of course, the

Soviet Union also fished in the troubled waters of anticolonial Arab bitterness and South African protest. A semiautonomous Palestinian state emerged alongside the demise of apartheid as possibilities only after the collapse of the Soviet Union, the Open Door rival superpower of the United States.

Colonialism went away, at least formally, like jim crow laws, almost everywhere. Former colonies eagerly became new nations. Economic national dependency and political inequality among nations replaced imperial and overtly racial forms of coercion and exploitation. Vestigial colonial remains in Hong Kong and Panama have been passing away in negotiated treaties. The lure and promise of nationalism were greater and more tangible than the alternative ideological visions of universal theories, such as Marxism, or even the promise of international or regional economic organizations such as the Organization of Petroleum Exporting Countries (OPEC), or the European Community (EC). Under the leadership of President Charles de Gaulle, France granted national independence to Algeria after a bitter struggle, and departed from its military alliance with the United States when it left the North Atlantic Treaty Organization (NATO) in 1966.

There are certainly well-known good reasons for the appeal of nations, in spite of their horrific failures in conflict resolution among themselves, their erection of vicious racial and ethnic mythologies and practices, and their questionable record at protecting their populations from abuse. Organized administratively as states, they do make efficient agencies for modern human society, no mean feat or small accomplishment. No matter whether democratic, authoritarian, militaristic, or clerical, in nations the mail is carried, train schedules (remember Mussolini) and airlines are organized, patents are granted, telecommunications systems are licensed, currencies and credit systems are underwritten, and economic processes are rationalized. Nations are an inspiration to artists, poets, and musicians and create a secular cultural haven in an otherwise lonely world. Nations form linguistic and cultural communities, extend political inclusion, offer their own image for self-worship, and are as understandably appealing as families made large. Racism makes few such positive claims for itself and has even fewer contemporary defenders. Nonetheless, these two have never been far apart, and they remain so. Because nationalism was regarded largely in positive terms and racism as a negative vestigial remnant of specific archaic practices, most Cold War studies of racism and nationalism have concentrated their analytical emphasis on economic, labor, and social issues, not the historic interrelationship of the two.[5]

Racism has been said to be a disorder, or an authoritarian breakdown in the inherently positive functions of the democratic nation. It has been described as dysfunctional, a cultural hangover. These were among the criticisms of racism that were most popular among scholars in the early years of the Cold War.[6] Racism was regarded by most of its critics in the postwar era as either a mad cultural aberration made worse by hard times, as in Germany, or as a vestigial remnant of the social divisions inherent in former colonial or slave-labor systems. To some, it was a device designed simply to divide the labor force. Hard reality, however, defied neat theory. Race, like nation, has been bigger and stronger than it was perceived to be. Legal racial categories for employment, use of public facilities, political rights, education, and residential location were enforced as innovative or continuing government policy in South Africa, the United States, Israel, Cuba (until 1959), Ireland, Great Britain, Australia, New Zealand, Latin America, and in most of the decolonizing world during the first generation after the death of Hitler.

Racism found, as it had in earlier historic periods, innovative institutional and legal forms. Once the age of formal colonialism came to an end in the course of the Cold War, the articulated legal social structures that had accompanied its long domestic and overseas history also came to an end. Nevertheless, the idea of race, which had been conceived in national expropriation and had grown up as collective self-identification in the unstable atmosphere of national rivalry and expansion, was as vital without jim crow and apartheid as ever. The old flag, the Stars and Bars of the American Confederacy, was actually revived after the Kennedy-Johnson era of civil rights legislation as a defiance against new threats to racial identity. Contentious racial immigration policies emerged in many European nations that spawned it, and racialized nationalism arose in the void of the collapsed ideological imperiums of Yugoslavia, Eastern Europe, and the Soviet Union. Murderous and sometimes genocidal racial battles for national political control emerged from ethnic differences and accompanied the establishment of new nation-states. Race and nation persisted as the linked foundations of collective public, social, and political identity.

Racism and nationalism never rested on logic or real scientific premises. They were both functional, historical opportunists willing to serve modernity's masters of economic stratification, expropriation, and administrative cohesion. Historically altered administrative and managerial needs influenced hierarchical relationships. In their colonies and on their plantations, conquerors and masters elevated some of their racinated subjects and bestowed on them authority denied to others. Intermediary racial categories were established to enable some to oversee and manage Dutch, Portuguese, English, French, Spanish, and American colonial ventures. In the earliest stages of the broad retreat of colonialism after World War I, there was an attempt by the departing authorities to leave behind sympathetic or compliant new national leadership, especially if the separation was negotiated with little or no armed conflict. Almost any regime was preferable to one that would impose economic restrictions on resources, markets, and labor sources.

The new Republic of South Africa, formed in 1948, was an old settler colony with roots in Portuguese, Dutch, and English imperial history. Legally institutionalized racial slavery and laws such as the Immorality Act of 1685, which prohibited marriage between Europeans and Africans, built a racially divided culture for the descendants of all the various people, including Asians, who had been brought into the region in large numbers to work sugar plantations and mills in the nineteenth century. Those who were the backbone of the politically successful National Party in 1948 had the most to gain from maintaining strict racial categories. Poor and struggling South Africans of Boer and English ancestry shared a common political objective in forming the new nation: their own guaranteed racial advantage. The Great Powers of the postwar world offered no objection to their plans. Neither the recent horrors of World War II, nor the creation of the United Nations, and the almost universally acknowledged scientific fallacy of the concept of race, prevented the new nation from establishing four legal racial categories, new laws regarding marriage, and, under the Group Areas Act, forced residential practices on the entire population to the distinct economic and political benefit of the small minority known as "white." Employment practices in public and private institutions made race the key to wage benefits, advancement, and jobs. Complex political and social adjustments, including new parliaments for "Coloreds" and "Indians" and a "Homelands" policy of resettlement, never completely succeeded in stifling almost continuous protest, strikes, and boycotts by its racial victims, no matter how much coercive violence was applied by the state and its freelance vigilante allies. The police killed sixty-nine demonstrators in the "Sharpeville Massacre" of 1960, and jailed or killed every popular protest leader they could find throughout this period. The horrible death of Stephen Biko in 1977 while in police custody sparked international protests, films, and songs.

Continuous racial brutality and growing international revulsion in an increasingly global economy and culture ultimately isolated and undermined racial minority rule in South Africa, as it damaged traditional forms of racial segregation in the American South. But it was not until the end of the Cold War and the final completion of regional decolonization that a new nonracial and democratic constitution was proclaimed in the administration of President Nelson Mandela in 1994. Should his government fail to achieve its stated universalist economic and social goals after a reasonable period of trial, or after his passing from the scene, there is no reason to doubt the potential for a reemergence of racial national politics, only this time with a democratically legitimized group in the position to exploit the mythology for itself. Past racial resentments and fears about the future of the nation have prompted a new outward trek of emigration of the formerly privileged in South Africa that will certainly increase if conditions for their well-being deteriorate.

The State of Israel was founded in the same year, 1948, in the tense withdrawal of Great Britain from its Middle Eastern empire. Historically there was never a nation in the region. It was a land of many people, faiths, and cultures from antiquity to modernity. Various empires, from Egyptian and Roman times to Moslem and Turkish, claimed political hegemony over the region, last of which were the French and English, who had divided it. Three great religions, Christianity, Judaism, and Islam, composed of people living all over the world, looked to Jerusalem as a center in the origins and development of their faiths. A nationalist movement known as Zionism was born among European Jews in the nation-building fervor of the 1890s. After the racial devastation and displacement of World War II, a huge and growing population of Jewish survivors sought refuge in the British Mandate of Palestine. They found little welcome elsewhere as their frustrated attempts to find safety before and during the war all amply testify. Exceptions were made for celebrities in the arts and sciences, and the well-to-do also had less trouble finding new homes. But hundreds of thousands of European Jewish refugees fought or found their way into Palestine and then fought English forces and, immediately following that, local Arab resistance to their establishment of the nation-state of Israel. The early Zionists did not envision a racially defined state. They did not envision Hitler either, or the racial implications of nation building in a homeland claimed no less fiercely by someone else.

Jews and Arabs were once placed in the same racial category of "Semite" by many of the nineteenth-century scientists who pondered such mysteries. In making the new nation the State of Israel, the nation builders also made new racial laws, categories, and distinctions for their own security and economic benefit. Palestinian Arabs were displaced from their homes and resettled both voluntarily and by coercion as refugees in camps. External Arab world assistance spurred Palestinian resistance and increased Israeli repressive measures and warfare in the Suez Crisis of 1957, the Six-Day War of 1967, the Yom Kippur War of 1973, and the invasion of Lebanon in 1982. The new nation of Israel, just as so many predecessor nations, grew up in warfare and territorial expansion that included the expropriation of land and cultural legitimacy from an indigenous population. Warfare and security measures were not the only contributors to a racially defined and divided state. Middle Eastern, African, and Asian Jews found social, economic, and employment discrimination in private and public institutions that favored their European and American immigrant coreligionists. Israeli popular culture increasingly turned defensively in the direction of religious authorities whose views of the state were less equivocal than those who expressed an interest in compromise with its enemies and a more ecumenical cultural policy among its own citizens. Those conservative religious and nationalist views coincided unsurprisingly with comparably harsh public and private racial attitudes and actions. The government of Israel launched brutal murderous air attacks on civilian Palestinian refugee camps in southern Lebanon because they were said to shield terrorists. An American immigrant, a man who was a medical doctor and a devoutly Orthodox Jew, carried out his own murderous assault on peaceful Moslems at prayer in a mosque not long afterward in 1996. Some religious Jews came to believe, and acted on the belief in 1996, that the murder of their own head of state was warranted if it might prevent the negotiated return of some Palestinian authority in conquered territory. A nineteen-year-old Israeli soldier who was off-duty walked into an open-air market in Hebron on January 1, 1997, and fired into eight Palestinian civilians with his automatic rifle. He was hoping to scuttle peace talks he believed were harmful to his nation. Violent independent action on the racial and territorial frontiers of authority is not new to this story; it has been part of it from the start and deserves greater reflection.

The Frontiersman

Portuguese, Spanish, Dutch, English, American, German, and other settler forces in the colonial outposts of national empires routinely exceeded official government or religious social, economic, or military restrictions. They went further than authorized, but usually in the same direction. In trade, farming, the exploitation of land and labor, and political and governmental practices, those at the edges of the new settlements took the biggest risks and had the most to gain or lose. The pioneer and mostly mythical cowboy who fought with, murdered, and displaced the Native American from the American frontier became revered cultural icons, heroic symbols of independent, self-reliant manhood. The real conquest of the American West was more systematically carried out by the U.S. Army on behalf of railroads and their linked interests with mining concerns and land barons. Afrikaners and Australians who trekked, slaughtered, and racially rationalized the expropriation of Bantus, Bushmen, and aboriginal people, or Israeli settlers in Palestinian territory, never thought of themselves as unpatriotic or as acting in a manner hostile to perceived standards of authority or legitimacy. To the contrary, these settlers were on the front lines of the goals and perceived destinies of their nations. *Gauchos,* who claimed the Pampas in Argentina and Uruguay, Spanish *conquistadores* in the Americas, the Portuguese and Dutch adventurers in Africa and Asia, and patriotic German police units in parts of Eastern Europe, all at times went beyond the law; sometimes, they were well beyond its reach. They were not acting in defiance of the law, but ahead of it, at times perhaps for their own purposes, but always in keeping with its intent as they understood and interpreted it.

It is among the most highly trained and highly socialized coercive forces of national law and public authority, the domestic police and the overseas or frontier military, that the most patriotic and racially assertive national cultural sentiments can be observed. The French military threatened the stability of the Fourth and Fifth Republics because so many of its officers expressed a militant racial and patriotic determination to hold on to Algeria that exceeded the will of the French national government. For many, it was impossible to imagine the French nation stripped of empire. It required the political leadership of a celebrated national military leader, General Charles de Gaulle, to negotiate the end of French colonial dominion in Algeria, and he did so at great risk to his own life and safety. Yizhak Rabin was not as fortunate, and was murdered by an individual who was part of an Israeli political and cultural movement that truly considered him less of a patriot than themselves. His successor, Benjamin Netanyahu, is moving with great hesitation and uncertainty toward some limited recognition of Palestinian autonomy. His disputed settlements are contemporary frontier outposts. Every fragile agreement seems tentative. Two fierce nationalisms confront each other in the same landscape. Racial and national violence share an emotional attachment to authority that inhibits the efforts of those who are outside positions of authority to bring under control.

Paternalism, Patriotism, Racial Violence

Sigmund Freud, ruminating about the massive, destructive, national violence of World War I, observed that "a belligerent state permits itself every such misdeed, every such act of violence, as would disgrace the individual."[7] Many individual soldiers never recovered from the horrors they experienced and the deeds they and their comrades did in war, especially as citizen-soldiers of the past 200 years. Their individual actions in war are often contrary to everything they have learned that enabled them to think of themselves as civilized. Examples of this postwar emotional trauma or "syndrome" are well known and now better understood. A newspaper front-page headline described "A JAPANESE GENERATION HAUNTED BY ITS PAST" and opened with a frightful lead sentence: "Nearly six decades have passed, but when Shinzaburo Horie sees a baby he still cringes inside, and his mind replays the indelible scene of himself as a young soldier in China, thrusting his bayonet through the chest of a Chinese infant."[8] Both Freud and the reporter could as easily have described acts of racial violence as Horie's national action. Racial lynching, burning, and mutilation are acts of violence similar to the Brooklyn-born murderous Israeli doctor Baruch Goldstein's assault on Moslem worshippers that have social origins and are often collectively carried out and condoned (*New York Times,* February 25, 1994). Now there is a monument to Goldstein in the disputed town of Hebron.

The nation-state was the legal authority from which racial expropriation, displacement, and murder originated. Coercive, nonreligious violence defined the nation as distinct from its feudal counterpart. Without a racially specified motivation and explanation, the torture and murder that race elicits would, as Freud said about national warfare, "disgrace the individual." Instead of shame or disgrace, the perpetrators of racial violence, like dutiful soldiers or quite ordinary people, most often seem proud of their deeds, expect the social approval of authorities in their communities, and at times include civic and police authorities in their ranks. Sometimes they truly are good ol' boys whose delinquent acts are perverse yearnings for the approval and affection of the Men whose authority they revere, the secular collective pillars of the community. Just as very young men make the most malleable soldiers for their nations, violent racial assaults or murders are often the acts of the young acting in indirect, or at times direct, obedience to the authority of their elders.

Henry Francis Hays, the son of Bennie Jack Hays, the titan of the Ku Klux Klan, and the organization's leader of southern Alabama, was convicted of a March 21, 1981, racial killing of a nineteen-year-old man in Mobile, Alabama. In the course of a subsequent (1987) lawsuit against the Klan that charged the killing was "part of a pattern of racial intimidation inspired by the top leaders of the United Klans," two Klansmen testified that their leader, Hays, aged seventy, described the hanged corpse of the beaten-to-death teenager as a "pretty sight" that would "look good for the Klan."[9] Included among the other defendants in the case were Frank Cox, the elder Mr. Hays's son-in-law. Bennie must have been very proud of his boys. The younger Hays was finally executed by lethal injection by the State of Alabama June 6, 1997. Another elated and patriarchical imperial wizard of the White Knights of the Ku Klux Klan, Samuel H. Bowers, boasted, according to his wife "smiling and jubilant," of a 1966 firebombing and murder: "Look at what my boys did to that [Vernon] Dahmer nigger for me" (*Newsday,* August 21, 1998, p. A19). The young, patriotic Israeli soldier who fired his automatic rifle into a peaceful Palestinian marketplace in 1996, or Dr. Goldstein, who killed twenty-nine and wounded about sixty, must have imagined pleasing at least some of their social peers, Orthodox rabbis, and paternal authorities. When a Jordanian soldier slaughtered a group of Israeli schoolgirls within a day or two of his monarch's public condemnation of Israeli settlement construction in a contested part of Jerusalem, King Hussein must have recognized the connection. The king could not have been ignorant of his own indirect responsibility and appeared sincerely sympathetic to the mourners at the funeral for the children. Klansmen and militia men everywhere may take on different names and racial targets; they are consistently patriotic and devoted soldiers out to please the paternalistic authorities of the nation or faith they revere.

Violent racists, acting alone or in organizations, invariably associate their actions with patriotism. They believe they are acting responsively to collective national social desires, as interpreted by those community leaders or social authorities who appear most legitimate. The anxious instability of nations in constant rivalry with one another is matched by the personal internalized insecurity of the racist. Racial assailants typically express fear of the loss of personal or collective group purity through the imagined intervention of the individual from the group whose projected antithetical behavior defines their own. To the Klansman, his victim posed a threat to an order that grew from an imagined personal and social purity. As a synthetic aristocracy, racial hierarchy is never secure. Any social or material gain or advantage achieved by those who have been stigmatized by race is perceived as a loss or setback to those whose authority rests in some part on their belief in their own racial superiority. Race and nation are played out at the high end of the emotional spectrum where violence and sexuality are located. When the enemy gains, the nation or race loses. Many Germans truly believed that Jewish bankers profited conspiratorially from their nation's defeat in World War I and were therefore responsible for it; indeed, that explanation, however specious, wrong, or simplistic, was emotionally satisfying to millions of ordinary Germans. Racial sexual myths evoke similar images of threatened losses to sexually more attractive and aggressive scheming rivals. As nations assume a part of their identity from their interaction with each other, racial awareness is likewise only possible when there is an Other, a people who can serve as an inverse or opposite collective to those who dominate them.

Patriarchal authority creates mythological bases for both race and nation. The story of national origins, leaders, and triumphal ideals in modern history is told in paternalistic language. The nation is the "fatherland," the population or citizenry is regarded as members of a family, and the national territory is a "homeland." People are not expected to like their nation or feel fondness toward it, but to pledge themselves to it, to love it. They are encouraged by every institutional authority and through every medium voice to be ready to die for it. George L. Mosse, in his book *Nationalism and Sexuality* (1985), makes the emphatic claim that "the idealization of masculinity [w]as the foundation of the nation and society" (p. 17).

The close association of government and patriarchal authority, insofar as it endows racial identity with emotional power and legitimacy, are frequently noted, as for example references to the American president as a "Great White Father." Additional research analysis along the lines of *The Authoritarian Personality* (1950) by Theodor Adorno et al. and Robin Wiegman's *American Anatomies: Theorizing Race and Gender* (1995) would undoubtedly sustain the closeness of racial, national, paternal, and religious behaviors as positive responses, not renegade behaviors, toward authority. The murder of Moslems at prayer by the Israeli medical doctor exceeds legal authority in much the same way as the action of a soldier who kills civilians in war, a racial lynch mob, Rabin's killer, or police officers who kill or brutalize a so-called racial or national public enemy in their custody. They go beyond the law because they are so driven by emotional ties to revered authorities. Those authorities usually back them up or cover for their excesses. The South African police killers of Stephen Biko, for example, were hardly outlaws. They may have sincerely thought of themselves as good officers out to please their boss, their neighbors, and their nation-state. Like so many patriotic citizens, they may have done their jobs too well. The safety and purity of their own social identity, their personal autonomy, were defined by the imagined antithetical reality of those whom they vilified and destroyed. Those who attack or brutalize racialized immigrants to their nation are imposing their own personalized resentments to state-imposed codes and regulations.

The Martinique-born Algerian psychiatrist Franz Fanon, in his essays in *The Wretched of the Earth* (English translation, 1965) and *Black Skin, White Masks* (English translation, 1965) and the historian Eugene D. Genovese in *Roll Jordan Roll: The World the Slaves Made* (1972), among others, have described the psychological consequences that result from social dominion in different settings, postwar Algeria and pre–Civil War America. Fanon described a world of racially colonized subjects and the psychologically damaging consequences of their condition. Genovese depicted historically grounded social behaviors such as theft with distinct emotional power: "Roast pig is a wonderful delicacy, especially when stolen" (p. 599). In both situations, the racialized group shared a contrived and unstable difference with the dominant group akin to that of rival nations with one stark exception: legitimacy. The racialized subject had no (or less) sanctioned autonomy, no (or less) independent legal position in the face of institutional authority. Possessors of legitimate identity, those within the paternal bond of the nation, feel little or no remorse when they attack in wartime or in racial encounters those outside that protective association. Racial dominion established a personal, paternal authority enforced by the power of the nation-state. The nation provided legitimate identity for expropriation. The nation's virtues were heralded as the antithesis of the vices of the racialized subject. The nation idealized itself in the process. The frontier genocidal experience against Native Americans formed part of the identity of the United States. The colonies contributed to the identity of their European colonizers, and Jews were vital in the creation of the identity of Germans. The racialized slave, servant, colonial subject, or genocidal victim gives up more than labor, land, or even life to the master whose nation constructs the coercive relationship. The idea of the modern nation-state itself is formed from the legitimacy of racially mythologized expropriation.

Sex Lies

Sexual mutilation and sexual imagery or motivation often accompany racial and national violence. Expression of sexual anger and fantasy about anticipated sexual danger were part of the racial conqueror's stock explanation for domination and the imposition of control. The conquered were depicted as wildly sexual, licentious and predatory, in contrast to the restraint, modesty, and civil decorum of those who murdered them on behalf of a civilizing mission. In spite of their vast differences the Irish, African, Native American, Asian, and Jewish victims of racial expropriation and conquest all shared a projected common sexual depravity, in contrast to the pristine, imagined virtues of their oppressors. Some imagined racial behavioral projections varied over the centuries, but the sexuality of those men, women, and children who were racinated was portrayed as a dangerous omnipresent threat. Legally or socially sanctioned sexual abuses of racinated men and women, and the destruction of innocent children, are well known and important qualities of racism that typically exceed the conventional parameters of ordinary state coercion or warfare. Such practices as legal sterilization or publicly sponsored syphilis experimentation, where treatment was deliberately and secretly withheld, for example, accompany rape and castration as manifestations of the sexual dimension of racism in the United States. Other national cultures present parallel sexually hostile transference and practices in racist circumstances.

Out with the Old, In with the New

Rape, mass murder, undifferentiated violence, sexual fantasy, and mutilation are but one part of the emotional and physical cost of collective identification with race and nation in modernity. The postwar era witnessed both the continuing expression of high-intensity emotions and innovative new opportunistic steps and turns in the double helix. Lynching and castration lost ground as the preeminent coercive weapon of racism, but were replaced by criminalization. Emmett Till was only thirteen when he was lynched by an enraged mob in Mississippi in 1953. No legal actions were taken against his murderers. During the next decade, civil rights activism, court decisions, and federal legislation put an end to some legal forms (called *de jure* to differentiate them from *de facto*) of exclusionary and differential racial practices. The cold-blooded assassination in 1963 of Medgar Evers, the prominent Mississippi leader of the National Association for the Advancement of Colored People, led to a series of murder trials and the eventual conviction of his killer, Byron De La Beckwith, almost thirty years later. Church bombings in Alabama that included the vigilante murder of children provoked a recognition of it as a dangerous threat to civil authority. Freelance violence beyond certain discreet limitations challenged the authority of the state. Vigilante racial violence in the American South in the mid-1960s generated its counterpart in the formation of the Black Panther Party and the Deacons for Defense and Justice. Some violent confrontations ensued with legal authorities who were naturally more protective of the traditional forms of racial coercion and control than those who fought them. Increased social conflict and instability threatened the legal authority of the state and nation. Alabama Governor George C. Wallace put his authority against that of the nation in his grandstand attempt to block the desegregation of the University of Alabama in 1963. If the nation could not impose control over its zealous racists or its racinated population, public confidence in government itself was threatened.

The torture and brutal murder of three civil rights workers in Mississippi in 1964 led to criminal action against those in the community who were involved. A year later, the president of the United States proudly signed a sweeping Civil Rights Act into law and declared, "We shall overcome." It seemed to many observers at the time as if a new day, free of racism, was dawning in the United States. But, like the hermit crab that outgrows its former home and scurries off to find a new and better fit, racial identity formed by the authority of the nation-state soon found congenial new ways to reaffirm its power.

The years 1965–69 were distinctive for many contentious challenges to authority in the United States. Civil rights activism was joined by anti–Vietnam War protest, and a revived and militant feminism. The breaking down of traditional racial codes built on segregation coincided with a contentious foreign policy marked by failure to achieve neocolonial objectives in the former French colony of Indochina. Malcolm X was killed in February 1965 before he was able to bring a human rights violation charge against the United States in the United Nations. Martin Luther King Jr. was murdered soon after he joined the battle for civil rights with organized labor and a condemnation of the Vietnam War. Some serious theologians proclaimed the death of God; minimal artists took color, line, and form out of painting; and some composers experimented with spare musical themes wherein silence played an increasingly important part. Every bastion of authority was under assault as Maoist-inspired Red Guards challenged elders, expertise, and all traditional elites. Richard Nixon narrowly gained the presidency in the election of 1968 in the midst of the most contentious political atmosphere in American history since the Civil War. He pledged to restore what he claimed a "silent majority" of Americans desired. Nixon began a process of racial initiatives, police and FBI interventions, selective enforcement policies, and judicial appointments that continued for more than a generation and through several administrations after his personal disgrace drove him from office.

By 1990, American prisons, courts, and law enforcement agencies regained control and were the chief coercive authorities responsible for a racialized criminal system and its vastly expanded inmate- and probation-restricted population. Police brutality in South Africa, the United States, and Israel have much in common. Sworn latter-day testimony, one dramatic Southern California videotape, and terrible Israeli military brutality all testify to the shift, with some important exceptions, away from racial mob or vigilante action to civil authority. Racism has always required the formal authority of the nation state. De facto racism requires institutional and legal authority no less than jim crowism or public fascination with a racially based celebrity murder trial. Outbursts of jealous teenage bat- or gun-wielding hooligans, police and prison guard real and imagined murderous excesses indicate the linked vitality of racial and sexual emotions in the United States after decades of legal desegregation. The government of the United States shed its overt segregation practices; on the other hand, the government of South Africa sought unsuccessfully to keep its formal racial structure intact. In the United States policy initiatives, legislative measures, and court actions successfully transferred most of the burden of physical enforcement from the federal government to state and local authorities and private institutions in the same period. Capital punishment, for example, notorious for its racially discriminatory application, was restored in many states by popular referendums or legislative action after a brief national hiatus in the mid-1970s, and it has been increasing in use ever since. It showed no signs of abating even after it was criticized as racist by a UN Commission on Human Rights Report in 1998 (*New York Times,* April 7, 1998, p. A17). The suburbanization of the nation and racial ghettoization of its cities completed the job of constructing a new racial realignment for the nation. Of course, there remains the open and incompletely answered question of the racial role of covert FBI and CIA actions with regard to political dissent, drug abuse, and selective law enforcement policy. There can be little doubt that these two shadowy agencies of national authority played significant roles in racial matters, whether through illegal surveillance and infiltration (as COINTELPRO documents revealed) or their association with illegal drug importation, distribution, and enforcement practices.

Pop Culture, Media Images

Race as a component of sexual fantasy and brutality, and as the foundation for imagined virtues and deficiencies kept its cultural hold on the public imagination in the Cold War era, but found new means of expression in the United States. Popular cultural images, purveyed globally through a massive telecommunications industry, took American racial myths far beyond the public of an earlier age. Music, film, sport, and dance became racially accessible on a commercial basis as never before. Where professional prizefighters, blackface minstrels, and radio voices had been, a new entertainment industry emerged. Brutal physical exertion in competitive games elicit childlike joys and behaviors. The entire range of human emotions is part of the vicarious pleasures of spectator sport and entertainment. The first American sports arena to open up racially to a national audience was boxing, a poorly regulated blood-and-guts sport notorious for its connection to gambling and well-organized (usually a euphemism for police protected) crime. Professional major league baseball was desegregated in 1947, a year before the Truman Executive Order moved in the same direction with the armed services and a year after the Supreme Court quietly barred segregated public facilities in interstate travel. More complete implementation of the interstate travel code awaited the celebrated "Freedom Rides" of the mid-1960s.

Changes in mass markets for cultural as well as material commodities and the end of the Cold War led to new turns in the racial/national helix. Sports, movies, televison, music, fashion, and travel practices put national trends ahead of regional parochialism throughout the nation. Within a few years, celebrities began to displace American economic and political leaders and the social elite as public figures of heroic dimension. Now, descendants of slaves could begin to amuse and entertain a mass, ultimately global, audience as fighters, singers, dancers, actors, and adult players of children's games with little restriction on their participation other than their abilities. There would be democracy at the box office, equal opportunity corporate endorsement contracts. No matter that these wondrous skills had little or no applicability in the workaday world or that only a few hundred positions were available at any given time in these extremely narrow fields. Celebrity work and celebrity life were synthetic and representational. Once, in the late nineteenth and early twentieth centuries, Social Darwinian dreams were fueled by rags-to-riches stories of great industrial fortunes made in a single generation. A half century later, corporate endorsement contracts by celebrities became the pathway to riches for the talented poor. Not much public reflection was given to the fact that most of this kind of employment, especially in sports, was a form of play. Nor did it matter that such careers were often short and ephemeral. The unimaginable wealth paid for the services of these few members of racialized groups served as an illusion of social and economic opportunity for all, while by every objective standard of measurement, the racial divisions of the nation stagnated or widened.[10]

Americans of every ideological outlook self-indulgently expressed enthusiasm for the heroic sports achievements of Jackie Robinson, Michael Jordan, and Tiger Woods, while the economic and social conditions of people just like them stagnated and declined during the period of their greatest notoriety. One author, a professor of Germanic languages at the University of Texas at Austin, John Hoberman, in his book *Darwin's Athletes: How Sport Has Damaged Black America and Preserved the Myth of Race* (1996), has argued that an obsession with the extraordinary physicality of athletic prowess was destructive to both its aspirants and to efforts to deracialize the culture. Many of the same criticisms are applicable to other areas of entertainment and popular culture. Human skills undoubtedly develop best when they are permitted to thrive. When they became the solitary allowable means of artistic or human expression for some groups, those skills increased in social importance as spiritual music did among American slaves, and jazz and *Hoop Dreams* did among so many of their descendants. Racially defined persons whose attributes helped reinforce mythological qualities that were imposed or projected by the dominant culture were as richly rewarded for their services as those made to carry the burden of negative mythologies were severely punished. Racial criminalization in the United States statistically increased apace with racial celebrity enrichment in the fifty years after World War II.

Codes, Language

The satirical humorist Lenny Bruce capped the racial dilemma faced by President Lyndon B. Johnson in a routine where he depicted the president awkwardly attempting to learn to say the word "Negro." Until about 1965, virtually all the words used to describe racially vilified people were disparaging and carried abusive, emotional tones. The United States is composed of many subcultures, religious groups, regions, and traditions. Racial identity exerts an important unifying national, cultural theme in the United States and does so in the form of debasement and shared agreement about vilification and hostility. This kind of cultural, racial debasement is directed toward those who have been delegitimized by the authority of the nation itself. Emotionally loaded racial jokes and language were the shared means of testing the common cultural assumptions of neighbors, friends, and associates.[11] At the highest corporate levels of the Texaco Company, this social bonding practice expressed through the use of vicious racial terminology was continuing in 1996. Only the victims sought to employ terms that were free of hostility, though they, too, used the prevailing words with a touch of irony and self-mockery. When it was formed in the Progressive era, the National Association for the Advancement of Colored People used terminology that reflected the multihued appearance of people in the period of racial slavery and its aftermath. As in Brazil, there were parts of the plantation South where slaves were more numerous than their masters. House servants and field hands in a coercive environment produced offspring of every tone and human type. The word *colored* may have been imprecise, but it covered without anger all those who were subjected to the same oppressive treatment, North or South. Public facilities designated separate areas and entrances for "colored only." The word *Negro* came into use as a more dignified term and became a standard in the era of civil rights struggle; public figures had to learn to use it, despite their lifelong custom toward blunt derision. Race, however, is inherently derogatory, as it functions mainly to create hierarchical legitimacy. Every attempt at taking the sting out of its terminology results in frustration. No racial term of identity can escape vilification.

Nationalism engendered an identification with Africa among many African Americans in the period of independence movements during the 1960s. As Zionism was born in the ethnic European nationalist upsurge of the 1890s, a racial nationalism harmonious with African decolonization affected terminology and identity in the 1960s. The term *African-American* fit consistently with other ethnic hyphenated groups, though it was inadequate for building political coalitions with Latin, Asian, and Native American groups that sought to combat racially exclusionary housing, employment, and educational policy in the United States. Some of the fashions of "Black Nationalism" expressed the desire to affirm an aggressive identity with movements for national independence and racial decolonization. Fashions, however, are known for their brevity. A political "Rainbow Coalition" was formed a few years later and soon fell apart. The government and mass media made use of the euphemism "minority" instead of speaking directly about race. Newspapers reported that more than half the children in the New York City public school system were minorities. The word lost all its meaning, and the courts failed to find a consistent constitutional application for voting reforms or the construction of political districts aimed at combating underrepresentation or racial gerrymandering.

Mythologies are not easily discarded by their own creators when they continue to serve the ends that called them forth. The idea of race affected many words within the language. Terms came to be associated with race by public figures and through public policy. *Welfare* became a racial term, as did *inner city,* especially when connected to *fraud* or *crime.* The nation's *drug war* was not against the costs and abuses wrought by alcohol, tobacco, or prescription medications, but aimed almost exclusively at drugs used by the racinated poor. In England the word *mugging* came into widespread use as a racial crime, no matter the description of the offender. Willie Horton's menacing image helped elect George Bush to the presidency in 1988, and gave the word *liberal* a racial body blow from which it has not recovered in American politics. Presidential candidate Michael Dukakis dodged the term; President Bill Clinton ran away from it.

The older European colonial term, *black,* was introduced widely in the United States, at first awkwardly and with some embarrassment by almost everyone who used it. It became a commonplace national term because racism, in spite of its repudiation by science, reason, and human decency, was a commonplace national reality. The word *ghetto* was absorbed into American usage after World War II as a way of referring to enforced racial residential segregation as practiced in Europe; it was used to describe a terrible and undemocratic thing done by fascists or other racial bigots in power. It soon became a neutral matter-of-fact term for explaining the reality of American community life, though everyone stuck in a ghetto was advised and encouraged to try and get out of it. No matter that public housing, mortgage policy, and state and local laws, political districts and zoning codes constructed such rigid racial community lines in the first place. Terminology that had traditionally been employed to describe hardship or social powerlessness fell into disuse. Words such as *slum* or *poor* fell away in media usage. There was no longer a *working class.* Entry into something called the *middle class* promised a destigmatized race-neutral American possibility found mostly in television situation comedies and advertising.

While a wide range of economic conditions prevailed, those who were racially stigmatized felt the barbs and exclusionary barriers of race regardless of their wealth. In South Africa as well, the national racial terminology resulted in odd linguistic contradictions. The laws of apartheid had constructed four elaborate legal racial categories: white, colored, Asian, and black, each with its complex legal restrictions and regulations. Chinese businessmen and residents in South Africa until the late 1980s were designated as Asians, but Japanese businessmen and diplomatic guests were accorded the higher status of "honorary whites."[12] George Orwell was not thinking specifically about race, though he could have been, when he observed in the essay "Politics and the English Language" the damage done to language by arbitrary authority.

Europeans

For the great and former European national empires, the end of colonial racism marked the beginning of innovative domestic forms. Paul Gilroy has studied the matter in Great Britain in his book, *There Ain't No Black in the Union Jack: The Cultural Politics of Race and Nation* (1987). Gilroy confirms its resilience when he notes: "Racism does not, of course, move tidily through time and history. It assumes new forms and articulates new antagonisms in different situations" (p. 11). Throughout the history of the British Empire, until 1948 there was an indivisibility among British subjects, whether found in Great Britain, the colonies, or the Commonwealth. After the passage of the British Nationality Act in 1948 a separate citizenship was designated for those in the Commonwealth as distinct from the UK and its colonies, but there were no legal restrictions on immigration. Racial restrictions and controls were under colonial administrative authority and enforceable under shipping legislation until the passage of the Commonwealth Immigrants Act of 1962, when an ancestral legacy became a requirement for migration to Great Britain from a Commonwealth nation.[13] This was similar to immigration restrictions based on national origins imposed by the United States after World War I. To this point, however, there were no explicit legal racial restrictions or barriers to immigrants to Great Britain from its colonies. The Labour government initiated the next step in a famous White Paper of 1965. Race relations in the nation would be improved, the paper argued, with "fewer numbers of black immigrants."[14] Once that die was cast, a new Commonwealth Immigration Act was passed in 1968 that extended the earlier ancestral requirement for entry into England, now called patriality, to the British colonies as well as to members of the Commonwealth. The European Commission on Human Rights found this to be racist and in violation of its codes, but the EC Council of Ministers took no action, and the act remained unimpeded. A comprehensive Immigration Act followed in 1971 that established a more uniform code for all patrials. The overtly racist intention of the newest law was proudly proclaimed by the Home Secretary, who declared: "The numbers, who qualify under the patrial clause, will be large, and the vast majority will be of European extraction. This is a fact."[15]

A vigorous, openly racist, and extremely nationalistic political movement emerged that coincided with England's immigration policies and restrictions. Enoch Powell, a minister in the Conservative government of Harold Macmillan from 1960 to 1963, coalesced public racial and national sentiment in a famous speech made in 1976. Powell warned that "the nation has been and is still being, eroded and hollowed out from within by implantation of unassimilated and unassimilable populations . . . alien wedges in the heartland of the state."[16] Further restrictive measures were added with the passage of the British Nationality Act of 1981. A year later, during the war with Argentina, Falkland Islanders 8,000 miles away were more closely identified as English citizens than former West Indians who were now resident citizens of London. The word *immigrant* became synonymous with *black* in England. Law enforcement and adherence to traditional authority were contrasted with fears of racial criminality. Disputes in schools erupted that were centered on "multicultural" issues because of alleged "antiracism." Urban riots in 1981 and 1985 were associated with race, and a conservative hegemony built on a "rhetoric of order" dominated the English governments of Conservative Prime Ministers Margaret Thatcher and John Major and influenced both major political parties for more than a generation.[17] The political fallout from the 1965 Labour initiative has an unknown divisive half-life.

European immigration policies varied from nation to nation and depended on economic and regional circumstances as much as colonial legacies. In almost every place, the legal issue of race and nation was used to the advantage of traditional centers of authority, political or religious, in the era of the Cold War and after. Legal "guest" Turkish workers in Germany, "green card" workers such as Mexicans in Texas or California, were attacked or vilified by racist gangs. Government actions, both legislative and coercive, were taken either to impose new restrictions or to establish order at the expense of those who were racinated. The courts also played an important role in racially restrictive immigration policy by their general

acceptance of the discretionary authority of the legislatures and "in particular in delimiting the scope for judicial review and permitting a devolution of
powers to immigration officers."[18] Californians sought to deny public
health, schooling, and other services to noncitizen children. Algerians in
France were more likely to share the experiences of Pakistanis or Indians in
England. The National Front, the neofascist French political party, led by
the overtly racist Jean-Marie Le Pen, won local elections in the areas of
greatest Algerian immigration after that colony won its independence in
1962, and with the onset of the highest postwar rates of unemployment
during the ten years beginning in the late 1980s.[19] Within Italy, some
northerners sought to curb the free mobility of southern Italians, while
others talked of secession and the creation of a new, racially purified Italian
state. The postwar preeminence of the debilitating effect of racism on union
solidarity and leftist organizations in the United States and a decolonizing
Europe led many analysts and critics to regard racism primarily as a divisive tool of capitalist governments and an extension of class conflict and
control, not as an inherent reciprocal component of nationalism.[20]

Conclusion

The peculiar energy of racism has always been internally focused, defined by
inverse national cultural characteristics and sparked into flaming intensity by
changing circumstances. There have been as many variations in the specific
expression and utilization of race as there have been expansive or emergent
nations among alien people. Each nation constructs its own distinctive form
of banking, currency, political organization, language, and cultural style.
Without wilderness frontiers to conquer, without jim crow controls, without
colonial subjects to rule, without scientific or intellectual rationalizations to
confirm them, race and nation, the great mythologies of modernity, survived
and prospered in the era of the Cold War. Plato once advised that those who
would seek to govern find good myths on which to build their authority (*The
Republic*, bk. IV, 425E–427D). Confucius observed: "If those at the top are
fond of the rites, the people are easy to direct" (*Sayings of Confucius*, XIV,
41). Race and nation have been of great service. Their rites and rituals have
flourished in the face of contradictory democratic ideals and resolutions
against them by the assembled representatives of the United Nations. Religion condemns them, but religious institutions have accommodated them.
Ideological imperiums in the Soviet Union or Yugoslavia that promised
material and human equality when racism and nationalism were in disgrace
could not offset their more compelling appeal and global power. The contemporary destiny of race and nation remains our final inquiry.

Chapter 8

Epilogue: Dusk and Dawn, 1991–2000

Summing Up

Throughout five centuries of modern history, the European nation gradually usurped and absorbed clerical and dynastic mythologies and put them to work confirming its ends: the wielding of power over economic relationships in human society. Secular laws and institutions established national categories of value, credit, social organization, and human differentiation. National citizenship legitimization, immigration rules, paper currencies, and passport regulations developed alongside jim crow and apartheid laws and codes. Mythologies of identity grew up with the authority of the laws that came forth from the power of governments and frontier conquerors who acted on their own and on behalf of their governments. From Cromwell to Hitler and beyond, the racial explanations of authorities for otherwise inexplicable arrangements became enduring and self-serving truths. "Our orders," said the Dutch East India Company to its overseas managers and administrators, "must be your laws." Repeated arguments on behalf of the rightness of those laws became enduring verities. Adherence to the laws of the nation required little coercion when they were perceived as built on an accurate reading of reality. The laws and the shared sentiments about them became cultural verities. It was Manifest Destiny, God's will.

These truths endured on their own as internalized codes to those who accepted and benefited from the power and authority of their leaders and the state. All those who were part of the nation were as united by their agreement about a commonly shared vision of reality as they were joined in common language, law, and custom. In the great sixteenth-century struggle with religious authorities for political hegemony in matters of wealth, the nation prevailed, and race became a legitimate category of human differentiation. National leaders placed a patriotic imprint on their every public

188

deed, most emphatically on actions that were confiscatory, murderous, and exploitative. Those who adhered to the authority of national leaders or felt some genuine protective advantage in doing so resonated with the collective emotional bonds formed by national legitimacy. Racists invariably identified themselves as the truest patriots. It was the most uncompromising critics of racism who suffered the charge of national disloyalty. Race and racial identity depend on the nation, and, as long as the latter commands allegiances and emotional loyalties, will continue to define and divide human populations.

Economic Integration

Now national leaders must respond increasingly to the will of multinational corporations that compete for global marketplace hegemony. What was once good for General Motors may no longer be good for the nation of its origin, and vice versa. The nation is being redefined by agreements such as the North American Free Trade Agreement (NAFTA) and the General Agreement on Tariffs and Trade (GATT), and by international financial bodies such as the World Bank and the International Monetary Fund (IMF). To the earlier functions of the nation are now added its services as an administrative agency and disciplinary structure for transnational corporate goals. Nations that impose environmental, labor, or tariff standards unsuitable to potential multinational investor groups risk serious consequences to their economic well-being. The strong social safety net and high wage and benefit system of European nations has fallen out of step with unfettered globalism and is suffering low growth and high unemployment rates as a punitive consequence. National leaders interpret corporate goals through a prism that is increasingly formed by a global marketplace. International human rights standards, once important in focusing public attention on abuses in the Soviet Union and apartheid in South Africa, may be waived, UN resolutions to the contrary notwithstanding, especially when colossal Chinese national interests and transnational corporate opportunities are at stake. On April 16, 1997, the *New York Times* reported the continuing frustration of the United Nations in attempting to take action on Chinese abuses. The newspaper noted that for the "seventh consecutive year . . . resolutions condemning its human rights record" were defeated (p. A11). The Chinese delegate Wu Jianmin said that "China had followed its own course for 5,000 years and would continue to do so." On economic issues, nations face corporate and investor actions, not moral or ethical resolutions.

The national political power to mediate with other nations and multinational corporations remains precious to those who contend for control. Manipulation of information, "spin doctoring," is an omnipresent part of political conflict, and racial or ethnic mythology is a mainstay of that discourse. Euphemistic language about "crime," "drugs," and "welfare" pollutes the public discussion because these terms are most often poorly disguised appeals to racially formed sentiments. Governing brings tangible rewards along with police and military power. Some political struggles that involve race go far beyond a degenerate discourse. They can become murderous and genocidal. The decline or fall of governments is often accompanied by civil conflict and war among groups contending for national power, as in Mobutu Sese Seko's mineral-rich Zaire or in the former USSR or Yugoslavia. News reports of overt anti-Semitism and unpunished racist attacks on Moslem businessmen in Moscow are current examples of the continuing energy of these mythologies. These ethnic conflicts take on the historical characteristics of racism when legal expropriation of property, life, or labor are carried out. Racism also becomes a component of these ethnic conflicts when cohesive national identity is formed at the expense of a degraded and delegitimized Other. In Rwanda and Burundi racial division in the struggle for national political power reached near-genocidal levels in 1994–95. Race and nation may remain enigmatic and analytically underserved, but at the end of 500 years as functional interrelated mythologies, they are as politically forceful as ever.

The human rights violation of legal racial oppression and discrimination is generally condemned, though no effective means of amelioration of its consequences is in sight. The United States delegate to the United Nations, William Richardson, reacted to a report of the UN Commission on Human Rights that condemned his nation's use of the death penalty for its racial "unfairness and arbitrariness" by saying that the report would simply "collect a lot of dust" (*New York Times*, April 7, 1998, p. A17).

Social and economic differentiation based on race actually has intensified in Europe and the United States, while politically overt and legally coercive measures have been alleviated. Indeed, racial identity appears today as forceful as ever inside most nations in aligning patriotic political support and redirecting class loyalties toward traditional national elites. Racism has always offered a synthetic aristocracy of blood. It has served as artificial class insurance to secure the loyalties of those on the way down or with little else to sustain their social status. The movement of investment capital and labor has become less easily subject to national restriction than at any other time in history. The social consequences of this mobility include racial differentiation. In Great Britain and Europe, one commentator has observed, the tendency is to "racialize the internal and international market for labor."[1] Regional national conflicts in Basque sections of Spain or in French Canada, for example, and internal political disputes in former European colonies in Africa and Asia, continue to evoke racial and ethnic rivalries. These disputes characterize the military and political struggles for the considerable internal authority that is still available to nations.

The Contemporary Dilemma

Race still depends on the legal authority of the nation. Neither humanitarian liberal nor hard-nosed conservative remedies alter the inherently oppressive and exploitative place of race, no matter how genuine the intentions; both sentiments form the ideological national political perspectives that twist the helix into adaptability through historic change. The ideological heirs of Thomas Jefferson's liberal concern for human rights and Alexander Hamilton's conservative economic nationalism carry on the racial national-ism of their founders. Whether associated with affirmative action, school busing to achieve desegregation, the creation of racially distinct political districts, or lifting or adding immigration restrictions, the nation responds to racial matters in racial terms and can realize only innovative or regressive racial outcomes. The next worst thing to the racial hostility of the nation for any human group may be its legal designation as a "protected category." Twenty-five years after the passage of the sweeping and liberal Civil Rights Act of 1964, the conservative Supreme Court imposed a raft of rulings that sharply curtailed the effect of the law. Congress responded with a new Civil Rights Act in 1990, which was vetoed by President George Bush. After a series of compromises, a new Civil Rights Act was signed into law by the Republican president the following year. Republicans and Democrats, liber-als and conservatives, from the earliest days of the Republic to the era of Reconstruction and through the Civil Rights struggles to our own time, have traded ideological sides and compromises on the nation's racial poli-cies. The Republican Party Platform on Civil Rights in 1944 led the Demo-crats into the postwar era, then fell behind in the Nixon years. Racial division, emotion, and identity appear to glide above the conventional ideo-logical debate, without regard to party, throughout the nation's history.

Israel continues to define itself as a nation in mythological racial opposi-tion to a large part of its indigenous population, the people of a new politi-cal minority district known as Palestine. Israel's internal politics is marked by ethnic and racial division as well. Hutu and Tutsi people in Rwanda and Burundi have made use of genocidal racial mythologies against one another in a terrible struggle for national political power. Supreme Court Justice Clarence Thomas, in the midst of contradictory rulings on the creation of minority voting districts, declared that it was the "tacit objective" of the

United States to establish "roughly proportional allocation of political power according to race."[2] If this view prevails, a rigid political division may secure racial separation and consciousness indefinitely.

How will new nation-states be formed in the remnants of Yugoslavia, the Soviet Union, or in those places still in a disputed aftermath of European colonial power in Africa or Asia? Who will draw the lines, how and where will they be drawn? Will they be proportional "according to race," as Judge Thomas envisions for his country? Cromwell's "Hell or Connaught," America's Indian reservations and racialized ghettos, South Africa's "Homelands," and Israel's policies toward Palestinians were all defended either as humanitarian or natural consequences of inevitable forces. They were, and are, simply racial provinces established by the legal authority of the state. The powerful loyalties formed by race and nation face less competition from class, religion, or ideology at the end of the twentieth century than they did at its beginning or midpoint.

The 1996 school controversy about the introduction of colloquial English, or Ebonics, into racially segregated Oakland, California, might have been anticipated. It is a conflict with ominous features for the future as well. Certainly the controversy is understandable, and it is not original. More isolated than ever and with less expectation or realistic hope of crossing the barriers to the dominant culture, millions of American children and adults have experienced a cultural isolation that is expressed in unique language. It is a racial language formed in a racial culture. That culture did not completely form itself, but was formed by the nation its identity antithetically served and still serves.

Children learn the language of the real world in which they live, not the one we might imagine they are in or wish for them. It becomes more difficult for their teachers to be understood and to win the trust of their students in the language they use, that of the hostile bigger world, the language of the public school and the police. Some teachers and school leaders in Oakland, California, tried sympathetically to legitimize their verbal interaction with the children by a formal recognition of some of their speech habits and through a sympathetic search for linguistic roots, hoping to get across to them. Critics quite naturally feared that any formal acceptance of a colloquial English would further isolate and condemn the children to a cultural marginality. The famous Kerner Commission warning of "two nations, separate and unequal" could be more formally realized and an existing gap made even wider. The discussion over Ebonics was a discussion of despair. Go with the standard English language forms, and the children exclude the teachers; go the other way and accept that the children are excluded. Like so much of the discussion of race, it is still a debate at the bottom of the well. The children need a different community, a perceived sense of inclusion and welcome into the bigger world, not the reaffirmation of their exclusion from it, which they must already sense. Unfortunately, the teachers cannot change the world, nor can they bear to lose contact with the children who are falling further away. Ebonics is one sad answer. Racially designated political districts are another.

There were twenty-six racially identified "minority" representatives in the House of Representatives in 1990. By 1994, that number had increased to forty-one, as a consequence of a process and approach with similarities to that of affirmative action.[3] On the state and local levels, courts found the underrepresentation of some groups to be a form of discrimination barred by the Civil Rights Law of 1964 and by subsequent legislative actions and court rulings that expanded the law's meaning. The Supreme Court, however, turned in the opposite direction in 1996 in rulings against minority districts in *Shaw* v. *Hunt* and *Bush* v. *Vera;* and in February 1997 a federal court ruled the Twelfth Congressional District of New York, a "mostly Hispanic" district, illegal "because race and ethnicity were the dominant factors used to draw it."[4] A panel of three federal judges ruled in the same month that the Third Congressional District, the first in Virginia to elect a "black member of Congress since Reconstruction, was unconstitutional because of being drawn too heavily along racial lines."[5] At the same time, other federal judges continued to order redistricting to counter political discrimination that diminished representation of racial or ethnic categories. In the same week as the Twelfth Congressional District was outlawed for its explicitly Hispanic construction, Federal Judge John Gleeson gave the Town of Hempstead, New York, seventy-eight days to abolish its at-large electoral system and create six districts for its Town Board. Gleeson ruled that the at-large system was racially discriminatory.[6] If one of the new six is constructed along the lines of the Third or Twelfth Congressional District, it too could be outlawed. Hempstead must create six new districts to assure minority representation, but apparently must not use explicit racial or ethnic criteria to do so.

Deliberate racial political representation, as Judge Thomas appears to welcome, can fix even more firmly a segregated housing and community culture by encouraging residential practices wherein racial identity can find formal legal expression and representation in government. Ebonics will flourish in such communities. Semiautonomous Palestinian regions under Israeli national authority are a bitterly contested compromise that are legally analogous to "minority districts" or "native homelands." As South Africa attempts to move away from the political segregation of "black townships" and "native homelands" in the 1990s, the United States and Israel may be constructing a new form of the same thing.

Affirmative action policies in the United States experienced setbacks similar to several rulings on minority districts. Courts decided during the 1990s that its ostensibly corrective remedies could themselves be discriminatory violations, while its officers and administrative agencies continued to collect and catalogue data into racial, ethnic, gender, and other categories in pursuit of their goals. What began in the 1940s as a struggle for universal civil rights became a complex porridge of nondiscrimination legislative, executive, and judicial actions and decisions fifty years later. Similar to the protective legislation and executive actions extended to labor as the United States moved toward war, and to the welfare and antipoverty policies continued thereafter, that which was offered by the federal government could as easily be modified or taken away. In all three areas—labor, welfare, and civil rights—government action secured slipping allegiances with creative responses that ultimately strengthened existing institutional authority. The measurable statistical gaps fell off at first, but actually grew dramatically between rich and poor, labor and management, and among those groups who were racially defined as the years of so-called protective policy legislation passed. Douglas Frasier, former president of the United Auto Workers, called for a return to the "law of the jungle" as preferable to the strangling effect of labor law as it evolved over fifty years from the passage of the National Labor Relations Act of 1935. The same regression could easily be seen as preferable to the tangles and inequities that have resulted in welfare and civil rights policy. Indeed, there are plenty of forceful advocates for just that on both sides of the debate.

By the close of the twentieth century both major political parties in the United States appeared to be congratulating themselves on the success of their termination of a half century of national welfare programs, powerful labor union organizations, and the conclusion of civil rights activism on behalf of racial justice. Coincidentally, both parties were awash in an embarrassing assortment of campaign contribution riches. They celebrated a cynical, material euphoria reminiscent of the Gilded Age that followed the failed hopes of a Reconstruction era a century earlier. National policy on the issue of race has been a central feature in every era of the nation's past, though the United States was not alone among nations in adapting innovative responses to social stratification that reinforced loyalty to dominant sources of authority and strengthened dependency on the state. The legal protection extended by national government brought about a dependency on the law and the authority of the state that was previously missing. What appears to be inconsistency in policy is actually the devolution of protection in the aftermath of a crisis of loyalty. Depression-era measures secured the loyalty of the unionized labor force for World War II. Once that crisis passed, the Taft-Hartley law began to rectify those concessions to labor. As big Cold War conflicts came to an end after the Vietnam War, the United States no longer needed to count on the military and political devotion of urban and rural communities that had been protected by civil rights legislation or assisted by antipoverty measures. "Benign neglect" became a Nixon-era civil rights program enunciated first by the Harvard professor of sociology, then New York senator, Daniel Patrick Moynihan. The same approach was taken toward antipoverty assistance, jobs programs, and welfare policy. The post–Cold War global marketplace prefers the lowest-cost labor resources it can find and eschews the expensive safety nets offered by universally available social welfare, health, or labor protection. England and the United States have moved faster and harder into the global winds and have trimmed their welfare and labor expenditures accordingly. There is no viable ideological or political alternative; only prison, workfare, and lower-than-subsistence wages for those cut from the welfare roles or the dole, or those held to abandoned (or frozen) minimum-wage standards. This contemporary response was consistent with national policies on economic frontiers and within colonies elsewhere regarding race for the last 500 years.

When W.E.B. Du Bois wrote *Dusk of Dawn* (1940) he was reflecting, at least in part, on the enormous changes he had witnessed since his observation in *Souls of Black Folk* (1903) that "the problem of the twentieth century is the problem of the color-line, the relation of the darker to the lighter races of men in Asia and Africa, in America and the islands of the sea" (p. 23). By 1940, it must have appeared to Du Bois as if a major shift was under way, at least in the United States. As that century comes to an end, both his prophetic remark and his novel seem too optimistic and short-sighted. His great intelligence undervalued the power of racial classification to transcend color and too narrowly confined the use of race to European colonial and plantation applications. Since his death on the eve of the monumental March on Washington in August 1963, racial conflict and division have been as destructive and as dominant in human relations as ever. The midcentury tilt toward democratic universal opportunity was as soundly reversed by a highly racialized crime and punishment system, and by every measurable racial economic index in the United States by the end of the twentieth century, just as the educational and political opportunities of Reconstruction were crushed nearly a century earlier.

At the end of 500 years, the nation has become the dominant form of political organization everywhere on earth. Where nations seek to expand their territory or hegemony over others, they employ racially derived explanations and mythologies for their acquisitions and ambitions for control. The great wars among nations were once battles among coequals for control of external colonial or strategic properties. Nations granted a legitimacy to the captured prisoners of each other's armies and civilian populations that was denied in their colonies and among their racinated subject populations. The Cold War was, ironically, a fifty-year era of peace among those nations, though most European nations faced colonial uprisings and wars with racial features. The French loss of Indochina and Algeria was marked by national political crisis and racial division. "No Vietcong ever called me nigger" was an expression of this racial dichotomy by many Americans unwilling to take part in the war in Vietnam. In every former colony or settler nation, and those still moving from one system to another, a racial legacy helps form new national identity.

With the end of the Cold War in 1989 and the passing of traditional colonialism, there is only a global marketplace and a world of nations. Inside the new and the old nations, groups contend for political power or maintain it by claiming they are the true racial inheritors of the national public destiny. "There ain't no black in the Union Jack" is only one expression of such sentiment. At the perimeters of the earliest national colonial conquests, racial identity continues to characterize the struggle for political autonomy or the remaining shards of national independence. When will Ireland finally be at peace with itself and England? From Africa to the Philippine Islands, resentments born of colonialism and racism continue to smolder. It is not very different in the Middle East, though there the colonial heritage was made more complex by lingering anti-Semitism, and an Israeli settler nation of racism's victims in the place of former French and English colonial powers. Hong Kong has ceased to be a wealthy outpost of the British Empire now that it has been absorbed into the nation of China. The Chinese nation, as the most populous on earth, has the potential to match its emerging economic power with racial arrogance. Social divisions within China and its dominance over economically dependent and less powerful neighbors can elicit the same racial codes and practices characteristic of every former great nation. When Japan enjoyed a brief episode of economic glory during the 1980s and early 1990s, there was a corresponding outbreak of racially arrogant rhetoric. America was falling behind, it was widely reported in Japan, because it was a "mongrelized" population. In contrast, the same pundits noted, the Japanese were a "pure" race. If China is to move into the ranks of the great nations of the new century, there can be little doubt that racial mythology will accompany that elevation.

South Africa enjoyed the leadership of Nelson Mandela. He sought to build a democratic and nonracial nation. His was a principled reaction to a long oppressive history of racial conquest, slavery, colonialism, and apartheid. The danger for Mandela, and especially his successors, is in the ability of the new government to deliver on the material side of its dreams and promises. Economic democracy and a more equitably shared prosperity are prerequisites for a society that would rid itself of racism. Only in isolated enclaves, such as Scandinavia or the Netherlands, can the glimmerings of these possibilities be discerned. Can South Africa, or any nation, adhere to the demands of international competition and successfully withstand its corollary social divisions? Many prosperous South Africans left the country soon after the elections that brought Mandela into the government. More have left since then. Hard times will prompt still more to leave. Those who remain are vulnerable to the stigmata of the former racial legacy, though those who left were its chief winners. Those who remain, since their options are more limited, can become the targets of a new racial majority seeking an outlet for the frustrations of failed expectations. A twenty-first-century racism with the descendants of Europeans on the receiving end of opprobrium is as palpable a reality in South Africa as Chinese or Japanese racial contempt could be for their Western counterparts.

Along with its Asiatic and African potential, at the end of 500 years the idea of race remains a powerful force in the ordinary political life and cultural identity of the nations of the world. Its sources of strength are not obscure. Everyday politics and great institutions are shaped by racial consciousness in Europe, the United States, the Middle East, the old colonial world of Africa and Asia, Australia and New Zealand, and the former Soviet Union and Yugoslavia. The emotional appeal and security offered by nationalism binds people to the authority of the mythologies of past and present leaders. National leaders (with the exception of Mandela) cannot, therefore, be expected to take the lead in the eradication of racism. Ironically, racism is typically regarded as a national issue, not as an inherent characteristic of nations.

Though leadership is understandably imperfect and fraught with contradictions on many matters within and among nations, most popular discontent with government figures about race is currently in the direction of excesses of patriotic emotion and racially antagonistic zeal. Rebelliousness is not marked by challenges to racism and nationalism. Self-identified patriots are not found in the forefront of the battle against racism. Rejected by most intellectuals and the scientific community, racism continues to find academic and empirically fortified defenders in almost every nation. The statistical consequences of racism are presented as proof of its premises by these contemporary empiricists. The great religions of the world have no place for race or racism but have excommunicated virtually no one from membership for espousing its sentiments or imposing its codes. Among many so-called fundamentalist faiths and sects are found the most simplistic expressions of devotion to racial and national mythologies. Religious orthodoxy has been a haven for every form of social exclusivity and intolerance. Social elites at the metropole or on the colonial frontiers have been the primary beneficiaries of race and nation. They can hardly be expected to bite the hand that feeds them. They will, of course, cluck disapprovingly at vulgar excessive expressions of their own racial sentiments. Elite-class snobbery finds the original socially exclusionary product invariably superior to the cheaper and physically more abusive working-class imitation. Indeed, it is in the highest circles where most of the prevailing public mythologies about race and nation have had their origins. Members of private clubs and institutional boardrooms, where people of social power gather, continue to favor those innovations and traditional responses to social challenges that serve them. They offer liberal and conservative solutions, as usual. Race and nation have been the foundations of the hegemony of national elites and, until adequate substitutes are found, continue to sustain them.

Possibilities for Tomorrow

As long as nations can impose their expropriating will on each other by force of arms or can act arbitrarily against the property or common humanity of groups of people, either internally or externally, racism will continue to fill the void formed by the unreason of those acts. International law that effectively disarmed the nation and set an enforceable global human rights standard could begin to do the job of curbing racism. Such law would have to bar the coercive alienation or separation of land, labor, or resources from the people who hold them. Privatization would have to be regulated and controlled to prevent the abuses and inequities whose justification is otherwise found in the irrationalities of racism. Universal standards for human rights would have to protect the material side of existence, wages and salaries, health care, and education with the same force of law as is now extended to the protection of privately owned property. The destructive force of race and nation flourishes in the absence of effective international law. The nation is the modern tribe or gang; its flag and race are its colors and clan; its laws define it and separate its people among themselves and from every other. There can be no racism without nationalism, no race without a nation. Race is defined by national law and depends on that law.

It has often been observed that good laws can help to make a good society. Good rules, properly enforced, make good games and good food and ensure efficient productive processes. A more completely global economy can precipitate a movement toward more universal labor standards. The news of abusive working conditions imposed by Nike contractors and other transnational corporation sweatshops and exploitative wage practices have evoked new calls for regulation and control. More exposure and more efforts to raise minimum human rights and employment standards are a real possibility. Limits on the autonomy of nations to violate human rights alone, as in criticism of China since the suppression of the 1989 Tiananmen Square demonstrations, will not end racism. Those human rights standards would have to be enlarged to include labor and material requirements of life so that racism could no longer provide any economic advantages to its purveyors. The attainment of wealth in Brazil is said to "whiten" or "bleach" its beneficiaries. Social privileges there accrue to those who are perceived as fair-skinned, sometimes without regard to their actual hue. The unearned and arbitrary advantages of identity associated with race sustain racism itself. When they are gone, along with the laws that protect those advantages and that identity, then, and only then, can the idea of race begin to fade away.

The floodgates of information and communication are just opening worldwide to ordinary people. Many cultural commodities are currently setting universal standards in entertainment and fashion. Films, sports, and music now reach into every corner of the globe. A universal European currency, the "euro," suggests that a time may be approaching when there will be a partial diminishing of national economic borders. Immigration controversies, along with the mobility of capital and production facilities, continue to reflect the uneven levels of wages and living conditions around the world. Reductions in the wide discrepancies of development and increases in international economic integration could, over time, take some of the bitterness out of immigration disputes. In the short run, immigration will continue to provoke sharp national and racial reactions. The current weaknesses of labor unions and their national focus of identity prevent them from taking a more progressive lead in international wage, investment, and immigration equity policy. Perhaps they will awaken to the possibilities of the Internet and follow the corporate money in new regional and international organizational initiatives.

Racism could lose more of its bite when there are no immigrants because there would be no hard borders or passports or "green cards" or "guest" workers to divide human society. Race could fade further from influence should the nation-states federate and move toward a more politically integrated human community, as the once disunited, ex-British, colonial North American states formed their national union and made laws together. Nations would have to sacrifice the very autonomy that allows for racism and war in exchange for the stability and economy their passing would bring. Nationalism might maintain its positive cultural qualities without racism, its rainbow of flavors and colors, only when the uneven distribution of wealth, political power, and human rights are mitigated by enforceable universal standards.

Perhaps the greatest obstacle to a race-free human community is the remaining control of warmaking violence in the hands of nations. That wild autonomy of discretionary deadly force continues to portray its internal and external victims as racial enemies when it takes something away from them. Peaceful conflict resolution built on reason, economic equity, and democratic participation may sound utopian, but it is the only alternative to the brutality and irrational violence of racism and nationalism. As the lone remaining superpower, the United States is in a real position to facilitate effective international conflict resolution without war.

There might be a time in the future when there could be peace among all the nations on earth and an end to racism. That will be a time when great cities such as Jerusalem, revered by the big three of Western religions, is not claimed as the exclusive property of one nation or race or faith but exists for all to see, visit, and inhabit. There would have to be an enforceable international standard for the protection of human rights that included economic and social justice as well. Rational terms and agreements hammered out democratically, in a global organization, could make such open cities and human rights guarantees possible someday. Speculation along these lines may seem wildly unrealistic right now. The racial and national alternatives are what we know. They have been with us for half a millennium. It is almost impossible to imagine a world without them. It is difficult to disagree with the distinguished social scientists Etienne Balibar and Immanuel Wallerstein, who remain pessimistic: "We observe that in traditional or new forms ... racism is not receding, but progressing in the contemporary world."[7] Nonetheless, race and nation are, in the end, identity formations that are historical phenomena, not an inevitability of human nature. They have been made, they can be unmade. As our creations, can we imagine ourselves without them?

Notes

Chapter 1. Introduction

1. John Dower, *War Without Mercy: Race and Power in the Pacific War* (New York: Pantheon Books, 1986), pp. 295–303.

2. The UN Educational, Scientific and Cultural Organization (UNESCO) published its first "Statement on Race" July 18, 1950, and followed it with a more scientific text, "On the Nature of Race and Race Differences," drafted by physical anthropologists and geneticists and published June 8, 1951. Both can be found in UNESCO's *Race and Science* (New York: Columbia University Press, 1969), pp. 496–506.

3. All twelve essays collected in Malcolm Cross and Keith Michael, eds., *Racism, the City and the State* (London: Routledge, 1993), show the strength and pervasiveness of racial division in the urban life of the United States, Great Britain, and France.

4. Cited in Louis L. Snyder, *The Idea of Racialism* (New York: Van Nostrand, 1962), p. 3.

5. Ashley Montagu, ed., *The Concept of Race* (New York: Free Press, 1964), p. 12.

6. M.C. Abercrombie, J. Hickman, and M.L. Johnson, *A Dictionary of Biology* (Harmondsworth, England: Penguin Books, 1951).

Chapter 2. No Nations, No Races: Premodern Formations of Authority and Cultural Identity

1. Edwin O. Reischauer and John K. Fairbank, *East Asia: The Great Tradition* (Boston: Houghton Mifflin, 1960), pp. 59–60.

2. Woodridge Bingham, Hilary Conroy, and Frank Ikle, *A History of Asia: Formation of Civilizations, from Antiquity to 1600,* vol. I (Boston: Allyn and Bacon, 1964), pp. 130–31.

3. Ibid., pp. 132–34. On the matter of Aryan *varnas* and color consciousness, see Ranbir Vohra, *The Making of India* (Armonk, N.Y.: M.E. Sharpe, 1997), pp. 24–25. An Indian author, Shashi Tharoor, in *India: From Midnight to the Millennium* (New York: Arcade, 1997), contends that "centuries of intermixing" gave India "perhaps the world's most hetero-hued population (with skin color often varying startlingly even within a single family)," p. 103.

4. Bingham, Conroy, and Ikle, *History of Asia,* p. 137.

5. Romila Thapar, *A History of India* (New York: Penguin Books, 1990), pp. 34–38. The sociologist Andre Beteille is emphatic: "No significant social unit in India—whether based on language, religion, or caste—is racially homogeneous; it is more common for physical and social differences to intersect than to overlap." This is

from his "Race and Descent as Social Categories in India," in John Hope Franklin's collection of essays, *Color and Race* (Boston: Houghton Mifflin, 1968), p. 170.

6. Dinesh D'Souza, *The End of Racism: Principles for a Multiracial Society* (New York: Free Press, 1995), p. 38.

7. Cited in Victor Tcherikover, *Hellenistic Civilization and the Jews* (Philadelphia: Jewish Publication Society of America, Magnes Press, 1966), p. 359.

8. Ibid., p. 374.

9. Ibid., p. 375.

10. Robert Miles, *Racism* (London: Routledge, 1989), p. 15.

11. Ibid., p. 13.

12. Henri Pirenne, *Medieval Cities, Their Origins and the Revival of Trade* (Garden City, N.Y.: Doubleday Anchor, 1956), p. 63.

13. Cited in Leon Poliakov, *The History of Anti-Semitism: From the Time of Christ to the Court Jews*, vol. I (New York: Vanguard Press, 1965), p. 42.

14. Robert S. Wistrich, *Anti-Semitism: The Longest Hatred* (New York: Pantheon Books, 1991), p. 23.

15. Poliakov, *History of Anti-Semitism,* pp. 46–47.

16. An excellent selection of such illustrations that span five centuries of Moslem history can be found in Bernard Lewis, *Race and Slavery in the Middle East: An Historical Enquiry* (New York: Oxford University Press, 1990). Though the author would not agree completely with my interpretation, readers may draw their own conclusions. For a glimpse of Christian depictions of people in the Moslem world, see Robert I. Burns, S.J., *Islam under the Crusaders: Colonial Survival in the Thirteenth-Century Kingdom of Valencia* (Princeton: Princeton University Press, 1973), pp. 318–19.

17. Sidney W. Mintz, *Sweetness and Power: The Place of Sugar in Modern History* (New York: Viking Press, 1985), p. 28.

18. Pirenne, *Medieval Cities,* pp. 126–27.

19. Ibid., pp. 139–46.

20. Boies Penrose, *Travel and Discovery in the Renaissance, 1420–1620* (New York: Atheneum, 1962), pp. 22–23.

21. J.H. Parry, *The Age of Reconnaissance* (New York: New American Library, 1963), pp. 22–24.

22. Ibid., p. 25.

23. Penrose, *Travel and Discovery,* pp. 29–30.

24. Doris M. Stenton, *English Society in the Early Middle Ages, 1066–1307* (Baltimore: Penguin Books, 1962), pp. 191–95.

25. Ibid., p. 198; Poliakov, *History of Anti-Semitism,* p. 203.

26. Poliakov, *History of Anti-Semitism,* p. 203.

27. Michael de Laval Landon, *Erin and Britannia: The Historical Background to a Modern Tragedy* (Chicago: Nelson-Hall, 1981), pp. 29–44.

28. Charles R. Boxer, *Four Centuries of Portuguese Expansion, 1415–1825: A Succinct Survey* (Johannesburg: Witwatersrand University Press, 1965), p. 6.

29. Parry, *Age of Reconaissance,* p. 163.

30. Penrose, *Travel and Discovery,* p. 50.

31. Boxer, *Portuguese Expansion,* p. 24.

32. Parry, *Age of Reconnaissance,* p. 164.

33. Boxer, *Portuguese Expansion,* p. 19.

34. Ibid.

35. Ibid., p. 9.

36. Anthony Smith, *National Identity* (Reno: University of Las Vegas Press, 1991), p. 51.

37. Cited in Tzvetan Todorov, *The Conquest of America: The Question of the Other* (New York: Harper & Row, 1984), p. 123.

38. Fernand Braudel, *Civilization and Capitalism, 15th-18th Century,* vol. 2, *The Wheels of Commerce* (New York: Harper & Row, 1979), p. 555.

39. Liah Greenfeld, *Nationalism: Five Roads to Modernity* (Cambridge: Harvard University Press, 1992), p. 31. I completely agree with Greenfield's location of the beginning of the modern evolution of nationalism and the state at 1500.

Chapter 3. The European Discovery of Race and Nation, 1500–1650

1. Cited in Robert Miles, *Racism* (London: Routledge, 1989), p. 24.

2. Cited in Anthony Smith, *National Identity* (Reno: University of Las Vegas Press, 1991), p. 1.

3. Boies Penrose, *Travel and Discovery in the Renaissance, 1420–1620* (New York: Atheneum, 1962), p. 75.

4. Cited in Charles R. Boxer, *Four Centuries of Portuguese Expansion, 1415–1825: A Succinct Survey* (Johannesburg: Witwatersrand University Press, 1965), p. 35.

5. Charles R. Boxer, *Race Relations in the Portuguese Colonial Empire: 1415–1825* (Oxford: Clarendon Press, 1963), p. 22.

6. Ibid., p. 23.

7. Cited in Tzvetan Todorov, *The Conquest of America: The Question of the Other* (New York: Harper & Row, 1984), pp. 127–29.

8. Ibid., p. 133.

9. Cited in Michael de Laval Landon, *Erin and Britannia: The Historical Background to a Modern Tragedy* (Chicago: Nelson-Hall, 1981), p. 63.

10. Ibid., p. 64.

11. Theodore W. Allen, *The Invention of the White Race,* vol. 1, *Racial Oppression and Social Control* (New York: Verso Press, 1994), p. 57.

12. Cited in David Beers Quinn, *The Elizabethans and the Irish* (Ithaca: Cornell University Press, 1966), p. 108.

13. Nicholas P. Canny. "The Ideology of English Colonization: From Ireland to America," *William and Mary Quarterly* 30, 3rd series (1973): 582–83.

14. Cited in Allen, *Invention of the White Race,* p. 63.

15. Ibid., p. 64.

16. Cited in Charles R. Boxer, *The Dutch Seaborne Empire: 1600–1800* (New York: Knopf, 1965), p. 96.

17. Ibid., p. 99.

18. Leon Poliakov, *The History of Anti-Semitism,* vol. 1, *From the Time of Christ to the Court Jews* (New York: Vanguard Press, 1965), p. 211.

19. Cited in Boxer, *Dutch Seaborne Empire,* pp. 98–99.

20. Boxer, *Portuguese Expansion,* pp. 50–51.

21. Boxer, *Race Relations in the Portuguese Empire,* p. 15.

22. Cited in Robert S. Wistrich. *Antisemitism, the Longest Hatred* (New York: Pantheon Books, 1991), p. 39.

23. Cited in Richard S. Dunn, *Puritans and Yankees: The Winthrop Dynasty of New England, 1630–1717* (Princeton: Princeton University Press, 1962), p. 11.

24. Boxer, *Race Relations in the Portuguese Empire,* p. 2.

25. Ibid., pp. 64–65.

26. Ibid., p. 86.

27. Ronald Sanders, *Lost Tribes and Promised Lands: The Origins of American Racism* (Boston: Little, Brown, 1978), pp. 164–65.

28. Stanley M. Elkins, *Slavery: A Problem in American Institutional and Intellectual Life* (Chicago: University of Chicago Press, 1968), p. 67.

29. George L. Mosse, *Toward the Final Solution: A History of European Racism* (New York: Fertig, 1978), p. xiv.

30. Boxer, *Portuguese Expansion*, pp. 42–43.

31. Sanders, *Lost Tribes*, p. 217.

32. Ibid., pp. 218–19.

33. Boxer, *Dutch Seaborne Empire*, pp. 217, 228–31.

34. Ibid., p. 229.

35. Ibid., p. 239.

36. Sanders, *Lost Tribes*, pp. 203–10.

37. Ibid., p. 258.

38. Poliakov, *Anti-Semitism*, pp. 237–45.

39. Cited in Allen, *Invention of the White Race*, p. 115.

40. Cited in Alden T. Vaughan, *Roots of American Racism: Essays on the Colonial Experience* (New York: Oxford University Press, 1995), p. 13.

41. Cited in James Muldoon, "The Indian as Irishman," *Essex Institute Historical Collections* 3 (October 1975): 280–81.

42. Vaughan, *Roots of American Racism*, p. 119.

Chapter 4. The Colors of Gold: Mercantile Empires, Great Nations, Reason and Racism, 1650–1800

1. Michael de Laval Landon, *Erin and Britannia: The Historical Background to a Modern Tragedy* (Chicago: Nelson-Hall, 1981), p. 132.

2. Theodore W. Allen, *The Invention of the White Race*, vol. 1, *Racial Oppression and Social Control* (New York: Verso Press, 1994), p. 51.

3. Maureen Wall, *The Penal Laws* (Dundalk: Dundalgen Press, 1961), p. 9.

4. The Penal Laws and Burke's sharp criticism of them are reviewed carefully in Allen, *Invention of the White Race*, pp. 81–90.

5. Stanley Elkins, *Slavery: A Problem in American Institutional and Intellectual Life* (Chicago: University of Chicago Press, 1968), p. 41.

6. Ibid.

7. Locke's statement is cited in Lawrence James. *The Rise and Fall of the British Empire* (New York: St. Martin's Press, 1994), p. 23. The Virginia law is in Alden T. Vaughan, *Roots of American Racism: Essays on the Colonial Experience* (New York: Oxford University Press, 1995), pp. 172 and 151.

8. Allen, *Invention of the White Race*, p. 89.

9. Louis Ruchames, ed., *Racial Thought in America*, vol. 1, *From the Puritans to Abraham Lincoln* (Amherst: University of Massachusetts Press, 1969), p. 71.

10. Lawrence James, *The Rise and Fall of the British Empire* (New York: St. Martin's Press, 1994), p. 24. Eric Williams, *Capitalism and Slavery* (Chapel Hill: University of North Carolina Press, 1994), pp. 32–33.

11. Vaughan, *Roots of American Racism*, pp. 18–19.

12. Ibid.

13. Cited in Allen, *Invention of the White Race*, p. 81.

14. Vaughan, *Roots of American Racism*, pp. 27, 29. Color characteristics are cited

in Louis L. Snyder, *The Idea of Racialism: Its Meaning and History.* (New York: Van Nostrand, 1962), p. 11.

15. Ibid., p. 19.

16. Charles R. Boxer, *The Dutch Seaborne Empire, 1600–1800* (New York: Knopf, 1965), pp. 216–17.

17. Cited in ibid., p. 221.

18. Ibid., pp. 230–31.

19. Ibid., p. 236.

20. Ibid., p. 241.

21. Cited in Charles R. Boxer, *Four Centuries of Portuguese Expansion, 1415–1825: A Succinct Survey* (Johannesburg: Witwatersrand University Press, 1965), p. 78.

22. Charles R. Boxer, *Race Relations in the Portuguese Colonial Empire: 1415–1825* (Oxford: Clarendon Press, 1963), pp. 49–51.

23. Vianna Moog, *Bandeirantes and Pioneers* (New York: George Braziller, 1964), p. 3. For Jesuit expulsions, see Boxer, *Race Relations,* pp. 94–97.

24. Boxer, *Race Relations,* pp. 54–55.

25. Ibid., p. 74.

26. Ibid., p. 71.

27. James, *Rise and Fall of the British Empire,* p. 123.

28. Cited in ibid., pp. 21–22.

29. J.H. Parry and P.M. Sherlock, *A Short History of the West Indies* (New York: St. Martin's Press, 1966), pp. 164–65.

30. Snyder, *Idea of Racialism,* p. 11.

31. Ibid., pp. 103–4.

32. Frank Tucker, *The White Conscience* (New York: Frederick Ungar, 1968), pp. 38–39.

Chapter 5. To the Ends of the Earth: Racism and Nationalism Rampant, 1800–1917

1. The great American historian Charles Beard depicted an overriding and self-serving economic motivation among the Founding Fathers in his book *An Economic Interpretation of the Constitution of the United States* (New York: Crowell-Collier and Macmillan, 1935). Beard's thesis may have some real flaws, but it generated its most serious controversy only when it encountered a Cold War era's need to envision the nation's founders in an idealized patriotic image.

2. The scholarly American federal judge A. Leon Higginbotham Jr., in two meticulously researched and written books, *In the Matter of Color: Race and the American Legal Process: The Colonial Period* (New York: Oxford University Press, 1978), and *Shades of Freedom: Racial Politics and Presumptions of the American Legal Process* (New York: Oxford University Press, 1996), makes the case the American legal process has played in "substantiating, perpetuating, and legitimizing the precept of (racial) inferiority" (*Shades,* p. xxv).

3. Cited in Michael Crowder, *West Africa under Colonial Rule* (Evanston: Northwestern University Press, 1968), p. 10.

4. Cited in Lawrence James, *The Rise and Fall of the British Empire* (New York: St. Martin's Press, 1994), p. 223. On H.M. Stanley, interested readers can consult his remarkable *Autobiography,* edited by his wife, Dorothy Stanley, and published originally in 1909, then reproduced as *The Autobiography of Henry Morton Stanley* (Boston: Houghton Mifflin, 1969).

5. James, *Rise and Fall of the British Empire*, p. 311.
6. Cited in Raymond F. Betts, *The False Dawn: European Imperialism in the Nineteenth Century* (Minneapolis: University of Minnesota Press, 1975), p. 99.
7. Philip Y. Nicholson, "George Dewey and the Expansionists of 1898," *Vermont History* 42, no. 3 (Summer 1974): 222.
8. See, for example, David Brion Davis, *The Problem of Slavery in the Age of Revolution, 1770–1823* (Ithaca: Cornell University Press, 1975).
9. This analysis is most thoughtfully explored in Edmund S. Morgan, *American Slavery, American Freedom: The Ordeal of Colonial Virginia* (New York: Norton, 1975).
10. Voltaire's remarks are from Robert S. Wistrich, *Antisemitism: The Longest Hatred* (New York: Pantheon Books, 1991), p. 45.
11. Cited in Thomas Gossett, *Race: The History of an Idea in America* (Dallas: Southern Methodist University Press, 1965), pp. 185–89.
12. Forrest G. Wood, *The Arrogance of Race: Christianity and Race in America from the Colonial Era to the Twentieth Century* (New York: Knopf, 1990), p. 220.
13. Ibid.
14. From Josiah Strong, *Our Country* (1885). Cited in Richard J. Hofstadter, ed., *Great Issues in American History*, vol. 2, *1864–1957, A Documentary Record* (New York: Vintage, 1960), pp. 184–87.
15. Cited in Betts, *False Dawn*, p. 219.
16. Cited in Louis L. Snyder, *The Idea of Racialism: Its Meaning and History* (New York: Van Nostrand, 1962), p. 69.
17. Ibid.
18. See for example, Franz Boas, *Race, Language, and Culture* (New York: Macmillan, 1940). This was originally a paper written for the U.S. government in 1911.
19. Snyder, *Idea of Racialism*, pp. 11–14.
20. Gosset, *Race*, p. 352.
21. From his remarks at Charleston, Illinois, September 18, 1859, as cited in Gosset, *Race*, p. 254.
22. Betts, *False Dawn*, p. 172.
23. F.S. Stevens, ed., *Racism: The Australian Experience, A Study of Race Prejudice in Australia*, vol. 1 (New York: Taplinger, 1972), p. 13. In this work, one of the authors, W.E.H. Stanner, observed in the Introduction: "Both nationalism and imperialism dined out on racial symbolism," and in the 1880s and 1890s the "racialist ideology was in high vogue" with frequent examples in the newspapers "of the frenetic extremes to which it could be pushed" (p. 13).
24. M.W. Daly, *Empire on the Nile: The Anglo-Egyptian Sudan, 1898–1934* (Cambridge, England: Cambridge University Press, 1986), pp. 3–4.
25. For an edited sampling of TR's racial and anti-Semitic views, readers should browse in the accessible Elting E. Morison, ed., *The Letters of Theodore Roosevelt*, 4 vols. (Cambridge: Harvard University Press, 1951).

Chapter 6. No Holds Barred: Race and Nation, 1918–1945

1. Sidney Osborne, *The New Japanese Peril* (New York: Macmillan, 1921), p. 162.
2. Lawrence James, *The Rise and Fall of the British Empire* (New York: St. Martin's Press, 1994), p. 401.
3. Robert O. Paxton, "The Uses of Fascism," *New York Review of Books* 43, no. 19 (November 28, 1996): 48.

4. James, *Rise and Fall of the British Empire*, p. 400.

5. Ibid., p. 419.

6. Gilbert Osofsky, *Harlem: The Making of a Ghetto* (New York: Harper, 1965), p. 183.

7. Eric Arnesen, *Waterfront Workers of New Orleans: Race, Class, and Politics, 1863–1923* (Urbana: University of Illinois Press, 1994).

8. For a fascinating and credible discussion of just how seriously a fascist coup was contemplated in the United States in 1932, see Gerard Colby Zilg, *Behind the Nylon Curtain: A History of the DuPont Family in America* (Englewood Cliffs, N.J.: Prentice-Hall, 1974).

9. A thorough summary of "Anti-Jewish legislation" is in Lucy S. Dawidowicz, *The War Against the Jews, 1933–1945* (New York: Holt, Rinehart and Wiston, 1975), pp. 48–69.

10. Ibid., pp. 68–69.

11. This is a primary argument presented in Daniel J. Goldhagen, *Hitler's Willing Executioners: Ordinary Germans and the Holocaust* (New York: Knopf, 1996). A somewhat different view is in Christopher Browning's *Ordinary Men: Reserve Police Battalion 101 and the Final Solution in Poland* (New York: Harper, 1993). Browning uses similar sources but finds that the circumstances, not their beliefs or national backgrounds, turned ordinary men into willing killers.

12. These important documents are found in Box 1346 of the Historic Cryptographic Collection in Record Group 457, National Archives, Washington, D.C., and were described in *Newsday*, December 15, 1996, p. 3.

13. Anthony D. Smith, *National Identity* (Reno: University of Las Vegas Press, 1991), p. 161.

14. John W. Dower, *War Without Mercy: Race and Power in the Pacific War* (New York: Pantheon Books, 1986), p. 203.

15. *Time*, March 1, 1943, p. 18.

16. Dower, *War Without Mercy*, p. 209.

17. Ibid., pp. 209–10.

18. John Rabe's diary and Iris Chang's book are described in the *New York Times*, December 12, 1996, p. A3, and December 15, 1996, where selections from the Rabe diary are included.

19. Cited in Dower, *War Without Mercy*, p. 99.

20. Ibid., p. 100.

21. War Labor Board Document, 1943, cited in Eileen Boris and Nelson Lichtenstein, eds., *Major Problems in the History of American Workers: Documents and Essays* (Lexington, Mass.: D.C. Heath, 1991), pp. 464–65.

Chapter 7. Cold War Watershed, 1946–90

1. Sigmund Freud, *The Standard Edition of the Complete Psychological Works*, vol. 22, *1932–1936*, ed. James Strachey (London: Hogarth Press, 1957), p. 207.

2. Cited in Roger Daniels and Harry H. L. Kitano, *American Racism: Exploration of the Nature of Prejudice* (Englewood Cliffs, N.J.: Prentice-Hall, 1970), p. 28.

3. Ian F. Hanley Lopez, *White by Law: The Legal Construction of Race* (New York: New York University Press, 1996), pp. 49–51. The prerequisite cases themselves are interesting as they reveal some of the inconsistencies and illogic of the concept of race. In *United States* v. *Thind*, 261 U.S. 204, 211 (1922), the Supreme Court gave up the attempt at anything scientific. "What we now hold," the decision proclaimed, "is that

the words 'free white persons' are words of common speech, to be interpreted in accordance with the understanding of the common man, synonymous with the word 'Caucasian' only as that word is popularly understood" (p. 90). Naturalization of Asian Indians became legally impossible, and the federal government began a process of denaturalizing at least sixty-five people from 1923 to 1927, one of whom committed suicide because of the humiliation.

4. For a critique of the enormous power wielded by the automobile-energy-industrial lobby, see Bernard Snell, *American Ground Transportation,* printed for the use of the Committee on the Judiciary, United State Senate Subcommittee on Antitrust and Monopoly (Washington, D.C.: Government Printing Office, 1974).

5. Two outstanding examples are Stanley B. Greenberg, *Race and State in Capitalist Development: Comparative Perspectives* (New Haven: Yale University Press, 1980); and Etienne Balibar and Immanuel Wallerstein, *Race, Nation, Class: Ambiguous Identities* (New York: Verso Press, 1991).

6. The intellectual reaction toward Hitler and anti-Semitism after World War II found a sociological voice in the controversial work of a group led by Theodor W. Adorno, Else Frenkel-Brunswik, Daniel J. Levinson, and R. Nevitt Sanford, *The Authoritarian Personality* (New York: Norton, 1969). Bigotry and racial or religious bias were problematic group and individual deficiencies in, for example, Gordon W. Allport, *The Nature of Prejudice* (New York: Addison-Wesley, 1954). Among various theories, Allport strongly argued the case for transference by the dominant group of its own negative traits to the subject group, but granted only two and a half pages to the "historical emphasis" (pp. 204–6) and concluded the section on "Theories of Prejudice" with the observation that it was a matter of "multiple causation" (p. 212).

7. Sigmund Freud, *The Standard Edition of the Complete Psychological Works,* vol. 14, *1914–1916,* ed. James Strachey (London: Hogarth Press, 1957), p. 279.

8. Nicholas D. Kristof, "Main Street Japan: Wounds of War," *New York Times,* January 22, 1997, p. A1.

9. *New York Times,* February 12, 1987, p. A23. The news of the final outcome of the criminal case was reported on the Associated Press wire and in *Newsday,* June 7, 1997, p. A13.

10. For a stark depiction of the racial divisions, economic inequities, and criminalization after nearly fifty years of nominal desegregation of government, the military, sports, and entertainment see, for example, Andrew Hacker, *Two Nations: Black and White, Separate, Hostile, and Unequal* (New York: Scribner's, 1992).

11. Though inconclusive on the big sociological and political issues, a good place to begin thinking about humor and slang is Walter P. Zenner, "Joking and Ethnic Stereotyping," *Anthropological Quarterly* 43 (1970): 93–113.

12. Immanuel Wallerstein, "The Construction of Peoplehood," in Balibar and Wallerstein, *Race, Nation, Class,* p. 80. Wallerstein is emphatic in describing the function of race: "Race, and therefore racism, is the expression, the promoter and the consequence of the geographical concentrations associated with the axial division of labour" (p. 80).

13. Abdul Paliwala, "Law and the Constitution of the 'Immigrant' in Europe: A UK Policy Perspective," in *Nationalism, Racism and the Rule of Law,* ed. Peter Fitzpatrick (Brookfield, Vt.: Dartmouth, 1995), pp. 81–82.

14. Ibid., p. 77.

15. Cited in ibid., p. 81.

16. Cited in Paul Gilroy, *There Ain't No Black in the Union Jack: The Cultural Politics of Race and Nation* (Chicago: University of Chicago Press, 1987), p. 43.

17. Ibid., pp. 12, 46, 48.

18. Paliwala, "Law and the Constitution," p. 91.

19. See, for example, Craig R. Whitney, "National Front Wins Control of a 4th City in Southern France," *New York Times,* February 10, 1997, p. 3.

20. One of the most compelling discussions of the formation of national identity that sharply differentiates its relationship to racism is Benedict Anderson's *Imagined Communities,* rev. ed. (London: Verso Press, 1991). Anderson claims that "the dreams of racism actually have their origin in ideologies of *class* [his emphasis], rather than in those of nation: above all in claims to divinity among rulers and to 'blue' or 'white' blood and 'breeding' among aristocracies" (p. 149).

Chapter 8. Epilogue: Dusk and Dawn, 1991–2000

1. Paliwala, "Law and the Constitution," p. 92.

2. Cited in Michael Eric Dyson, *Race Rules: Navigating the Color Line* (New York: Addison-Wesley, 1996), p. 221.

3. Ibid., p. 219.

4. Clifford J. Levy, *New York Times,* February 27, 1997, p. A-1.

5. *New York Times,* February 8, 1997, p. A7.

6. Isaac Guzman, *Newsday,* February 28, 1997.

7. Etienne Balibar and Immanuel Wallerstein, *Race, Nation, Class: Ambiguous Identities* (New York: Verso Press, 1991), p. 9.

Bibliography

Adorno, Theodor W., Else Frenkel-Brunswick, Daniel J. Levinson, and R. Nevitt San-
ford. *The Authoritarian Personality.* New York: Norton, 1969.
Alba, Richard D. *Ethnic Identity: The Transformation of White America.* New Haven:
Yale University Press, 1990.
Allen, Theodore. *The Invention of the White Race,* vol. 1, *Racial Oppression and Social
Control.* London: Verso Press, 1994.
Allport, Gordon. *The Nature of Prejudice.* New York: Addison-Wesley, 1954.
Alter, Peter. *Nationalism.* New York: Edward Arnold, 1989.
Ambrose, Stephen E. *Undaunted Courage: Meriwether Lewis, Thomas Jefferson and
the Opening of the American West.* New York: Simon and Schuster, 1996.
Anderson, Benedict. *Imagined Communities: Reflections on the Origin and Spread of
Nationalism.* London: Verso Press, 1983; revised, 1991.
Anderson, Warwick. "The Trespass Speaks: White Masculinity and Colonial Break-
down." *American Historical Review* 102, no. 5 (December 1997): 1343–70.
Andrews, George Reid. *Blacks and Whites in São Paulo, Brazil, 1888–1988.* Madison:
University of Wisconsin Press, 1991.
Anthias, Floya, and Nira Yuval-Davis. *Racialized Boundaries: Race, Nation, Gender,
Colour and Class and the Anti-Racist Struggle.* London: Routledge, 1992.
Appiah, Anthony. *In My Father's House: Africa in the Philosophy of Culture.* New
York: Oxford University Press, 1992.
Aptheker, Herbert, ed. *W.E.B. Du Bois: Against Racism: Unpublished Essays, Papers,
Addresses, 1887–1961.* Amherst: University of Massachusetts Press, 1985.
Arnesen, Eric. *Waterfront Workers of New Orleans: Race, Class, and Politics, 1863–
1923.* New York: Oxford University Press, 1991.
Balibar, Etienne, and Imannuel Wallerstein. *Race, Nation, Class: Ambiguous Identities.*
New York: Verso Press, 1991.
Ballhatchet, K. *Race, Sex, and Class under the Raj: Imperial Attitudes and Policies and
Their Critics, 1793–1905.* London: Weidenfield and Nicolson, 1980.
Baker, John R. *Race.* London: Oxford University Press, 1974.
Banton, Michael. *Rational Choice: Theory of Racial and Ethnic Relations.* Bristol:
S.S.R.C. Research Unit on Ethnic Relations, 1977.
———. *Race Relations.* New York: Oxford University Press, 1967.
———. *Racial Theories.* Cambridge: Cambridge University Press, 1987.
———. *Racial and Ethnic Competition.* Cambridge: Cambridge University Press, 1988.
———. *Racial Consciousness.* London and New York: Longman, 1988.
Banton, Michael, and Jonathan Harwood. *The Race Concept.* New York: Praeger, 1967,
1975.
Barkan, Elazar. *The Retreat of Scientific Racism: Changing Concepts of Race in Britain*

and the United States between the World Wars. New York: Cambridge University Press, 1992.

Barzun, Jacques. *Race: A Study in Superstition.* New York: Harper, 1938, 1965.

Bastide, Roger. "Color, Racism, and Christianity." In *Color and Race,* ed. John Hope Franklin. Boston: Houghton Mifflin, 1968.

Belich, James. *The New Zealand Wars and the Victorian Interpretation of Racial Conflict.* Montreal and Kingston: McGill/Queen's University Press, 1989.

Bell, Derrick. *Race, Racism and American Law.* 3rd ed. Boston: Little, Brown, 1992.

———. *Faces at the Bottom of the Well: The Permanence of Racism.* New York: Basic Books, 1992.

Bettelheim, Bruno, and Morris Janowitz. *Dynamics of Prejudice: A Psychological and Sociological Study of Veterans.* New York: Harper, 1950.

Berkhofer, Robert F. Jr., *The White Man's Indians.* New York: Knopf, 1978.

———. *Social Change and Prejudice.* New York: Free Press, 1964.

Betts, Raymond F. *The False Dawn: European Imperialism in the Nineteenth Century.* Minneapolis: University of Minnesota Press, 1975.

Bingham, Woodridge, Hilary Conroy, and Frank Ikle. *A History of Asia: Formation of Civilizations, From Antiquity to 1600.* Vol. 1. Boston: Allyn and Bacon, 1964.

Blackburn, Robin. *The Making of New World Slavery.* London: Verso Press, 1997.

Blakley, Alison. *Blacks in the Dutch World.* Bloomington: Indiana University Press, 1993.

Blauner, R. *Racial Oppression in America: Essays in Search of a Theory.* New York: Harper, 1972.

Boas, Franz. *Race, Language, and Culture.* New York: Macmillan, 1940.

Bolt, Christine. *Victorian Attitudes Toward Race.* London: Routledge and Kegan Paul, 1971.

Bonacich, Edna. "A Theory of Ethnic Antagonism: The Split Labor Market." *American Sociological Review* 37 (1972).

———. "Advanced Capitalism and Black/White Relations in the United States: A Split Labor Market Interpretation." *American Sociological Review* 41 (1976).

Boston, Thomas D. *Race, Class, and Conservatism.* Boston: Unwin Hyman, 1988.

Boxer, C.R. *Race Relations in the Portuguese Colonial Empire, 1415–1825.* Oxford: Clarendon Press, 1963.

———. *The Dutch Seaborne Empire, 1600–1800.* New York: Oxford University Press, 1965.

———. *Four Centuries of Portuguese Expansion, 1415–1825: A Succinct Survey.* Johannesburg: Witwatersrand University Press, 1965.

Braudel, Fernand. *Civilization and Capitalism, 15th–18th Century.* 3 vols. New York: Harper & Row, 1979.

Breen, T.H., and Stephen Innes. *Myne Own Ground: Race and Freedom on Virginia's Eastern Shore, 1640–1676.* New York: Oxford University Press, 1980.

Brown, Richard Maxwell. *Strain of Violence: Historical Studies in American Violence and Vigilantism.* New York: Oxford University Press, 1975.

Browning, Christopher. *Ordinary Men: Reserve Police Battalion 101 and the Final Solution in Poland.* New York: Harper Perennial Edition, 1993; original copyright, 1992.

Brunschwig, Henri. *French Colonialism, 1871–1914.* New York: Praeger, 1964.

Burleigh, Michael, and Wolfgang Wippermann. *The Racial State: Germany, 1933–1945.* Cambridge, England: Cambridge University Press, 1991.

Bunche, Ralph J. *A World View of Race.* Port Washington, N.Y.: Kennikat Press, 1968; originally published in 1936 by Associates in Negro Folk Education.

Burns, Robert I., S.J. *Islam under the Crusaders: Colonial Survival in the Thirteenth-Century Kingdom of Valencia.* Princeton: Princeton University Press, 1973.

Canny, Nicholas P. "The Ideology of English Colonization: From Ireland to America." *William and Mary Quarterly* 30 (1973): 575–98.

Carter, Gwendolen. *The Politics of Inequality: South Africa Since 1948.* London: Thames and Hudson, 1958.

Cashmore, E. *The Logic of Racism.* London: Allen and Unwin, 1987.

Cell, John. *The Highest Stage of White Supremacy: The Origins of Segregation in South Africa and the American South.* New York: Cambridge University Press, 1982.

Chang, Iris. *The Rape of Nanking: The Forgotten Holocaust of World War Two.* New York: Basic Books, 1997.

Chase, Alan. *The Legacy of Malthus: The Social Costs of the New Scientific Racism.* New York: Knopf, 1977.

Cheyette, Brian. *Constructions of "the Jew" in English Literature and Society: Racial Representations, 1875–1945.* Cambridge, England: Cambridge University Press, 1993.

Cloutier, Norman R. "Who Gains from Racism? The Impact of Racial Inequality on White Income Distribution." *Review of Social Economy,* 45, no. 2 (October 1987): 152–62.

Cohen, William B. *The French Encounter with Africans: White Response to Blacks, 1530–1880.* Bloomington: University of Indiana Press, 1980.

Conrad, Earl. *The Invention of the Negro.* New York: Paul S. Erikson, 1969.

Cook, Anthony E. *The Least of These: Race, Law and Religion in America.* New York: Routledge, 1997.

Coon, Carleton S. *The Origin of Races.* New York: Knopf, 1962.

Cox, Oliver C. *Caste, Class and Race: A Study in Social Dynamics.* New York: Doubleday, 1948.

Cross, Michael, and Michael Keith. *Racism, the City and the State.* London: Routledge, 1993.

Crowder, Michael. *West Africa under Colonial Rule.* Evanston: Northwestern University Press, 1968.

D'Souza, Dinesh. *The End of Racism: Principles for a Multiracial Society.* New York: Free Press, 1995.

Day, Beth. *Sexual Life between Whites and Blacks: The Roots of Racism.* London: Collins, 1974.

Daly, M.W. *Empire on the Nile: The Anglo-Egyptian Sudan, 1898–1934.* Cambridge, England: Cambridge University Press, 1986.

Daniels, Roger, and Harry H.L. Kitano. *American Racism: Exploration of the Nature of Prejudice.* Englewood Cliffs, N.J.: Prentice-Hall, 1970.

Davidowicz, Lucy S. *The War Against the Jews, 1933–1945.* New York: Holt, Rinehart and Winston, 1975.

Davis, David Brion. *The Problem of Slavery in Western Culture.* New York: Cornell University Press, 1966.

———. *The Problem of Slavery in the Age of Revolution, 1770–1823.* New York: Cornell University Press, 1975.

Davis, Horace B. *Toward a Marxist Theory of Nationalism.* New York: Monthly Review Press, 1978.

Davis, James F. *Who Is Black? One Nation's Definition.* University Park: Pennsylvania State University Press, 1991.

Degler, Carl. "Slavery and the Genesis of American Race Prejudice." *Comparative Studies in Society and History,* II, 1959.

————. *Neither Black nor White; Slavery and Race Relations in Brazil and the United States.* New York: Macmillan, 1971.

Dehejia, Vidya. *Indian Art.* London: Phaidon Press, 1997.

Doob, Leonard. *Patriotism and Nationalism: Their Psychological Foundations.* New Haven: Yale University Press, 1964.

Dower, John. *War without Mercy: Race and Power in the Pacific War.* New York: Pantheon Books, 1986.

Du Bois, W.E.B. *Dusk of Dawn: An Essay toward an Autobiography of a Race Concept.* New York: Harcourt Brace, 1940.

————. *Souls of Black Folk.* New York: Modern Library, 1996.

Duffy, James. *Portuguese Africa.* Cambridge: Harvard University Press, 1957.

Dunham, Barrows. *Man Against Myth.* New York: Hill and Wang, 1968.

Durkheim, Emile, and Marcel Maus. *Primitive Classification.* Translation and Introduction by Rodney Needham. Chicago: University of Chicago Press, 1963.

Dyson, Michael Eric. *Race Rules: Navigating the Color Line.* Reading, Mass.: Addison-Wesley, 1996.

Elkins, Stanley M. *Slavery: A Problem in American Institutional and Intellectual Life.* Chicago: University of Chicago Press, 1968.

Eze, Emmanuel Chukwudi, ed. *Race and the Enlightenment: A Reader.* Cambridge, England: Blackwell, 1997.

Ezekiel, Raphael S. *The Racist Mind: Portraits of American Neo-Nazis and Klansmen.* New York: Viking Press, 1995.

Ezorsky, Gertrude. *Racism and Justice: The Case for Affirmative Action.* Ithaca: Cornell University Press, 1991.

Fanon, Frantz. *The Wretched of the Earth.* New York: Grove Press, 1967.

————. *Black Skin, White Masks.* New York: Grove Press, 1967.

Feagin, Joe R. "The Continuing Significance of Race: Antiblack Discrimination in Public Places." *American Sociological Review* 56 (1991).

Fehrenbacher, Don Edward. *Slavery, Law, and Politics: The Dred Scott Case in Historical Perspective.* New York: Oxford University Press, 1991.

Fernandez, Florestan. *The Negro in Brazilian Society.* New York: Columbia University Press, 1969.

Fields, Barbara Jeanne. "Ideology and Race in American History." In *Region, Race, and Reconstruction: Essays in Honor of C. Van Woodward,* ed. J. Morgan Kousser and James McPherson. New York: Oxford University Press, 1982.

————. "Slavery, Race and Ideology in the USA," *New Left Review* 181 (May/June 1990): 95–117.

Fischer, Claude S., et al. *Inequality by Design: Cracking the Bell Curve Myth.* Princeton: Princeton University Press, 1996.

Fitzpatrick, Peter, ed. *Nationalism, Racism, and the Rule of Law.* Aldershot, England: Dartmouth Press, 1995.

Frankenberg, Ruth. *White Women, Race Matters: The Social Construction of Whiteness.* Minneapolis: University of Minnesota Press, 1993.

Franklin, John Hope, ed. *Color and Race.* Boston: Houghton Mifflin, 1968.

————. *Race and History.* Baton Rouge: Louisiana State University Press, 1989.

Fraser, Steve, ed. *The Bell Curve Wars: Race, Intelligence, and the Future of America.* New York: Basic Books, 1995.

Frazier, E. Franklin. *Race and Culture Contacts in the Modern World.* Boston: Beacon Press, 1957.

Frederickson, George M. *Black Image in the White Mind: The Debate on Afro-American*

Character and Destiny, 1817–1914. New York: Harper & Row, 1971.

———. *White Supremacy: A Comparative Study in American and South African History.* New York: Oxford University Press, 1981.

———. *The Arrogance of Race: Historical Perspectives on Slavery, Racism and Social Inequality.* Middletown, Conn.: Wesleyan University Press, 1988.

———. *Black Liberation: A Comparative History of Black Ideologies in the United States and South Africa.* New York: Oxford University Press, 1995.

Fuentes, Carlos. *The Buried Mirror: Reflections on Spain and the New World.* New York: Houghton Mifflin, 1992.

Geller, Ernest. *Nations and Nationalism.* Oxford: Basil Blackwell, 1983.

Genovese, Eugene. *The World the Slaveholders Made: Two Essays in Interpretation.* New York: Random House, 1969.

———. *In Red and Black: Marxian Explorations in Southern and Afro-American History.* New York: Random House, 1971.

———. *Roll, Jordan, Roll: The World the Slaves Made.* New York: Random House, 1972.

Genovese, Eugene, and Elizabeth Fox-Genovese. *Fruits of Merchant Capital.* New York: Oxford University Press, 1983.

Germani, Gino. *Authoritarianism, Fascism, and National Populism.* New Brunswick, N.J.: Transaction Books, 1975.

Gibbons, Luke. "Race Against Time: Racial Discourse and Irish History." In Robert Young, ed., "Neocolonialism." *Oxford Literary Review* 13 (1991): 95–117.

Gilmore, Glenda E. *Gender and Jim Crow: Women and the Politics of White Supremacy in North Carolina, 1896–1920.* Chapel Hill: University of North Carolina Press, 1996.

Gilroy, Paul. *There Ain't No Black in the Union Jack: The Cultural Politics of Race and Nation.* Chicago: University of Chicago Press, 1987.

———. *The Black Atlantic: Modernity and Double Consciousness.* Cambridge: Harvard University Press, 1993.

Glass, James M. *"Life Unworthy of Life": Racial Phobia and Mass Murder in Hitler's Germany.* New York: Basic Books, 1997.

Gobineau, A. de. *Essay on the Inequality of Human Races.* Translation by A. Collins. New York: Howard Fertig, 1967.

Goldberg, David T., ed. *Anatomy of Racism.* Minneapolis: University of Minnesota Press, 1990.

———. *Racist Culture: Philosophy and the Politics of Meaning.* Oxford, UK: Blackwell, 1993.

Goldfield, Michael. *The Politics of Color: Race and the Mainsprings of American Politics.* New York: New Press, 1997.

Goldhagen, Daniel Jonah. *Hitler's Willing Executioners: Ordinary Germans and the Holocaust.* New York: Knopf, 1996.

Goodman, Paul. *Of One Blood: Abolitionism and the Origins of Racial Equality.* Berkeley: University of California Press, 1998.

Gosset, Thomas. *Race: The History of an Idea in America.* Dallas: Southern Methodist University Press, 1965.

Gould, Steven Jay. *The Mismeasure of Man.* New York: Norton, 1981.

Greenberg, Jack. *Race Relations and American Law.* New York: Columbia University Press, 1959.

Greenberg, Stanley. *Race and State in Capitalist Development: Comparative Perspectives.* Connecticut: Yale University Press, 1980.

Greenfield, Liah. *Nationalism: Five Roads to Modernity.* Cambridge: Harvard University Press, 1993.

Group for the Advancement of Psychiatry. *Us and Them: The Psychology of Ethnonationalism.* New York: Brunner/Mazel, 1987.

Guillaumin, Colette. *Racism, Sexism, Power and Ideology.* New York and London: Routledge, 1995.

Gutman, Herbert G. *The Black Family in Slavery and Freedom, 1750–1925.* New York: Pantheon Books, 1976.

Hacker, Andrew. *Two Nations: Black and White, Separate, Hostile, Unequal.* New York: Scribner's, 1992.

Hakluyt, Richard. *Voyages and Discoveries.* Baltimore: Penguin Books, 1972.

Handlin, Oscar. *Race and Nationality in American Life.* New York: Doubleday, 1957.

Handlin, Oscar, and Handlin, Mary F. "Origins of the Southern Labor System." *William and Mary Quarterly* 7, 3rd series, no. 2 (April 1950): 199–222.

Hannaford, Ivan. *Race: The History of an Idea in the West.* Washington, D.C.: Woodrow Wilson Center Press, 1996.

Harris, Abram L. *The Black Worker: The Negro and the American Labor Movement.* New York: Atheneum, 1968.

Harris, Marvin. *Patterns of Race in the Americas.* New York: Walker, 1964.

Hartman, Chester, ed. *Double Exposure: Poverty and Race in America.* Armonk, N.Y.: M.E. Sharpe, 1997.

Hechtor, Michael. *Internal Colonialism: The Celtic Fringe in British National Development, 1536–1966.* London: Routledge and Kegan Paul, 1975.

Hernton, Calvin. *Sex and Racism.* London: Andre Deutsch, 1969.

Herodotus. *The Histories.* Baltimore: Penguin Books, 1964.

Herrnstein, Richard J., and Charles Murray. *The Bell Curve: Intelligence and Class Structure in American Life.* New York: The Free Press, 1994.

Hess, Robert. *Italian Colonialism in Somalia.* Chicago: University of Chicago Press, 1966.

Higginbotham, Leon. *In the Matter of Color: Race and the American Legal Process, the Colonial Period.* New York: Oxford University Press, 1978.

———. *Shades of Freedom: Racial Politics and Presumptions of the American Legal Process.* New York: Oxford University Press, 1996.

Hill, Herbert. *Black Labor and the American Legal System: Race, Work, and the Law.* Washington, D.C.: Bureau of National Affairs, 1977.

Hoberman, John. *Darwin's Athletes: How Sport Has Damaged Black America and Preserved the Myth of Race.* Boston: Houghton-Mifflin, 1996.

Hobsbaum, Eric. *Nations and Nationalism Since 1870.* Cambridge: Harvard University Press. 1990.

Hochschild, Jennifer L. *Facing Up to the American Dream: Race, Class, and the Soul of the Nation.* Princeton Studies in American Politics: Historical, International, and Comparative Perspectives. Princeton: Princeton University Press, 1995.

Hoeg, Peter. *Smila's Sense of Snow.* New York: Delta, 1993.

Hoetink, H. *Slavery and Race Relations in the Americas: Comparative Notes on Their Nature and Nexus.* New York: Harper & Row, 1973.

Horseman, Reginald. *Race and Manifest Destiny: The Origins of American Racial Anglo-Saxonism.* Cambridge: Harvard University Press, 1981.

Holt, Thomas R. *The Problem of Freedom: Race, Labor, and Politics in Jamaica and Britain, 1832–1938.* Baltimore: Johns Hopkins University Press, 1992.

Horowitz, Irving Louis. *Taking Lives: Genocide and State Power.* 3rd ed. London: Transaction Books, 1982.

Hughes, Michael. *Nationalism and Society: Germany, 1800–1945.* London: E. Arnold, 1988.

Hutchinson, Earl Ofari. *The Assassination of the Black Male Image.* New York: Simon and Schuster, 1996.

Huttenback, Robert. *Racism and Empire: White Settlers and Colored Immigrants in the British Self-Governing Colonies, 1830–1910.* New York: Cornell University Press, 1976.

Ignatieff, Michael. *Blood and Belonging: Journeys into the New Nationalism.* New York: Farrar, Straus and Giroux, 1993.

Ignatiev, Noel. *How the Irish Became White.* New York: Routledge, 1995.

Israel, J.I. *Race, Class and Politics in Colonial Mexico, 1610–1670.* New York: Oxford University Press, 1975.

Israel, Jonathan. *The Dutch Republic; Its Rise, Greatness, and Fall, 1477–1806.* New York: Oxford University Press, 1995.

James, C.L.R. *The Black Jacobins: Toussaint L'Overture and the Santo Domingo Revolution.* New York: Vintage, 1963.

James, Lawrence. *The Rise and Fall of the British Empire.* New York: St. Martin's Press, 1994.

Jennings, Francis. *The Invasion of America: Indians, Colonialism, and the Cant of Conquest.* Chapel Hill: University of North Carolina Press, 1975.

Jensen, Arthur. "How Much Can We Boost IQ and Scholastic Achievement?" *Harvard Educational Review,* February 1969, pp. 1–123.

Jordan, Winthrop. "Modern Tensions and the Origins of American Slavery." *Journal of Southern History* 28 (1962).

———. *White Over Black: American Attitudes toward the Negro, 1550–1812.* Chapel Hill: University of North Carolina Press, 1968.

Katznelson, Ira. *Black Men, White Cities: Race, Politics, and Migration in the United States, 1900–1930, and Britain, 1948–1968.* New York: Pantheon Books, 1976.

Kedourie, Elie. *Nationalism.* 3rd ed. London: Hutchinson, 1966.

Kelly, Robin. *Hammer and Hoe: Alabama Communists during the Great Depression.* Chapel Hill: University of North Carolina Press, 1990.

Kennedy, Randall. *Race, Crime, and the Law.* New York: Pantheon Books, 1997.

Kerner, Otto. *Report of the National Advisory Commission on Civil Disorders.* New York: Bantam Books, 1968.

Kiernan, V.G. *The Lords of Human Kind: Black Man, Yellow Man and White Man in an Age of Empire.* London: Serif, 1995; originally published 1969.

King, James. *The Biology of Race.* New York: Harcourt Brace Jovanovich, 1971.

Kirby, John B. *Black Americans in the Roosevelt Era: Liberalism and Race.* Knoxville: University of Tennessee Press, 1980.

Kolchin, Peter. *American Slavery, 1619–1877.* New York: Hill and Wang, 1993.

Kovel, Joel. *White Racism: A Psychohistory.* 2nd ed. New York: Columbia University Press, 1984.

Kuper, Leo. *Genocide.* Harmondsworth, England: Penguin, 1981.

Landon, Michael de Laval. *Erin and Britain: The Historical Background to a Modern Tragedy.* Chicago: Nelson-Hall, 1981.

Leone, Bruno. *Racism: Opposing Viewpoints.* Minneapolis: Greenhaven Press, 1978.

Lepore, Jill. *King Philip's War and the Origins of American Identity.* New York: Knopf, 1997.

Levine, Robert. *Race and Ethnic Relations in Latin America and the Caribbean: Dictionary and Bibliography.* Metuchen, N.J.: Scarecrow, 1980.

Lewis, Bernard. *Race and Slavery in the Middle East.* New York: Oxford University Press, 1990.

Lewis, David Levering. *W.E.B. Du Bois: Biography of a Race, 1868–1919.* New York: Henry Holt, 1993.

Litwack, Leon. *Trouble in Mind: Black Southerners in the Age of Jim Crow.* New York: Knopf, 1998.

Lopez, Ian F. Haney. *White by Law; The Legal Construction of Race.* New York: New York University Press, 1996.

Lusane, Clarence. *Race in the Global Era: African Americans at the Millennium.* Boston: South End Press, 1997.

MacDougal, Hugh. *Racial Myths in English History.* Hanover, N.H.: University Press of New England, 1982.

McNeill, William H. *The Rise of the West: A History of the Human Community.* Chicago: University of Chicago Press, 1963.

Mann, Michael. *The Sources of Social Power.* Vol. 1. Cambridge, England: Cambridge University Press, 1986.

Marable, Manning. *How Capitalism Underdeveloped Black America.* Boston: South End Press, 1983.

Marx, Anthony. "Race Making and the Nation State," *World Politics* 48 (January 1996).

Mason, Philip. *Prospero's Magic: Some Thoughts on Class and Race.* London: Oxford University Press, 1962.

Massey, Douglas S., and Nancy A. Denton. *American Apartheid: Segregation and the Making of the Underclass.* Cambridge: Harvard University Press, 1993.

Mead, Margaret, Theodosius Dobzhansky, Robert Light, and Ethel Tobach, eds. *Science and the Concept of Race.* New York: Columbia University Press, 1968.

Miles, Robert. *Racism.* London: Routledge, 1989.

Mills, Charles W. *The Racial Contract.* Ithaca: Cornell University Press, 1997.

Mintz, Sidney W. *Sweetness and Power: The Place of Sugar in Modern History.* New York: Viking, 1985.

Montagu, Ashley. *Man's Most Dangerous Myth: The Fallacy of Race.* New York: Oxford University Press, 1974.

———. "Intelligence of Northern Negroes and Southern Whites in the First World War." *American Journal of Psychology* 58 (1945): 161–88.

Moog, Vianna. *Bandeirantes and Pioneers.* New York: George Braziller, 1964.

Morgan, Edmund. *American Slavery, American Freedom: The Ordeal of Colonial Virginia.* New York: Norton, 1975.

Mosse, George. *Toward the Final Solution: A History of European Racism.* New York: H. Fertig, 1978.

———. *Nationalism and Sexuality: Respectability and Abnormal Sexuality in Modern Europe.* New York: H. Fertig, 1985.

Mudimbe, V.J. *The Invention of Africa: Gnosis, Philosophy, and the Order of Knowledge.* Chicago: University of Chicago Press, 1988.

Muldoon, James. "The Indian as Irishmen." *Essex Institute Historical Collections* 111 (1975): 267–89.

Myrdal, Gunnar. *An American Dilemma: The Negro Problem and Modern Democracy.* 2 vols. New York: Harpers, 1964; originally published 1944.

Nairn, Thomas. *The Break-Up of Britain: Crisis and Neo-Nationalism.* 2nd ed. London: Verso Press, 1981.

Naison, Mark. *Communists in Harlem during the Depression.* Urbana: University of Illinois Press, 1983.

Nash, Gary B. *Race, Class, and Politics: Essays on American Colonial and Revolutionary Society.* Urbana: University of Illinois Press, 1986.

———. *Red, White, and Black: The Peoples of Early North America.* Englewood Cliffs, N.J.: Prentice-Hall, 1992.

Nash, Gary B., and Richard Weiss. *The Great Fear: Race in the Mind of America.* New York: Holt, Rineheart and Winston, 1970.

Nemai, Sadhan Bose. *Racism, Struggle for Equality, and Indian Nationalism.* Calcutta: Firma KLM, 1981.

Netanyahu, Benzion. *The Origins of the Inquisition in Fifteenth Century Spain.* New York: Random House, 1995.

Nicholas, Lynn H. *The Rape of Europa: The Fate of Europe's Treasures in the Third Reich and the Second World War.* New York: Vintage, 1995.

Noel, Donald, ed. *The Origins of American Slavery and Racism.* Columbus, Ohio: Charles Merrill, 1972.

Oakes, James. *The Ruling Race: A History of American Slaveholders.* New York: Knopf, 1982.

Olender, Maurice. *The Languages of Paradise: Race, Religion, and Philology in the Nineteenth Century.* Cambridge: Harvard University Press, 1992.

Omni, Michael, and Howard Winant. *Racial Formation in the United States: From the 1960's to the 1990's.* 2nd ed. New York: Routledge,1994.

O'Reilly, Kenneth. *Black Americans: The FBI Files.* New York: Carroll and Graf, 1994.

Osborne, Sidney. *The New Japanese Peril.* New York: Macmillan, 1921.

Oshinsky, David M. *Worse Than Slavery: Parchman Farm and the Ordeal of Jim Crow Justice.* New York: Free Press, 1996.

Osofsky, Gilbert. *Harlem: The Making of a Ghetto.* New York: Harper, 1965.

Pagliaro, Harold, ed. *Racism in the 18th Century.* Studies in Eighteenth Century Culture, vol. 3. Cleveland: Case Western Reserve University Press, 1973.

Parry, J.H. *The Age of Reconnaissance.* New York: New American Library, 1963.

Parry, J.H., and P.M. Sherlock. *A Short History of the West Indies.* New York: St. Martin's Press, 1966.

Paliwala, Abddul. "Law and the Constitution of the 'Immigrant' in Europe: A UK Policy Perspective." In *Nationalism, Racism and the Rule of Law,* ed. Peter Fitzpatrick. Brookfield, Vt.: Dartmouth, 1995.

Patai, Raphael, and Jennifer Patai Wing. *The Myth of the Jewish Race.* New York: Scribner's, 1975.

Patterson, Orlando. *Slavery and Social Death.* Cambridge: Harvard University Press, 1982.

Paxton, Robert O. "The Uses of Fascism." *New York Review of Books* 43, no. 19 (November 28, 1996).

Pearce, Roy Harvey. *Savagism and Civilization: A Study of the Indian and the American Mind. Baltimore:* Penguin, 1975.

Penrose, Boies. *Travel and Discovery in the Renaissance, 1420–1620.* New York: Atheneum, 1962.

Pfaff, William. *The Wrath of Nations: Civilization and the Furies of Nationalism.* New York: Simon and Schuster, 1993.

Phillips, Ulrich Bonnell. *American Negro Slavery.* Louisiana: University of Louisiana Press, 1918.

———. *Life and Labor in the Old South.* Boston: Little, Brown, 1929.

Pirenne, Henri. *Medieval Cities, Their Origins and the Revival of Trade.* Garden City, N.Y.: Doubleday Anchor, 1956.

Poliakov, Leon. *The History of Anti-Semitism: From the Time of Christ to the Court Jews.* Vol. 1. New York: Vanguard Press, 1965.

———. *The Aryan Myth: A History of Racist and Nationalist Ideas in Europe.* Translated by Edmund Howard. New York: Basic Books, 1974.

Polo, Marco. *The Travels.* New York: Penguin Books, 1958.

Posel, Deborah. *The Making of Apartheid, 1948–1961: Conflict and Compromise.* Oxford, England: Oxford University Press, 1991.

Pulzer, Peter. *The Rise of Political Anti-Semitism in Germany and Austria.* New York: Wiley, 1964.

Quadagno, Jill. *The Color of Welfare.* New York: Oxford University Press, 1994.

Quarles, Benjamin. *The Negro in the Making of America.* New York: Collier Books, 1964.

Quinn, David Beers. *The Elizabethans and the Irish.* New York: Cornell University Press, 1966.

Rabinowitz, Howard. *Race Relations in the Urban South, 1865–1900.* New York: Oxford University Press, 1978.

Rathzel, N. "Germany: One Race, One Nation?" *Race and Class* 3, no. 32 (1990): 31–48.

Reich, Wilhelm. *The Mass Psychology of Fascism.* New York: Simon and Schuster, 1970.

Reischauer, Edwin O., and John K. Fairbank. *East Asia: The Great Tradition.* Boston: Houghton Mifflin, 1960.

Rex, John. *Theories of Race and Ethnic Relations.* Cambridge, England: Cambridge University Press, 1986.

———. *Race and Ethnicity.* Milton Keynes, England: Open University Press, 1986.

Roediger, David. *The Wages of Whiteness: Race and the Making of the American Working Class.* London and New York: Verso Press, 1991.

———. *Towards the Abolition of Whiteness: Essays on Race, Class, Politics and Working Class History.* London: Verso Press, 1994.

Rosenberg, Daniel. *New Orleans Dockworkers: Race, Labor, and Unionism, 1892–1923.* Albany: SUNY Press, 1988.

Ruchames. Lois, ed. *Racial Thought in America.* Vol. 1. *From the Puritans to Abraham Lincoln.* Amherst: University of Massachusetts Press, 1969.

Russell, Katheryn K. *The Color of Crime: Racial Hoaxes, White Fear, Black Protectionism, Police Harassment, and Other Macroaggressions.* New York: New York University Press, 1998.

Said, Edward. *Orientalism.* New York: Pantheon Books, 1978.

———. *Culture and Imperialism.* London: Chatto and Windus, 1993.

Sanders, Ronald. *Lost Tribes and Promised Lands: The Origins of American Racism.* Boston: Little, Brown, 1978.

Sartre, Jean-Paul. "Portrait of the Anti-Semite." *Partisan Review,* no. 13 (1946).

Segal, Ronald. *The Race War.* New York: Viking Press, 1966.

Seton-Watson, Hugh. *Nations and States: An Inquiry into the Origins of Nations and the Politics of Nationalism.* London: Methuen, 1977.

Shirer, William. *The Rise and Fall of the Third Reich.* New York: Simon and Schuster, 1959.

Simone, Timothy M. *About Face: Race in Postmodern America.* New York: Autonomedia Press, 1989.

Skidmore, Thomas E. *Black into White: Race and Nationality in Brazilian Thought.* New York: Oxford University Press, 1974.

Small, Stephen. *Racialised Barriers: The Black Experience in the United States and England in the 1980's.* London: Routledge, 1994

Smedley, Audrey. *Race in North America: Origin and Evolution of a Worldview.* Boulder, Colo.: Westview Press, 1993.

Smith, Anthony. *Theories of Nationalism.* 2nd ed. London: Duckworth, 1983.

————. *National Identity*. Nevada: University of Las Vegas Press, 1991.

Smith, Arthur L. *Hitler's Gold: The Story of Nazi War Loot*. Oxford, England: Berg, 1989.

Sniderman, Paul M., and Thomas Piazza. *The Scar of Race*. Cambridge: Belknap Press of Harvard University Press, 1993.

Snowden, Frank. *Before Color Prejudice: The Ancient View of Blacks*. Cambridge: Harvard University Press, 1983.

Snyder, Louis L. *The Idea of Racialism: Its Meaning and History*. New York: Van Nostrand Reinhold, 1962.

————. *The Meaning of Nationalism*. New York: Greenwood Press, 1968.

Solomos, John. *Race and Racism in Contemporary Britain*. London: Macmillan, 1989.

Sowell, Thomas. *The Economics and Politics of Race*. New York: Morrow, 1983.

————. *Race and Culture*. New York: Basic Books, 1994.

Sparks, Allister. *The Mind of South Africa*. New York: Knopf, 1990.

Stanton, W.R. *The Leopard's Spots: Scientific Attitudes toward Race in America*. New York: Harper & Row, 1960.

Stenton, Doris M. *English Society in the Early Middle Ages, 1066–1307*. Baltimore: Penguin Books, 1962.

Stepan, Nancy. *The Idea of Race in Science: Great Britain, 1800–1960*. New York: Archon, 1982.

Stevens, Frank S. *Racism: The Australian Experience, a Study of Race Prejudice in Australia*. 2 vols. New York: Taplinger, 1972.

Sullivan, Patricia. *Days of Hope: Race and Democracy in the New Deal*. Chapel Hill: University of North Carolina Press, 1966.

Takaki, Ronald. *Iron Cages: Race and Culture in Nineteenth-Century America*. New York: Knopf, 1979.

Tarn, William Woodthorpe. *Alexander the Great*. Boston: Beacon Press, 1956.

————. *Hellenistic Civilization*. Cleveland: World, 1961.

Tcherikover, Victor. *Hellenistic Civilization and the Jews*. Philadelphia: Jewish Publication Society of America, Magnes Press, 1966.

Thapar, Romila. *A History of India*. New York: Penguin Books, 1990.

Tharoor, Shashi. *India, from Midnight to the Millennium*. New York: Arcade, 1997.

Thorton, John. *Africa and Africans in the Making of the Atlantic World, 1400–1680*. Cambridge, England: Cambridge University Press, 1992.

Tinkler, Hugh. *Race, Conflict and the International Order*. New York: St. Martin's Press, 1977.

Thompson, Leonard. *The Political Mythology of Apartheid*. New Haven: Yale University Press, 1985.

Todorov, Tzvetan. *The Conquest of America*. New York: Harper, 1982.

————. *On Human Diversity: Nationalism, Racism and Exoticism in French Thought*. Translated by Catherine Porter. Cambridge: Harvard University Press, 1993.

Tonroy, Michael. *Malign Neglect—Race, Crime, and Punishment in America*. New York: Oxford University Press, 1997.

Torres, Gerald. "Critical Race Theory: The Decline of the Universalist Ideal and the Hope of Plural Justice—Some Observations and Questions of an Emerging Phenomenon." *Minnesota Law Review*, no. 75 (1991): 993–1007.

Tucker, Frank H. *The White Conscience*. New York: Frederick Ungar, 1968.

Turner, E.R. *The Negro in Pennsylvania, 1639–1861*. New York: Arno Press, 1969; originally published 1911.

UNESCO. *The Race Question in Modern Science: Race and Science*. New York: Columbia University Press, 1969.

Van den Berghe, Pierre. *Race and Racism, a Comparative Perspective.* New York: Wiley, 1967.

Vaughan, Alden T. *Roots of American Racism: Essays on the Colonial Experience.* New York: Oxford University Press, 1995.

Vohra, Ranbir. *The Making of India: A Historical Survey.* Armonk, N.Y.: M.E. Sharpe, 1997.

von Eschen, Penny. *Race Against Empire: Black Americans and Anti-Colonialism, 1937–1957.* Ithaca: Cornell University Press, 1997.

Wagley, Charles, ed. *Race and Class in Rural Brazil.* 2nd. ed. New York: Russell and Russell, 1973.

Walvin, James. *Black Ivory: A History of British Slavery.* London: HarperCollins, 1992.

Ware, Vron. *Beyond the Pale: White Women, Racism and History.* London: Verso Press, 1992.

West, Cornell. *Prophecy and Deliverance! An Afro-American Revolutionary Christianity.* Philadelphia: Westminister Press, 1982.

———. "Race and Social Theory: Towards a Genealogical Materialist Analysis." In *Towards a Rainbow Socialism,* ed. Mike Davis et al. London: Verso Press, 1987.

———. *Race Matters.* Boston: Beacon Press, 1993.

Weston, Rubin. *Racism in United States Imperialism.* Columbia: University of South Carolina Press, 1972.

Wiegman, Robin. *American Anatomies; Theorizing Race and Gender.* Durham, N.C.: Duke University Press, 1995.

Wilson, William J. *Power, Racism, and Privilege: Race Relations in Theoretical and Sociological Perspectives.* New York: Macmillan, 1973.

———. *The Declining Significance of Race: Blacks and Changing American Institutions.* Chicago: University of Chicago Press, 1980.

Williams, Eric. *Capitalism and Slavery.* New York: Russell and Russell, 1961.

Williams, Patricia J. *The Alchemy of Race and Rights.* Cambridge: Harvard University Press, 1991.

Williamson, Joel. *The Crucible of Race.* New York: Oxford University Press, 1984.

Winant, Howard. *Racial Conditions: Politics, Theory, Comparisons.* Minneapolis: University of Minnesota Press, 1994.

———. "The New International Dynamics of Racism." *Poverty and Race* 4, no. 4 (July/August 1995).

Wistrich, Robert S. *Anti-Semitism: The Longest Hatred.* New York: Pantheon Books, 1991.

Wood, Forrest G. *The Arrogance of Faith: Christianity and Race in America from the Colonial Era to the Twentieth Century.* New York: Knopf, 1990.

Wright, Winthrop. *Café con leche: Race, Class, and National Image in Venezuela.* Austin: University of Texas Press, 1990.

Young-Bruehl, Elizabeth. *The Anatomy of Prejudices.* Cambridge: Harvard University Press, 1996.

Young, Robert J.C. *White Mythologies: Writing History and the West.* London and New York: Routledge, 1990.

———. *Colonial Desire: Hybridity in Theory, Culture and Race.* New York: Routledge, 1995.

Zahar, Renate. *Franz Fanon: Colonialism and Alienation; Concerning Franz Fanon's Political Theory.* New York: Monthly Review Press, 1974.

Zenner, Walter P. "Joking and Ethnic Stereotyping." *Anthropological Quarterly* 43 (1970): 93–113.

Zilg, Gerard Colby. *Behind the Nylon Curtain: A History of the DuPont Family in America.* Englewood Cliffs, N.J.: Prentice-Hall, 1974.

Index

Philip Y. Nicholson was born in Philadelphia and educated in the public schools there. He received a B.S. degree from Temple University (1962) and an M.A. in History from the University of Pennsylvania (1964). His Ph.D. in History was awarded by the University of New Mexico (1971). He has been a member of the faculty at Nassau Community College since 1967, and President of his faculty union, the Nassau Community College Federation of Teachers (NYSUT, AFT), since 1987. He has been married to Linda since 1963; they have three children, Andrew, Jennifer, and Peter.